# High Tea and the Low Down

An American's Unfiltered Life in the UK

## Claire Craig Evans

Publisher's Cataloging-in-Publication Data provided by Five Rainbows Cataloging Services

Names: Evans, Claire Craig, author.

Title: High tea and the low down : an American's unfiltered life in the UK / Claire Craig Evans.

Description: Peoria, IL : Claire Craig Evans, 2023.

Identifiers: ISBN 978-1-961542-00-6 (paperback) | ISBN 978-1-961542-01-3 (ebook) | ISBN 978-1-961542-02-0 (audiobook)

Subjects: LCSH: Women--United States--Biography. | Americans--England--Biography. | Moving, Household. | Emigration and immigration--Biography. | England--Description and travel. | BISAC: BIOGRAPHY & AUTOBIOGRAPHY / Personal Memoirs. | BIOGRAPHY & AUTOBIOGRAPHY / Women. | TRAVEL / Europe / Great Britain. | HUMOR / Topic / Travel.

Classification: LCC CT275.E93 A3 2023 (print) | LCC CT275.E93 (ebook) | DDC 920.72--dc23.

Visit Claire's website at www.teawithclaire.com

*To Ben*

# Contents

# Author's Note

T HIS BOOK CONTAINS MY imperfect recollection of true stories. I've reconstituted dialogue and altered chronology to make my life less confusing, though feeling confused is an authentic American-in-the-UK experience. I also tweaked a few names and details to avoid the wrath of the guilty.

# Introduction

*Cantabit vacuus coram latrone viator. (The empty-handed
traveler will sing in the face of the highwayman.)*

– Juvenal, Roman satiric poet

AFTER ABOUT A YEAR of dating, my British boyfriend Ben and I
were boarding a red-eye Air India flight from Chicago O'Hare to
Heathrow. He'd invited me to meet his family in Cornwall, the furthest
southwest county in England. I'd never met any of my dates' families
before, much less flown to a foreign country to do it. Ben was one of the
nicest people I'd ever known. We were completely *simpatico*. My future
happiness hinged on this trip, and no amount of Tums could calm my
stomach. Worse, Hurricane Ernesto was dissipating over Quebec near our
flight path. We were in for a bumpy ride.

I stepped across the jet bridge and took a deep breath. I smelled curry
and fear.

Ben had left me in charge of airline tickets, and I found ultra-cheap ones on Air India from Chicago to Delhi, stopping over in London. The olfactory assault of vindaloo was making me nauseous. Ben had the opposite reaction—like most Brits, he loved a good curry. He figured even airplane curry would be a step up from what passed for Indian cuisine where we lived in Peoria, Illinois.

We sat in seats stamped with permanent butt prints and upholstered in a pattern way older than me. As we entered the remnant of the hurricane, the back of the old Airbus creaked and shimmied, making sleep impossible. The plane rattled like there were dice in the walls. The sound made me think it would be up to chance whether we actually made it to London. I'd taken Dramamine, but the flight attendants were not familiar with the concept of Sprite.

I was elated to escape our curry coffin when we landed at Heathrow nine hours later. It was around eight in the morning local time. I sprang into the baggage hall and started scouting for my favorite megalithic piece of Samsonite. I was traveling heavy—I had gifts for Ben's family, a wardrobe option for every possible season, all my best shoes, and an outfit to wear to a wedding near the end of our ten-day UK stay. One by one, all the people on our flight found their bags and left. Ben dutifully waited by my side with his suitcase. I willed every piece of new luggage on the belt to be mine, but I was being orbited by random pieces of disappointment. I panicked like a child left behind after school. After an hour of anxiety, I suspected my luggage wasn't coming to Cornwall with me.

For the first time ever in my travels, I descended into the funk that came with knowing I'd spent more than twenty-four hours wearing the only pair of underwear in my immediate possession. I would rather gnaw off an arm than cry in public, but I couldn't stop a hot tear from running down my cheek. My brain replayed the scene in Emma Thompson's *Sense and*

*Sensibility* where Marianne Dashwood is confronted by the rogue who broke her heart and his new fiancée. Her sister Elinor takes Marianne by the arm and leads her elsewhere with the same words Ben used.

"Come away."

He handed me a bottle of cold Really Light Ribena blackcurrant squash he'd procured from a nearby shop. Fruity beverages were one of my love languages. It was an enticement to rejoin reality. But if I left Heathrow without my bag, I'd lose touch with the alternate universe in which Air India merely misplaced my luggage behind a giant cart of tarka daal.

The truth was that my bag was gone. I filed a lost baggage claim and wrenched myself toward the rental car counter. I'd not even met Ben's parents yet and was living a luggage-free nightmare. I held it together in denial until we set off in the hire car.

As Heathrow faded behind us, I was uncommonly quiet. It was a long drive to Falmouth, six hours on a good day. Ordinarily I'd be distracted by the novelty of cars whizzing past on the left or the rolling, sheepy landscape of what the unofficial national hymn "Jerusalem" called "England's green and pleasant land." I'd usually narrate everything I saw, but I couldn't speak. I'd had no sleep and hours of nausea in the tail of a spice rocket. My nerves were shot and I was in mourning.

Ben's mobile phone pinged with a text message. He was driving, so he suggested I read it out to him.

"Pain arriving from the west. Safe travels. Love, Nun."

I felt confused and validated at the same time.

Ben sighed. "She means rain." He received many nonsensical texts from his "nun," better known as mum. She hadn't quite mastered predictive text and made a habit of hitting send before proofreading. We laughed and it felt like old times, when I had a variety of clean underwear to choose from.

Ben made a pit stop at a roadside Marks & Spencer. I thought we were just getting tea and coffee, but he presented me with a beautiful bouquet of peach roses he'd purchased on the sly. It was a small gesture, but it made me think that maybe things were going to be okay. I was with a thoughtful man who loved me, and he would guide me through the unknown. In particular, he would help me find new underwear. I was a fiercely independent person and I was mad at myself for feeling vulnerable. Luggage loss through jet-lagged lenses had me getting misty over everything, including radio ads for mobile phones. I teared up again as we carried on down the M5 past Bristol.

Armed with a fresh perspective and fresh underwear thanks to ASDA (the British equivalent of Walmart), I was ready to meet "Nun." She was petite, and a blonde like Ben. Best of all, she was delighted to meet me. She occasionally broke into song mid-sentence, painted impressive landscapes, and played in local handbell choirs. She was endearing.

Thankfully, the airline drove my wayward suitcase down to Cornwall by courier the next day. It smelled of masala, and my shoes had been awarded platinum frequent-flier status, thanks to their trip to Delhi. The rest of the trip was relaxed and scenic, full of new experiences and free blackberries on public hedges. It added to my impression of England as an enchanted island where somewhat mysterious women with dewy complexions made jam in thatched cottages with millennia-old lichen attached. But things are not always as they seem.

# Part One:

## Preparing for Departure

*It is better to travel hopefully than to arrive.*

– nineteenth-century saying

## Searching for Mr. Darcy

I NEVER DATED MUCH, for a few reasons. My formative years were spent mostly mute, which puts a damper on getting to know anyone. I was very driven and interested in my own education, and I got the wild hair to try law school. After all, I liked to read and write, and I had opinions. Three years of law school seriously filled my schedule, and some of the personality types I found there were as comfortable as a wayward cheese grater. Once my legal career began, I found myself wondering if I'd ever meet anyone that didn't make me chafe. I didn't spend time in bars or gyms. I knew I would hate dating another lawyer because I'd rather knit

with dental floss than argue. (One might point out that being confronta-
tional is a large part of lawyering, so it was inevitable I wouldn't last in that
line of work.) To make things worse, I spent my lawyering days talking to
dockets full of driving-under-the-influence (DUI) defendants. People in
court-ordered drug or alcohol rehab didn't comprise the best dating pool.
When it came to my prospects, I remembered the old chestnut of financial
planning: "Past performance is the best predictor of future success." If I
ever wanted to meet boyfriend material, I needed to revisit the idea that
fate would magically put the right person in my current path. But courage
came slowly, like a pint glass filled from a dripping tap.

By late summer 2005, my levels of personal boldness had reached un-
precedented heights. I started dabbling in the scary world of online dating
after reading one too many articles crowing that dating was merely a numbers game. I had no success with any other theory, so to be sporting, I rea-
soned I should try this statistical approach before dismissing the entirety
of online men as geeks, super weirdos, or worse, just looking for their next
victim. Sometimes I thought I was undateable, but I didn't want to jump
to that conclusion without some evidence. Some parts of my legal training
were helpful, after all.

Through copious research, I developed an internet dating strategy.
(Whenever faced with any sort of problem, such as improving the R-value
of my attic space or the best treatment for plantar fasciitis, my habit was to
read as much as possible.) First, I would never let two weeks of emails tran-
spire without actually meeting an online acquaintance face-to-face. This
way, they wouldn't have time to spin a web of outrageous lies about their
Nobel Peace Prize, rich Uncle Peregrine in Borneo, or patents on pieces of
home cleaning equipment. It would also edit out those men who sounded
fine on paper, but suffered sphincter failure when it came to forming words
in the presence of a real, live female. I'd transcended my fear of speaking

to strangers in journalism school, and I had no sympathy for people who couldn't carry on a live conversation. Thanks to the overabundance of men who appeared in online dating profiles, I received so many "winks" that it felt like I was running my own personal HR department. I considered drafting a "Thank you for your interest, but we have no available positions at this time" letter to be polite, but decided against it for dread of the double entendre.

I T DIDN'T HELP MY morale that the first online date I met for lunch was indeed a super weirdo. In person, he was an extremely well-photographed computer programmer only interested in prattling on about his various trips to wine country in an irritating nasal tone. I felt like I was right there with him in whine country. The depth of my boredom gripped me like a coma. I secretly patted the underside of our lunch table, hoping for an ejector button. His parting shot was, "I'm out of town on business this week, so don't freak out if I don't call you right away." I concealed my eye roll reflex, bid him *bon voyage*, and fled on foot. Two hours later, he emailed with a request for me to join him on an eight-week pottery course. My mind went to a repulsive scene out of the movie *Ghost,* and I sought a trusted female opinion on whether I was overreacting. She put words to my feelings. "He's trying to lock you into a two-month date," she said.

With Mr. Whine Country as my muse, I wrote what I called the "digital crotch kick." Cruel, perhaps, but I had to look out for my own interests. I'd wasted years already. I didn't have time for men who made me want to risk my own arrest. A digital crotch kick was a quick, sharp email that got to the point—not interested. I wasn't overtly mean, but I wasn't afraid to point out that "we just didn't click." Click elsewhere.

Unfortunately, I was forced to use the digital crotch kick on my next date as well, a child psychologist who looked like an extra from the wedding scene in *The Godfather*. We met in the height of summer at an outdoor ice cream place. I'd hardly touched my cone when a Little League baseball team approached from the parking lot. With ninja-like dexterity, my date dove behind a large trash receptacle. Wasps buzzed around his head but he held his position flawlessly. Clearly, he'd done this before. I stared in disbelief, but then thought twice. I didn't want to admit I actually knew this person.

"I don't like to encounter patients outside a clinical setting," he whispered. I'd be damned if I wasted perfectly good ice cream, so I sat on my own until the team dissipated. He finally emerged from hiding, and without missing a beat, went on to tell me a seven-minute moral fable that he liked to use with clients "in session." Once I'd escaped, I assumed he thought I fell into a patient category and was luckily undateable. The next day, he sent a message inviting me to go camping. *What would happen if we spied Boy Scouts?* I was outraged and so was the group of friends I used for opinions.

"Camping on date two? But you couldn't even cope with the Pequot Motor Inn when you had an actual bed!"

*Exactly.* A digital crotch kick was in order.

M Y NEXT CANDIDATE WAS an engineer who worked for a defense contractor developing rocket engines. He drove a shabby minivan he bought from his ex-girlfriend's father. Over a burger, he gleefully explained how he was working on an interface between his satellite navigation system and various radio station signals that would enable him to automatically change radio stations as he drove. I was trying to follow the logic but couldn't help myself.

"Isn't that called the seek button?" I asked. He said nothing and glared at his pile of fries.

I didn't like my record thus far, and fully realizing I may qualify as a nerd as well, I extended an olive twig and went out with him a second time. Once again, he was so interesting that I begged off early so I could feed my reality television addiction: *Regency House Party*, a UK Channel 4 series that aired on American PBS.

*Regency House Party* was a jumble of real-life, eligible, prosperous young men, and young women with and without means. They dressed in Regency-garb, and the producers assigned them a persona and, for the women, a chaperone. They were under the watchful eye of the house's prim butler. I was glued to my television when one of the female chaperones struck up a May-December relationship with a much younger gentleman meant for her young charge. Everything got hopelessly exciting when a footman and scullery maid were caught by the butler *in flagrante delicto* on the penultimate evening of their stay. The chaperones tried to facilitate a suitable match before the summer-long house party ended, all while adhering to the Regency rules of dating.

I was rapt with episode synopses like: "*As the end of the party approaches, old quarrels rise to surface and the chaperones fall out in spectacular style by throwing the fine china at each other.*" My favorite part was when the producers, posing as "the estate," hired a professional hermit to live in a hut on the property, scare people, and lust after a kitchen maid. Perhaps this was a foreshadowing of our brief relationship's demise, but my date was nothing lost compared to missing my weekly episode.

After his bungle lining up another date and letting me hang out to dry, I was nearing a firm digital crotch kick. Before I could hit send, I had a message in my inbox saying Rocket Man had just broken up with his girlfriend before our first date and he "wasn't ready to get back on the horse again." Naturally, I was flattered by the equine analogy.

It had occurred to me that if these were my vetted picks, the best I could find, then perhaps I was being a bit too ruthless with my criteria and not long enough on patience. This was the mindset that led me to date a PhD candidate in mycology for an entire summer. He was a nice enough guy, but it was painfully obvious that he and his mold specimens were intimidated by me. All my prior dates knew I was a lawyer, but I never experienced such a fear reaction from anyone before. Despite the continual clamminess, he continued to ask me out and I continued to accept. I overlooked the severely wilted bouquet he had retrieved from the grocery store half-price rack, complete with sale tag. He made frequent language errors like Amy in *Little Women*, and it took every ounce of my willpower not to correct them. There was a big difference between the words "fetid" and "fecund." I let the malaprops slide, paid my own way everywhere, and continued extending the benefit of the doubt like tissues for a perpetually runny nose. The last straw was his tendency to just make up words and use them with nauseating frequency. My stomach lining and loyalty to the English language couldn't take any more, so after three months, I administered the crotch kick.

I was a bit upset after that one, not for the company I'd lost, but for what I had failed to gain after more than a year of auditions. There was one last card to play, but it took me five months to think about using it.

From time to time, I trolled other websites' personals, just in case the one I subscribed to attracted a disproportionate share of freaks and wackos. I had noticed a man back in May who mentioned he was looking for someone with a sense of "humour" because he was 3,000 miles away from his friends and family. I re-examined his picture. He was a serious-looking blond guy with pronounced bone structure. He posted pictures of himself effortlessly running a road race and listed fitness as one of his interests. For a change, I was intimidated. My personal mantra was that I only ran when chased. I had battled the sugar monkey for years, and although I had lost some weight, I certainly would never be classed as "sporty." I was interested in theoretical fitness but I hated to sweat. He was probably looking for some reedy companion to run the Boston Marathon. However, unlike the vast majority of the ads I read, I could tell English was his first language and I approved of his use of commas. I saved his profile for a rainy day when I had more nerve and weighed fifteen pounds less.

Admiring Mr. Sporty's in-home Power Bar buffet couldn't possibly be worse than Mr. Mold's torture by "non-wordboarding." There was a bit of a catch. I could only contact Mr. Sporty if I belonged to his chosen online dating service, and I drew the line at throwing good money after bad to access yet another pool of dork wits. Usually, daters had to subscribe to the service in order to communicate. But the service Mr. Sporty was using offered an escape—for any reason, I could cancel within forty-eight hours. I schemed to join, drop him an irresistibly witty message with my outside email address, unjoin, sit back, and hope he restricted his missives to words actually found in the Oxford English dictionary. If he had my personal email address, we could send messages for free. But the moment he misplaced a modifier, I was abandoning the rickety online dating ship and getting onboard the Morton, Illinois, Young Singles Supper Club, if it even existed.

In my methodical review of online dating literature, I'd read that it was a bad idea to use your real name in your email address, just in case your potential date moonlighted as a stalker. It worked in the case of a pushy guy who insisted on meeting for coffee without enough written exchanges for me to gauge his literacy. Thanks to the magic of Google and my above-average knowledge of where to locate public-access criminal records, I found coffee dude had a felony drugs conviction and lost his license for multiple DUI offenses. Besides the very real possibility that I might be personally called on to revoke his probation and send him to the clink, I would presumably be driving us everywhere. That sounded like no fun at all. I didn't hesitate to dispatch a digital crotch kick.

I sent the daunting, sporty man what felt like an electronic message in a bottle on a Wednesday. Much to my delight, I had a reply by Thursday evening. My email address used my *nom de plume* from years ago, Skippy Dubois. "Isn't Skippy a brand of peanut butter? Dubois is probably some place in Indiana where it's made..." He was British, but he was clearly up to speed on American savory condiments.

I was surprised to read, "I'm sure you understand the argument of wanting to meet different people, but I should warn you I'm an engineer (listens for screams)." He embraced his potential to skew geeky, and that on its own wasn't a dealbreaker. I'd been steeped in a bit of geeky myself when I began my undergraduate degree in mechanical engineering before switching to journalism. The final clue that I'd be happier in a field that strung words together vs. machine parts was thermodynamics.

With shocking prescience, he concluded his first message with, "Anyway, you've got my email, so feel free to run my name through the register of freaks and wackos or whatever PC name they give it these days." How could he read my mind? But I was thwarted in my online dredge because all his hypothetical baggage was in a foreign country. I'd just have to scour his messages for red flags—requests to make deposits into a Nigerian bank account, musings on his mansion in Romania, or details about his mother in Azerbaijan who'd been on a wait list for an appendectomy for the past twenty years.

So far, he'd lamented a repair bill for a *Miami Vice*-era Lotus he bought that spring, before he learned that Lotus stood for, "Lots of trouble, usually serious." It didn't fit that a con artist would solicit charitable donations to save his flashy sports car. I was partly to blame for motorhead chit-chat—I listed on my profile that I subscribed to *Car and Driver*. It was technically correct. I ordered it for my dad for Christmas one year, and when my parents temporarily redirected their mail to my house during a move, I saw the subscription label had my name on it. I thumbed through an issue in desperation when I tired of the Land's End catalog or the nutritional label on various cereal boxes. Was I the type of con artist *he* should avoid?

My outside reconnaissance proved inconclusive. I found quite a few pictures of him running in races, and he wasn't keeping stride with a synthetically enhanced, spandex-wrapped woman who bought self-tanner by the firkin. It was safe to carry on correspondence.

A strand of long, entertaining emails ensued, primarily themed around my approaching thirtieth birthday, aka "Black Tuesday." He had recently entered that decade, but I loathed the number. When I was a girl, I remember thinking I would have my entire life figured out by age twenty-five. That hadn't happened, and thinking about my new age left me sullen and wanting, mostly chocolate.

My mother was completely unsympathetic. This was ironic, coming from the woman who observed her fiftieth birthday by unceremoniously running her newly-minted American Association of Retired Persons card through the shredder. For her, it was deviant behavior; it implied she was not interested in any of the goods and service discounts membership afforded, which couldn't be further from the truth. My family wasn't flush with cash, and her habit was to make the most of what we had. Ordinarily, she was the type of person who wore out her brake pads scouting neighborhood garage sales. As a kid, I lost track of the times I was forced to use a coupon at a fast-food outlet and claim I was a separate customer to get the discount.

In the run-up to the dreaded "three-zero," I spent the preceding weekend with my good friend Georgie. She suggested we visit a western bar, where she took a shine to a random cowboy named Randy. They did the Texas two-step while I sipped a mean mango margarita. I'm still not clear why she ran over and told me we had to flee immediately—something about a confusing incident with Randy once they fired up a smoke machine on the dance floor. For most of the weekend, we existed in fleece and pajamas, watching Bridget Jones movies. As an outing, we buttered up an associate at her local Clarins cosmetics counter and scored a truckload of free samples. The weekend was therapeutic, but I still couldn't shake the general melancholia brought on by entering a new decade. My mother was candid. "Shut up, kid," she said. "I have shoes older than you."

Mr. Sporty, now known as Ben, didn't mince words. He sent a Dr. Phil therapy e-card, where an animated version of the doctor himself threatened in his Texas twang that if I didn't snap out of my funk, he would "unleash a can of whoop-ass" on me. Weren't Brits legendary for their reserve? It was the most direct and least likely card I thought he would send me. Maybe Ben and Dr. Phil had a point. How annoying.

I was getting unnerved by so much practically anonymous smart humor. I thought Ben was probably forwarding all my emails to Richard Curtis, screenwriter of *Four Weddings and a Funeral*, for drafting proper replies because building a 1/32 scale replica of the *Red October* submarine in his bathtub took up all his free time. Of course, I had no evidence that he was really that nerdy, but he did have a PhD in thermodynamics, my academic Achilles heel. When he offered his phone number, my female pride kicked in. I countered with mine and a good time to call. He took the bait and rang the next evening.

It had been four years since I studied abroad in London for the summer. Besides my PBS Britcom training, I had seen every Hugh Grant film ever made. I genuinely enjoyed digestive biscuits, despite the name. (It helped if they were covered in chocolate.) I steeled myself with these bolstering thoughts and waited.

When the phone finally rang, my stomach dropped, but things got easier after a few minutes of stumbling through niceties. Ben was not a natural chatter, as I was by then, but I found him to be just as interesting live as in writing. His field of expertise was engine development. He divulged some unlikely but delightful revelations. For example, he was the proud owner of a one-a-day "You Know You're a Redneck If..." desk calendar, and squirreled away the redneck-isms he found most amusing in his files. Strangely, his brief time in the Midwest cultivated an appreciation of chicken fried steak. He did tell me how disappointed he was when a waitress offered him a biscuit with dinner in the States, and he received what he would call a scone instead.

His family lived in Cornwall, which was on the short list of places I wanted to visit someday. I'm not terribly loud by nature, and when I mentioned my volume control was naturally low, he expressed surprise. "I thought most Americans were set on eleven," he said. That was a *Spinal Tap* reference I actually knew. Our senses of humor, no matter the spelling, were in sync. I was out of practice listening to a live English accent; I found that sometimes I was so busy listening to the way he said something as opposed to what he actually said, I would need a few seconds for accent and meaning to catch up to each other. Despite my mental processing speed, we blathered on for at least an hour.

After I had a chance to reflect on our conversation, I deemed him enter-taining and quirky, attributes that I liked to think I had myself. He was still enigmatic. On a wittiness level, it was possible that I was outclassed. Despite the bright spots, I was still on the lookout for dealbreakers. A close friend had just broken up with her engineer boyfriend because he spent far too much time working on his robot in the basement.

We met for a drink on date one, and he actually looked like his online pictures minus the sportswear. He dressed well and he collected cufflinks, which was unusual for a man my age. He handed me a much kinder birthday card, and he declined my offer to pay for my own drink.

I was delighted when he wrote me the next morning to ask me to dinner that weekend. He brought his bright red Lotus, but parked it against the flow of traffic on the wrong side of the street. As a traffic prosecutor, I resisted the urge to inquire about his illegal parking technique because we were leaving for dinner in minutes. At the end of the meal, I made a point of pulling out my wallet. Unfair, perhaps, but I find generosity attractive. I didn't expect it, but I always appreciated it. I rehearsed a polite line: "May I help you with that?"

To me, the perfect answer was, "Oh, no. Put your wallet away," with bonus points if he was offended by the mention of a contribution.

He stared at the bill. I became concerned because I was rooting for him.

"I can't believe it," he said to the restaurant at large. "It's just so cheap!"

I sat there trying to process the significance of this comment. I would start with the worst-case scenario.

"You mean, me?" I could feel my left eyebrow lifting. Thank goodness I never aspired to learn poker.

He looked at me, horrified.

"*No*, don't be mad. Eating out in this country."

"I'm glad we cleared that up."

He went on to reveal what colored his American experience. He was being paid by the English subsidiary of his US employer, who deposited pounds sterling into his UK bank account. The moment he transferred money from his UK account to his US bank, the funds doubled, thanks to the near two-to-one dollar-to-pound exchange rate. In fact, a fellow expat had saved up to transfer a large sum British bank account to American soil. He used the money he made in the currency conversion to buy a new Mazda Miata. It was a high time to be an Englishman a thousand miles west of New York. Americans ate out more, as well, so the law of supply and demand dictated bargain-basement biscuits, even if we had gotten it all wrong and actually served him scones.

Somewhere in the handful of early dates, he invited me to his house before we went to see a movie. It was a small and charming Cape Cod on an exclusive lane, high on a bluff. I gazed out the front windows to take in panoramic views of the Illinois River, the view everyone in Peoria coveted but few could afford. He confessed his employer was covering his rent. Inside, he kept a tidy house decorated with potted palms and running medals. His walls were filled with interesting pictures of Cornish sailboats, old race cars, and the architect Frank Lloyd Wright's drawing of his masterpiece house "Fallingwater." He showed me where deer had completely decimated his potato crop that summer. I spied an ironing board next to a row of neatly pressed French cuffed work shirts in the basement laundry room. Not a single robot in sight.

Our relationship evolved based on a series of extremely good times. In fact, the dialogue of our dates was so entertaining that I thought I should write it down. Neither of us were dating experts, but we managed an impressive effort. He always offered me strong British black tea with milk before we went out for dinner or to see a movie, which I found endearing.

One evening several months into our acquaintance, I seemed a bit pre-occupied as we sipped PG Tips tea with milk and caught the tail end of the original *Antiques Roadshow* on BBC America. I was trying not to squirm—I was wearing a top that was ever so slightly more revealing than my standard issue, but I could sense that I was using my wrap sweater as camouflage with obsessive-compulsive frequency. Granted, my self-exposure tolerance levels have always been microscopic.

"Is something wrong?" I knew the game was up.

I looked at the television. The appraiser was caressing and scrutinizing every inch of a priceless Dutch turkey platter from the 1400s. This was a parallel to my present situation.

"For me, cleavage is like the company china."

He looked a bit puzzled. To be fair, bachelors in their early thirties rarely possessed company china.

"You don't take it out very often. But when you do, you tend to worry about it the entire time."

He nodded with understanding and thought for a moment.

"Well, in that case, perhaps I should flip you over and inspect your bottom for a mark of quality."

I knew my jaw dropped. Worse yet, I had no reply. I was in the presence of a razor wit. From that point forward, Ben commanded my respect.

In time, Ben found a new job that would let him stay in the US longer than his anticipated two-year stint, and I gathered I was the reason why.

Our existence together was riddled with culture and language gaps. Even when we were copacetic, I did notice his inability to suffer fools. I didn't have a lot of sympathy for fools myself after years of working with so many criminal defendants.

As his unofficial American cultural tour guide, I was surprised how much Ben enjoyed American Halloween, a much bigger deal in the States than in the UK. He bought Reese's peanut butter cups to mix in with the gross gummy eyeballs and squidgy candy body parts he planned to offer trick-or-treaters. To add to the festivity, he answered the door impaled. He took joy in engineering a T-shirt with fake blood, a severed play sword, and a coat hanger.

One Halloween evening, I happened to be chatting to Ben on the phone as he anticipated the arrival of two young siblings he referred to as Simba and Simba. The prior year, both the sisters had shown up at his door dressed as Simba from *The Lion King* because they got into a dust-up over who was going to be king. The Simbas' mother had introduced the girls to Ben by their ultra-preppy Christian names, but names were not Ben's strong suit. In his defense, the sisters looked remarkably alike. Their mother was hard to miss—whenever she saw Ben, she had a habit of bustling over and breaking into the worst imitation of a British accent he had ever heard. He thought it was right up there with Dick Van Dyke in *Mary Poppins*. Surely she had no idea that she sounded less like the Queen and more like a fishwife straight out of London's East End.

"Oi... OI! Piss off, you little scamps!"

My ear hurt from the blasting receiver. I had witnessed Ben buy stale peanut brittle from a sad-looking little girl who turned up fundraising last week, so he couldn't be completely mean and grumpy when it came to kids.

"Ben, you can't treat those kids that way. They're your neighbors! What will their mother think?"

"Claire, I gotta go." I heard a dial tone.

My heart sank. This was a clear violation of one of my three keeper indicators. Number one was saying "bless you" when I sneezed, but short of driving us to an open field just after harvest, it was hard to conjure a sneeze on demand to administer this test. Numbers two and three were showing kindness to children and small animals, respectively. I was busy envisioning my hypothetical break-up speech when the phone rang.

As it turned out, the bane of Ben's existence had returned to his home turf, literally. He had been fighting a secret but losing battle with a small gang of raccoons. Raccoons aren't found in the UK, so their destructive tendencies were all new to him. He had been waking up to a ravaged front garden, as he called the front yard. Until recently, the source of the destruction was a mystery. He returned home long after dark one night, and the motion-sensitive flood light snapped on to reveal a gang of raccoons zealously ripping his lawn from its roots like over-worn carpet to look for the tasty grub worms beneath.

The turf war had escalated. While on the phone with me earlier, Ben spied that the gang had snatched a garbage bag from outside his back door. In fact, the ring leader was dashing across the back garden with the bag in its jaws, provoking the scamp comment. Simba and Simba's mother would not be filing an emergency order of protection after all.

I entered the UK for the first time with the impression that the English were painfully polite. I had evidence this was true when I heard a woman apologizing to a mannequin when she accidentally bumped it. The real truth was more nuanced. Certain infractions were never defensible. Cutting in line, known by the Brits as queue jumping, earned piercing laser glances from fellow queue dwellers. (That sort of heathen probably didn't de-scale the teakettle, either.) It might even provoke a stranger to comment. At first, I thought the comment would be an interpersonal olive branch, gently pointing out that someone else might have been ahead of the queue jumper. After a few more stints in line, the real remark was typically, "Oi! Mind the queue, you fat cow!"

—*elle*—

S OMETIME IN THE FIRST six months of our acquaintance, we happened to stroll through Best Buy, surveying inexpensive CDs, and
on the way out, we cut through household goods. I planned on powering
through to the exit, but strangely, I saw Ben drawn to the Dyson vacuum
cleaners on an endcap display. We were still in the stage of voluminous
information gathering, or at least I was, so I paid special attention to his
strong likes and dislikes. He shimmied closer to the Animal model, like he
was hanging out with an old friend.

One of my baby boomer coworkers gave me a bit of antique advice—I
should study up on my date's hobbies so I could engage in delightful
conversation about them, and thus, seem even more attractive. I preferred
to study just because I was nosy. I thought of two points. First, I was
highly suspect of a man who vacuumed as a hobby. Second, the thought
of vacuuming was so abhorrent to me, I knew there was no way I could
overcome my loathing to learn about the joys of Dyson's patented tornadic
suction. In my conspiracy-theory mind, I would likely learn he used to
work as a well-loved houseboy for a traveling band of Australian drag
queens who insisted on complete floor-surface dirt removal. I was already
starting to get disgusted with him for his presumably checkered past when
an overconfident saleskid approached.

"Looking to buy a vacuum cleaner? Those Dysons, they're the best."

Ben gave a solemn nod in agreement, with the air of an ultra-tidy Bud-
dhist monk. Surely his nonverbal reply would deflect the saleskid's attention and give Ben more quality time with something he loved. The ploy
didn't work.

"If you've got questions about how they work, just let me know."

Ben looked irritated. Maybe he wasn't used to American customer service standards and construed helpfulness as smothering. He glared at the
saleskid until he beat a retreat, then muttered something about patents.
Between the accent and the muttering, I wanted to make sure I heard him
correctly so I asked him to repeat himself.

"I don't *need* an explanation," he huffed. "I'm on the patent for this
nozzle." He pointed to the small tool ideal for cleaning upholstery and
small cushions.

Was this some version of a nerdy pickup line? I did find brains attractive,
but Ben was fairly low-key in flaunting his academic cred. I barely managed
to get out of him that he was a PhD. He was on a short list of very smart
people I'd had the privilege to know, but I wasn't sure if he was serious. He
explained that his doctoral thesis in combustion studied burning natural
gas in tornado formations to increase the efficiency of commercial drying
ovens. In other words, he was an expert on fire tornados. At his prior job,
Dyson hired him to do research because of its interest in developing root
cyclone technology in vacuum cleaners. He had moved on to researching
other things for Dyson, including air flow vents on vacuum cleaner heads
that didn't stick to the cushions.

If this explanation was fabricated for my benefit, it was the best cover
story in the universe. I took copious mental notes. Upon my return home, I
headed straight for my old friend Google and found the US Patent Office's
website. I knew that patent law class would come in handy someday. One
search of Ben's name in the inventor field turned up that he indeed was
listed as co-inventor on a patent for the very part we were staring at earlier.
Given that I'd had to extract this vacuum story myself, I noted the lack of
ego for someone so capable. It explained a lot. I'd witnessed Ben using his
Dyson canister vacuum, a fairly serious piece of domestic equipment for a

thirty-something bachelor. He was as fast in swapping out the attachments as an elite sniper clicking together a high-performance rifle.

B EN WAS ESPECIALLY THOUGHTFUL about opening car doors. He
didn't think of it every time, but I noted a pattern of opening, noted
in my mental files. We had been dating almost two years when not only
did he open the car door for me, but he actually got into the passenger's
seat before I could. I stood at the side of the car, confused, and saw him
slap his forehead. He confessed—every time he had opened the door, he'd
forgotten he was in the United States and would be driving on the left
side of the car, not the right like back home. To avoid looking foolish
switching sides at the last minute, he covered his error by letting me in.
It was chivalry by mistake, but it didn't warrant full deductions either. At
least he made himself useful while standing at the wrong door. Engineers
appreciate efficiency.

We had our differences, to be sure. One study in contrast was our respec-
tive lawn care standards. I arrived at Ben's house one weekend afternoon to
find him personally pushing and pulling a hefty water-filled drum across
his front lawn, trying to even out the surface after the raccoons had done
more overnight excavation. In the heat of the summer, his approach was a
lot of work.

"You know, those were meant to be towed behind lawn tractors," I
offered helpfully. I figured he would welcome the chance to use a piece
of engine-driven equipment, but his look soured. His exercise habits were
slipping since he spent more time with me. Also, I noticed he picked the
most difficult way of solving problems, like showing up in person at offices
when a phone call would suffice.

"Tractors are for fat, middle-aged American men obsessed with new
ways to grill chicken and beer simultaneously." Ben was quick to mow

down chefs who grilled their chicken carcasses stuffed with open beer cans, but he'd just bought a beer can chicken grilling rack for himself the week before. Like chicken fried steak, American redneck meat recipes were hard for him to resist. In any event, I didn't revisit the topic.

Ben was appalled at the state of my lawn, which I got around to mowing once a month or so, depending on what was on television. I looked forward to autumn leaf gathering like a trip to a prisoner of war camp. I could tell his urge to tidy my lawn was irresistible as he would excuse himself to "use the bathroom" and turn up raking a half hour later. In fact, we developed a reality show concept based on his self-imposed experience of tending my lawn. "On this week's episode of *Monster Thistle...*"

Right before Easter in year two, Ben said he had a surprise for me. He drove me to Home Depot and went to the customer service desk to claim an item he had purchased earlier. The clerk wheeled out a brand-new, bright yellow, self-propelled Lawn Boy push mower. Although I loathed the task it was designed for, it was an extremely generous gift. I was so simultaneously touched and repulsed, I cried at the cart return as he hoisted it into my Jeep.

I was not quite so touched by several of his other "practical" gifts. For our first Christmas, he gave me a book called *The Know-It-All*. It turned out to be an interesting account of one man's obsession with reading the Encyclopedia Britannica. Ben defended his selection by remembering I had told him that I did the same as a child, but it was a risky choice for an easily offended, mildly neurotic girl he hadn't known long. While useful, I found his practical gifts not nearly as much fun as jewelry or chocolate. He objected to flowers because they died, so I was gifted the occasional houseplant and whimsical indoor garden gnome to dangle from the pot's edge. Instead of chocolates, he gave me an excellent pair of Dr. Scholl's gel insoles because I was on my feet all day in court.

One of his gifts was a small, round package that completely defied all guessing as to its contents. The tag was addressed, "To Claire and her Jeep." I ripped into it to reveal a miniature, pop-up "rubbish bin" that he felt my vehicle lacked. My father saw it and burst into guffaws.

"You've seen the inside of that car? Good luck getting her to use it!"

"Thanks, Dad," To my horror, the talking continued.

"We pulled an entire Hefty bag of empty drink cans from underneath her front car seats when she was in college," my mother chimed in. I glared at her next.

"Why bother—her car is one big mobile recycling bin!" Ben added, cracking up everyone in the room but me.

After not quite two years had flown by in a long-running series of good dates, Ben gave me a beautiful engagement ring. I appreciated that gift and accepted without a second thought. No one else was willing to tolerate my mobile recycling bin on a long-term basis.

# A Tale of Two Weddings

### (Separated by a Common Language)

Once upon a time, there was an American lawyer[1] and a British engineer[2] who were separated by a common language, but were to be united in matrimony. They compromised on many things - she brewed him decent tea,[3] and he iced all her favo(u)rite beverages[4] - but to meet in the middle of Peoria, Illinois and Falmouth, Cornwall for a wedding ceremony was a cold, wet proposition.[5] Plans to shift the continents together have proven unsuccessful.[6] It wasn't hard to compromise on having two parties.

Our favo(u)rite American citizens[7] and subjects of Her Majesty[8] are invited to two ceremonies.

On Saturday, August 2, 2008, at 4:30 p.m., Claire Craig and Ben Evans will be married[9] at Sacred Heart Church[10] in Peoria, Illinois, surrounded by flat land and volumes of corn.[11]

On Saturday, August 30, 2008, at 4:30 p.m., they will renew their vows at the National Maritime Museum[12] in Falmouth, Cornwall, UK, surrounded by the sea and volumes of Cornish pasties.[13]

**Please save the dates on your calendars and plan to join us at the location(s) of your choice.**

_ele_

## Now Approaching the Island

I DIDN'T HAVE TO be a queen of deduction to figure out that, by marrying an Englishman on a short-term assignment to an American company while still on UK payroll, there might come a day when the source of his income would want him back. He was an expensive American houseguest. Besides ditching the felons, I thought moving to the UK would be a green and pleasant adventure. Thankfully, I had some UK experience to prop up my confidence about moving back with him.

_ele_

IN MY LAW SCHOOL era, I had spent the summer of 2001 studying abroad in London. I chose to visit during the nicest weather of the year, which factored into my liking the place as well as I did. I loved practically every minute, despite living four flights up in Dickensian student accommodation. There were times toward the end of my stay where all I wanted was a very tall iced tea, an abomination to most Britons. I also missed driving my convertible on the right side of the road in reliable sunshine. They sold convertibles in England, but surely the interiors got waterlogged by the constant threat of what BBC weather reports called "sharp showers."

I read all the guidebooks and watched all the *Rick Steves' Europe* episodes I could get my hands on. I learned that Americans threw around the terms English and British interchangeably, but British technically referred to anyone who came from any of the three smaller countries (England,

Scotland, and Wales) that made up the big island of Great Britain. (Although not on Great Britain, the people of Northern Ireland are also "British," even those who feel more Irish. But that's a whole other can of worms.) I stumbled upon a small dictionary of Cockney rhyming slang, which I quickly dismissed as graduate-level Britishness I wasn't ready for. At first, I was shocked that in Cockney rhyming slang, "Yanks" are "septic tanks." It dawned on me that the rest of the world stereotypes Americans as loud, demanding, and consuming more than their fair share of the world's resources, including ice. The guidebooks hinted that Americans weren't necessarily loved and cherished wherever in the world they decided to travel. I was not terribly worried about drawing negative attention to myself. I had a naturally quiet voice, and I would remember to recycle.

The prospect of spending those three months without some of my US must-haves made for an interesting game of Tetris in my suitcase. For years, I consumed an alarmingly large amount of cold beverages. At this point of my life, I could not cope without Country Time Lemonade mix. I had read all the UK brands would be different, and there was no guarantee Country Time would be six hours ahead. It was just as important as buying the right comparative law text, so I squirreled a couple of stupidly heavy Country Time containers into the corners of my case.

I had pre-trip jitters—I had never been responsible for navigating by myself in a foreign country before, so I studied all the ways to get from Heathrow to my dorm, on the University College London (UCL) Bloomsbury campus. I had copious notes about where in Heathrow I should pick up a particular, numbered double-decker bus, where it would drop me in North London, and how I would find my way on foot from the bus stop to my dorm, several blocks away.

I flew Virgin Atlantic from Chicago to Heathrow on a cheap student fare. The service was stellar and the miniature strawberry-and-cream with white chocolate ice cream bars were delightful. I was not as delighted when a child of about ten vomited orange juice on my jeans right after breakfast. I recovered and felt the buzz of international travel take hold.

As I wound my way out of Heathrow to ground transportation amongst unfamiliar announcements, I felt someone watching me. A young woman about my age had gotten off the same flight and kept herself about twenty paces behind me at any moment. When I paused at an overhead sign, she caught up and engaged me in conversation long enough to realize we were headed for the same destination.

"We should take a cab," she said. Her bloodshot eyes darted and her tone was demanding. She rummaged through her carry on and finally produced cigarettes. She lit one urgently.

I had spent weeks researching my budget travel strategy. Who was this frazzled stranger to glom onto me and start barking out my movements like a smokey general? I politely explained that many guidebooks said a Hackney cab was one of the most expensive ways to get into Central London. I was not deviating from my bus plan. My empathic tendencies absorbed energy from others, and I felt like a paper towel sent to clean up gallons of spilled, sour milk. I spied the bus I needed, and I was grateful for the excuse to part ways.

In hindsight, ten pounds of Country Time lemonade mix wasn't a good time for anyone when it came to hoicking my megalithic Samsonite into the bus luggage corral. I climbed to the upper deck, relaxing in the knowledge my plan was working until I spied the nervous general stub out her cigarette and get on the same bus at the last minute. I prayed she wouldn't be brave enough to climb the stairs and find a seat near me.

To get into the center, the bus took the major London ring road, the M25. My overtired mind would forget where I was for just a moment, and I would look up to see a torrent of small cars rushing toward us on the "wrong" side of the road. I caught myself bracing and cowering a few times, so I couldn't imagine how the nervous student was faring.

We arrived at the Hotel Russell just north of Russell Square, the nearest bus stop to the UCL dorm. I knew exactly where to get off, but I wasn't sure I could stifle the urge to tell the general exactly where to get off if she made any more demands. Getting myself to my destination was all I could handle, so I sped off the bus and down the sidewalk as fast as I could with a piece of seventy-pound luggage in tow. I oriented myself on the fly thanks to my Michelin spiral-bound pocket atlas of London. I had almost memorized the map of my new neighborhood.

I learned later that the general had successfully arrived, but locked herself in her room and smoked for the next two days to aid in her recovery.

I planned to keep quiet until I had a chance to watch London work, but I failed to account for the company I kept. A small group of my fellow American students joined me on a preliminary outing. We were scouting the route to school without being too obvious with our maps. We had collective volume, shorts, and Nikes that made blending in a lost cause. On the underground train system otherwise known as the Tube, we bantered away while the locals (given away by their impressive shoes) followed the commuter code—speak to no one and dive deep in a newspaper. Some locals had broken form and fanned themselves with their reading material, as summertime temperatures of 75°F can easily lead to temperatures of 82°F or so on the Tube.

We struggled with temperatures in the forecast. The US is one of the last bastions of the Fahrenheit scale. I'd been told 82°F (or 28°C) was the temperature statistically proven to cause mass fainting amongst old ladies at the Royal Cornwall Agricultural Show. It was like the State Fair with hot tea. UK summers were wardrobe conundrums because mornings were cold and shorts were a bit too ambitious at 9 a.m.

Frank from Ohio was a gregarious young Italian-American student with uncontrolled volume and temperature. He regretted his jeans decision and blasted it to everyone on the train.

"Man! The minute I get home, I have got to change out of these pants!"

Thanks to my years of Britcom viewing, I recognized his transatlantic language bomb. I covered my face with my hands and peeked through my fingers for the emergency exit. The usually unflappable locals flashed wry smiles and lowered their papers to take in the person who had said, in Britspeak, that for unknown and best undisclosed reasons, he required a fresh pair of underwear.

The learning curve was steep, but I was an attentive student. Despite American urban legend that England was an ice-free country, it was available in drinks if I requested it. When it came, it was probably one or two puny cubes, half melted by the time the bar staff passed the drink to me. There wasn't a nationwide moratorium on deep refrigeration. Rather, the UK simply did not subscribe to the concept of the free refill, let alone the thirty-two ounce Big Gulp. Ice watered down a drink and wasn't the ever-important "value for money." As thrifty as they were, British consumers felt outraged to pay for water unless it was fizzy or still and in a bottle. The rare exception to this rule was the TGI Fridays on Leicester (pronounced Lester) Square, where we could order profuse amounts of truly iced tea. The waitstaff listened for Americans and kept the free refills coming. After all, we were big tippers.

I walked from Bloomsbury to Trafalgar Square every day that summer, surrounded by the beauty of English pigeons. I found them attractive, especially the ones with a necklace of opalescent feathers that gleamed when they waddled into a sunny patch. Surely some innocent child had petitioned his mother to take one home, but they got a bad rap as "flying rats." London pigeons were immense creatures the size of small chickens,

well-fed on Burger King bun tidbits and shattered Ben & Jerry's waf-
fle cones. (They didn't object to the infiltration of American fast-food
chains.) Their tiny heads almost clucked as they waddled amongst edible
debris. On my student budget in pricey London, I had no doubt the
pigeons of Leicester Square ate much better than I did.

As opposed to expatriates who created litanies of what they miss from
their homeland, I tried to find new things to relish. I was addicted to cold
beverages and fruit, and no culture on earth combined the two as well as
the British. I struggled to drink my usual quantities of imported Country
Time lemonade, tempted by the wondrous selections of fruity refreshment
in the Marks & Spencer food hall on Oxford Street. There was pear and
ginger, elderflower cordial, blackberry and apple, mandarin, blackcurrant,
and a dizzying array of citrus offerings. My beverage dependence included
two new drugs: Lilt and Ribena. Lilt was a pineapple/grapefruit crush soda
manufactured by Coca-Cola, but cruelly unavailable in the United States.
Ribena was a black currant drink, available either in pre-mixed form or
highly concentrated syrup for diluting. It was high in vitamin C, so I had
the perfect excuse to go on a Ribena bender when a foreign cold struck.

—————·ℓℓ·—————

B EN AND I WERE married less than six months before our UK reloca-
tion plans began to crystallize. He had extended his American tour
to not quite five years, but his employer expected him to return to the UK.
He would have needed to convert his blanket work visa to a green card to
stay in the US much longer. Some Brits did this once they got used to living
in the States. It was easy to understand why, given the UK's high cost of
living and lower wages. As the US economy weakened after the financial
crisis of 2007–2008, international employees were even more expensive to
keep in the US after half a decade.

I agreed to entertain living in England, feeling confident about experiencing a new culture while putting my life lessons in ice and fruity beverages to good use. Even so, we did not know the day or the hour until about
six weeks before his British employer wanted him back.

In thirty-two years I had never lived more than a few hours away from
my family and I knew it would be difficult. In fact, it was hard to avoid
feeling disloyal to them, but at the same time, Ben's family was thrilled to
have him back in their country. It felt a bit like a war that we were doomed
to lose because someone's family would always be terribly far away.

For as much as I disparaged the felons at work, there were times it was
hard to get excited about quitting my fairly stress-free job as an assistant
state's attorney. It had taken many years for me to feel confident in most
of the unpredictable situations work threw me daily. I supervised another
younger attorney and had a legal secretary. I'd never not worked. I was
relieved to learn that a UK spouse visa would allow me to work, but the
major impediments were my American law degree and my specialty.

"An American criminal lawyer in the UK is about as useful as a chocolate teapot," Ben told me on a day I was feeling especially wary of leaving my career behind. I put on a brave face, but unfortunately, he was right. The seven years I'd spent on my degrees in addition to my body of experience didn't count for much in England's pleasant pastures. The equivalent of my job was something called a crown prosecutor for the Crown Prosecution Service, a UK government agency. It was a specialist area, and I could understand why recent graduates who grew up in the UK system would know far more about the job than I did. From what I could tell, it was theoretically possible for me to become qualified to work in the UK as a foreign-trained solicitor, but my prospects were slim. My specialized knowledge didn't translate well at all, especially in a down job market. I was anxious about finding something to do, especially since I didn't want to be a lady who lunched or a stay-at-home mum without children. We didn't even have pets.

On the other hand, I was ready to leave the felons behind. I had grown cynical since law school, largely due to DUI defendants who had the audacity to wear fleece Corona beer pajama bottoms to the hearings where we checked in on their community service and drug or alcohol treatment. A defendant representing himself called his mother to the stand as a character witness. When the bailiff called her, she was asleep on the benches and wearing a bright orange "Honorary Oompa-Loompa" T-shirt. I saw defendants—who breathalyzed more than three times the legal alcohol limit to drive—pass out on the courthouse's marble staircase en route to their hearing. Once in a while, a defense attorney with a morning court call would show up glassy-eyed and smelling a bit too much like peppermint schnapps. It could be depressing, especially when a young lawyer couldn't even manage to show up to his own DUI hearing without blown pupils. He said he knew he smelled of "cough medicine." I had a particularly heavy case go down that year where a defendant committed five DUI offenses in a relatively short timespan. Thanks to mandatory minimum sentencing, he received twenty-two years in prison for what was a Class X (a very serious) felony, and that meant he would probably die there, especially without access to the drug that had pickled him for the majority of his adult life.

I might be able to cross-train my skills in the UK, just as I had learned to handle what were mostly uncontested divorces for our local legal aid charity. I worked for women who had the misfortune of being married to drug addicts, jailbirds, alcoholics, or all-around deadbeats. We rarely could find and serve the soon-to-be ex-spouse, so getting them divorced and away from these men was a snap.

Once in a while, the case didn't go as planned. A very nice black woman wanted nothing more to do with her drug-addled husband. She had never been to court before, and I suggested she wear something appropriate, perhaps what she wore to church? She came to her divorce hearing wearing head-to-toe gold lamé, including matching shoes. She looked like a pair of Liberace's parlor curtains. As the time approached for our hearing, I waited with her in nervous anticipation of whether her deadbeat husband would show up. We had service by publication, but we couldn't physically locate him. Naturally, hearings where we accused the spouse of cruelty and drug use went much more smoothly if the perpetrator didn't bother to attend. At about one minute until the hearing was due to start, she nudged me and pointed out a small man approaching at a quick pace. She sighed, and we headed into court, where at least there were bailiffs to break up any urges to kill each other.

As expected, proving the grounds for her divorce was more annoying in his presence, but not more complicated. His credibility was undermined by the chunky home-confinement bracelet clearly visible around his ankle, a sign he was out on bond but generally not allowed to leave home without permission. I needed to work quickly. I didn't want the judge to continue an incomplete hearing, interrupted by the deputies bursting in to escort her husband to the county lock-up for violating home confinement. In our evidence portion, I had to ask my client about her husband's bad habits to prove they amounted to mental cruelty and unreasonable behavior.

"Did your husband ever make a habit of using illegal drugs in your presence?" I asked once she was sworn and on the stand.

The poor woman looked confused, despite my best efforts to prepare her. She looked at me for the answer only she could give. After several seconds' silence, she replied.

"Do *you* smoke crack in a pipe?"

This wasn't the hypothetical she meant to ask, emphasizing my habits versus whether a crack pipe qualified as illegal drugs. My eyebrows lifted halfway up my forehead. I looked at the judge. He looked as bemused as I did. He merely raised his shoulders and arms in a massive shrug of his black gown. I asked more questions. My client became reasonably confident that yes, one did smoke crack in a pipe, and her husband did that around her all the time. I had just managed to get her officially divorced when her ex asked the judge for a note to give to the home confinement officers. As if on cue, sirens started howling in the background. I told her that we shouldn't stick around to hear the answer and we left the court building by the quickest route possible.

Maybe working in a pastoral English tea shop serving Earl Grey and cake wouldn't be so bad.

We had to ship the contents of our home across the Atlantic by cargo container in six weeks' time, so I began giving possessions away like a woman whose days are numbered. We had a fire sale to rid ourselves of excess furniture, and our local Goodwill became a de facto second garage for all the things that used to be stored in ours. It was painful, but I pared down my inventory of sixty-five business suits to a mere dozen. A British expat friend of ours called his girlfriend's house a "bird's nest," the British female equivalent of a bachelor pad. My bird's nest had a master closet twice the square footage of my master bathroom. It had its own heating registers, with enough room for 120 business suits and a small refugee camp. If I was moving to an entirely new country, it would be important not to set myself up for failure by suffering through completely inadequate closet space. After we got married, I had moved from my house into Ben's place. I loved the river views but hated his puny 1930s closets. I had made inventory reductions just to move in with him—my collection of various real and fake designer handbags and shoes would have nearly filled a Buick. (My single-girl aunt still held the record for completely filling my grandpa's Buick LeSabre with shoes during her house move fifteen years earlier.) During my fall from closet heaven to the hell of Ben's storage space, I discovered that the four-foot hanging rail he cleared for me was not only insubstantial from a pure volume perspective, but that something under the rail left my dresses looking like tissue paper carnations. As the dam of frustration burst, I dove in and ferreted out a large plastic container holding an enormous, remote-controlled race car. I sputtered with rage and stomped off to accost him. I started to brim with tears. Would this radical change in hanging space be my new life in the UK? It was too much to ask.

"Here, take *this!*" I yelled as I shoved the container at him. He glanced around, likely for an escape route.

"I can't take it anymore, Ben. I have nowhere to hang my dresses..."

I dissolved into sniffing and phlegm. Emotional outbursts of this magnitude were relatively rare, so his eyes were wide and stunned. This only annoyed me further.

"Well, *say* something!"

"I had no idea you'd need room to hang your dresses." I'd seen such earnest expressions of horror before in photos of bomb blast survivors. His analytical, engineer mind was now recalculating his previous closet clear-out to account for longer hanging items.

Ben still owned the semi-detached (duplex) house in England he lived in before he moved to the States five years earlier, but when I asked if we'd move there, he didn't give me a definite answer. His house was on a busy street in an Italian neighborhood in Peterborough called Old Fletton. Seventy miles due north of London, Peterborough (pronounced Peter-burrah) was a fairly ancient city containing Bronze Age and Roman forts, and a magnificent medieval cathedral, the final resting place of King Henry VIII's first wife, Catherine of Aragon. It was home to some industry and retail distribution hubs, thanks to its proximity to motorways and its central location. In his absence, Ben's house had been let out to a family with two boys. I had seen pictures and knew for a fact one room was painted blood red and another minty green. There were only two closets in the entire house, so Ben still had giant wardrobes amongst his furniture that had held his clothing collection back home. The house in Peterborough had on-street parking and a garden shed, but no garage. I was starting to think that semi was short for semi-civilized. There was no air conditioning, basement, or forced air heating. Radiators that needed "bleeding" populated every room. The closet fracas got Ben thinking.

"We won't live in my house," Ben whispered to my mother over Easter dinner. "I don't think Claire would like living there."

I was trying not to be a fusspot, but I was greatly relieved when she conveyed this little nugget. The plan was to leave his tenants in situ and rent a house for ourselves, which we would find after we moved. We could live for six weeks on the company dime at the Marriott in Peterborough. Ben had tried to warn me not to expect closet space in any house we considered, but after all, he had been gone nearly six years. A lot could have changed. Maybe there'd been an English closet revolution, not covered in the mainstream press, where erstwhile citizens burned their old wardrobes and insisted on custom built-in closets as a sign of basic habitability and human rights. In the meantime, he had successfully persuaded me to acquire a beautiful antique wardrobe, just in case.

Ben was mindful of my sacrifices, but was reminded again of how much I was giving up during a series of dinners with a friendly American who had lived in England for the better part of six years. She was full of advice that left me perplexed. According to her, I would find England completely devoid of what she considered to be life's essentials, specifically Tampax tampons, iodized salt, and Old El Paso taco seasoning. During one of our dinners/lecture series, we were interrupted by her five-year-old child whimpering for attention and acting brutish toward his infant sibling. Without comment, his mother dug deep in her moving van of a handbag and placed a large, nylon serving spoon on the restaurant table. The offender's eyes widened with alarm, as if he had been silently threatened with unspeakable war crimes. We said nothing, but later, Ben questioned the musings of a woman who governed her children by kitchen utensil. I repeated her advice and he scoffed.

"Women in England have periods, too."

Granted, her pronouncements were nonsensical, skewing to paranoid, but she had lived in the UK for the better part of a decade. I gave her the benefit of the doubt and bought the family size Old El Paso shaker and Morton salt, just in case things had really gone to pot in the years Ben had been away. I wasn't about to import a year's supply of feminine products, even though they might come in handy should a luggage handler get rough with the suitcase that held our smuggled raspberry port. I planned to be a mule, but with far less street value.

I'd read about the infamous "Life in the UK" test, a controversial piece of the immigration puzzle that was required for citizenship. Starting in 2007, I couldn't apply for a long-term spouse visa without passing that exam as well. My provisional spouse visa was good for two years and nine months, but the thought of getting deported thereafter was never far from my mind. The test covered wide-ranging knowledge of UK culture and history. I was especially frightened because it had a 70 percent pass rate, just like the Illinois bar exam. Worse, an entire news desk's staff at the *New Statesman*, a UK political and cultural magazine, took the test as an experiment and failed. Critics from all sides wrote heaps of complaints in the press: it was impossible to test for "Britishness," the history facts were superficial and just plain wrong, and it was sexist in its lines of questioning. The mere fact that British people complained wasn't a slam dunk that anything was truly wrong—it looked like complaining, known in the UK as whinging (pronounced WIN-jing) was a national right and pastime. I would need to spend my time picking up breadcrumbs of UK history and culture if I had any hope of staying with Ben permanently.

Besides the "Life in the UK" test, the thought of driving in the UK unleashed a fountain of acid in my stomach. My first try at driving on the left was during a family visit. We took our hire car out late at night in rural Cornwall. As a criminal prosecutor, I knew minimizing witnesses was an excellent move. I heard Ben gritting his teeth as I consistently misjudged distance and bounced off the curb. Driving on the opposite side of the car reset everything I knew about how to keep it from careering around like a wayward pinball. Luckily, I was not hunted down by Interpol for unreported hubcap damage.

I was dutifully informed by another returned American expat that I needed driving lessons if I ever wanted to pass my UK driving test. Canadians could just swap their driving licenses for a UK version, but apparently, the UK Driving Agency was unwilling to bury the musket after the American Revolution. I had a year to pass the test. The average driver took twenty lessons before presenting for the exam. I had been driving for the better part of twenty years, I argued, but made no headway with my adamant expat advisor. Instead, he gave me a wry, "You'll see" smile, and I consoled myself with a massive, iced beverage from the specialty drinks menu as we dined in Peoria. I cherished driving home from work on the right, relishing my comfort zone while the clock ticked down to departure.

I couldn't change the motor vehicle code, but to put myself in a UK frame of mind, I began listening to as much Blur and Oasis as I could stand. I practiced boiling Ben's tea kettle with only the water we needed. So much for rampant American consumerism. I would get on absolutely fine.

I was grateful that much of becoming an expat would be handled for me. Ben's company took care of my provisional spouse visa. I was really looking forward to the prospect of having someone else pack my stuff. The company was paying for "full removal" in Britspeak, so I wouldn't really have to touch a thing, or so I thought. They sent along a chirpy man to survey our stuff, including the basement of doom where we stored all our wedding presents. He confidently declared they would need two days to pack, so I gave notice at the state's attorney's office and carried on offloading excess stuff. Finally, I was ready for the experts.

On the morning of our move, three hardy women arrived in a small truck, armed with dozens of flat-packed boxes, reams of tape, and spools of bubble wrap the size of hay bales. They proceeded to bubble wrap every piece of furniture in the house, and despite our attempts to contain them to rooms that were completely ready to pack, they strayed into no-fly zones. Thank God Ben was at work when I caught a sixty-plus-year-old woman wrestling to remove the pedals on the very expensive, carbon-fiber bike he had used in Ironman Brazil. The last person to touch it was a professional Brazilian bike mechanic named Paulo. Both Ben and Paulo would have been horrified to see her molesting it. I was sure that burly men would show up at any minute to wrap, say, the piano. I passed through the dining room, and to my utter shock and horror, two of the most certainly post-menopausal women I'd seen lately had deadlifted it. It was allegedly in the corner, completely bubble wrapped.

"We've been doing this since we were eighteen, sweetie," the bike mangler said, responding to my look of horror. "Anybody ready for a smoke?"

Our menopausal packing crew's favorite pastime was lamenting the two-day estimate the man in a suit had provided, sneering incredulously every time one of them mentioned it to each other. I did marvel at their speed, but puzzled over why they felt the need to disassemble an already collapsible laundry drying rack if they were so pressed for time. They were paid by the hour, but there would be no one but us on the other end to reassemble their handiwork.

Following their departure, the burly men with the truck showed up and packed everything into a series of smaller trucks. The cargo container that would hold it for its transatlantic journey wouldn't fit down our narrow, winding lane. Should they get it wrong, a semi would have just a few feet before our bluff ended and open air began. It was a wonderful location for viewing the river below, but a moving company's worst nightmare.

The burly men's favorite pastime was lamenting how heavy the burly women had made the dish pack boxes, especially the ones in the basement. They were down a flight of steep stairs and loaded with our beloved square, white plate set that wouldn't fit in Ben's shallow, 1930s wooden kitchen cabinets. To ease their pain, we offloaded a small fortune of Ben's considerable wine collection to the movers as tips. The company would not pay to ship alcohol after some oenophile ruined it for everyone—urban legend said he shipped his entire wine cellar abroad and incurred a heinous bill in import duty that the company ultimately paid. We kept the best of his cellar by giving it to my parents, who had their teeth cleaned more frequently than they drank alcohol. Ben bid *adieu* to his Chateauneuf du Pape, confident he'd see it again one day.

The movers were gone, and so were mostly all our earthly possessions for the next six weeks. We had that same amount of time reserved in Peterborough's Marriott, and a ticking six-week timer to find a house that would accommodate it all before the company stopped paying our hotel bill. It was best not to bite off too much at once. We had just packed up our entire life, wished my family well, and we had worn ourselves thin winding down our American existence.

There was one priority item left on our lengthy to-do list. We went to Club Med Turkoise on Turks and Caicos, watched lizards on the beach, and tried not to think about our house contents now floating somewhere in the north Atlantic.

# Part Two:

## Landfall

*There is a certain relief in change, even though it ebb from bad to worse; as I have found in traveling in a stagecoach, that it is often a comfort to shift one's position and be bounced in a new place.*

– Washington Irving, American writer and historian

## Just Marriotted

FOR ALL THE APPEAL a jet-setter lifestyle holds, one part they can keep is living out of a suitcase. We learned our cargo container crossed the ocean in two weeks' time instead of the six we were expecting, but the moving company was happy to store it for a few more weeks as we were technically homeless.

We got a quick air shipment of things we would need right away. I'd had the foresight to pack pots, pans, and towels as our bare necessities. Using the focus of hindsight, these things really aren't necessary until you actually have a house to live in. Another bit of madness was my insistence on taking a particular brand of diet shake so I could carry on the weight-reduction campaign I had successfully launched before we knew about our location change. Packing the bathroom scale in my carry-on luggage was a bit much, especially after more than a month of eating out began to take its toll. I detected a few eye rolls from Ben, especially when my carry-on contents provoked a fairly rigorous round of questioning by an unintelligible customs official at the Turks and Caicos airport. Thankfully, I looked more like a bake-off winner than a drug kingpin.

The Peterborough Marriott hotel was the hub around which arriving and departing expats congregated. We ran into an American Ben knew from the States, along with his wife, who were on their way back to the US after a few years of island living. We lamented our lengthy hotel stay to what we thought were sympathetic ears.

"But you'll definitely make Silver this year, if not Gold!" the man's wife said. I didn't understand her point. I knew it wasn't an Olympic year, despite having a shot at winning a medal for overpacking.

She was referring to our preferred Marriott customer status. We were gaining Marriott rewards points at the speed of light, but losing a bit of our souls in the process. I felt irrationally ungrateful. After all, I was the best stabled homeless person I knew.

This hotel contained a large, outdoor courtyard that every room overlooked. A mammoth willow tree grew at its center, and a warren of rabbits had established an estate under its considerable root structure. I started calling it Longear. It fit the naming conventions of other local places I'd seen on the map: Crowland, Dogsthorpe, Eye Green. Late afternoon was rabbit happy hour, with my all-time record for most rabbits sighted in one place set at twenty-seven. I was unemployed, so I watched a lot of rabbits and daytime television in those days. Thanks to various cooking shows, I was horrified to learn how common it was to include rabbit in any number of country stews. I had to change the channel out of respect for my neighbors.

I tried to get out long enough each day to make sure the cleaning staff knew I actually left. I preferred a travel companion, and it was intimidating to be out on my own so much while Ben was at work. He had the company rental car and I wasn't brave enough to drive on my own just days after my arrival anyway. Occasionally I took the bus to places of interest, but I found walking paths got me to interesting places without spending bus fare. One took me to a small lake that gave sailing lessons. Along the way, I passed ponies at a riding stable who happily crunched through the pits of wild plums they would pluck from the damson trees on the public footpath. I occasionally had to dodge horses, as the footpath doubled as a bridleway.

Six weeks was a long time to live in a hotel. I missed making my own toast. Everyone from dining to maintenance addressed me by name without any prompting. I found it disturbing that housekeeping straightened the already folded stacks of underwear I'd just brought back from the laundromat. I became fully conversant with every item offered on the breakfast buffet. I needed a vocation, so I made it my personal mission to "helpfully" give a breakfast debriefing to those hapless Americans who occasionally passed through. My buffet patter was roughly as follows: beans were a surprising, but legitimate, part of a full English breakfast, and nothing like the sugary, smokey baked beans of most American barbecues. Black pudding was gross and not even worth trying unless a person approved of blood as a seasoning agent. Conversely, Alpen cereal was earthy but darned tasty. Try to avoid UHT long-life milk. In the words of a semi-famous television quote from the sitcom *Father Ted*, "There's no demand for that because it's shite." Fried bread would probably kill you in the end and I was surprised Americans hadn't thought of it long ago. Finally, Marmite was a sticky, black yeast spread sampled at their peril. Even the marketing campaign admitted you either loved it or hated it. How it ever got past test marketing stumped me.

Stress levels soared during the six weeks that our hotel stay and cargo storage would be gratis. Ben was only free outside business hours, so we spent every weekend traversing any areas that looked to have promising homes to let. Our colossal rental Volvo station wagon was a liability, though I didn't remember that model looking nearly so large in the US. Ben thought I could handle it with a bit of practice, but he'd learned his lesson by letting me practice maneuvering it near a farm outbuilding. To his horror, we found that indeed, I could hit the broad side of a barn with a large Swedish car that could host its own smorgasbord. No one in the UK drove a car that big. It just didn't fit in Britain's shrunken car park spaces. After one incident where Ben himself nearly got the thing stuck in a narrow ramp of a multi-story car park (Britspeak for parking ramp), we downsized to a little silver Skoda that looked a bit larger than a child's toy. It made a wind-up sound when accelerating between gear shifts, which prompted me to look for the clockworks. Unlike the Volvo, it had a manual transmission. I could drive a manual, but shifting with my left hand while simultaneously sitting on the right side of the car and driving down the left side of the road felt like I had landed squarely in an alternate reality where tea flowed in the rivers. Ben sensed it was best not to rush me into driving alone or he'd risk a mental break not unlike the remote-control car incident that seemed like a lifetime ago.

We refused to pay £30 per day ($45 US) to gain access to the internet at the hotel, even when the company got the bill, so I compiled a list of local watering holes with free wi-fi. I was primary house hunter as my new occupation. My search revealed a series of homes that rented for astronomical amounts and had main room sizes that paled compared to my old walk-in closet. I kept reading about the "bijou" proportions of some properties on the rental market. "Bijou" was UK estate agent code for minuscule.

I was starting to think that England was the real-life Lilliput. Everything had shrunk – the roads, the homes, the furnishings, the clothes, the washing machines, the milk jugs, most of the cars, and the car parks to put them in. Clothes shopping was difficult for someone who boxed in a higher weight class. Garment construction was either cheap or really elaborate. Either way, sizes were small and prices exorbitant. I was expecting friendly Mr. Humphries, from the Britcom *Are You Being Served,* to pop out around a clothes rack and sashay over to help, but finding a shop assistant was like winning the National Lottery. The lines were so long, I knew why waiting was part of British DNA. Shop workers didn't spring into action to help like I remembered in the US. Even the shoe sizes were two smaller than my foot used to be. I didn't mind this particular Lilliputian experience too terribly.

Our most disheartening house tour was of a bungalow (Britspeak for ranch house) in a good location with decent room sizes, but with a layout conceived by someone who spent his later years at an asylum. Ben reckoned that despite the two-car attached garage, it was geometrically impossible to put a car in the garage with less than a fifty-point turn. Worse yet, the master bedroom was connected to the garage for all those times that the first thing you wanted to do upon returning home was tumble through the door and fall into bed. Upstairs, there were steeply inclined dormer bedroom ceilings sure to produce clouds of obscenity and concussions on sleepy mornings when I forgot I was living in a children's playhouse. We furrowed our noses and returned to the lettings office to decline, only to learn this madman's playground was already let. Like so many other properties, it was snapped up less than a half hour after the "To Let" listing appeared online.

As I scouted for properties to rent in the more upmarket countryside settings, I would occasionally come across an ad that touted a "shepherd's hut" somewhere on the premises. One picture was of a very nice little cabin on wheels, with a curved roof and a cast iron stove inside. These could be the UK equivalent of "man caves" or "she-sheds," or potential home offices if they were extra fancy. Apparently, the selling point was their versatility and that was reflected in the rent.

"For that price, is the shepherd included?" I asked Ben.

"Maybe. We could put him to work herding your shoes."

I never quite got the allure of a shepherd's hut or their price tags. To my mind, shepherd's huts were fairly bougie and not the image I was going for. I rolled my eyes and ruled out any listing that included one.

I also discounted a 1930s bungalow in a desirable, small market town location. The estate agent hadn't shared that it was sketchily rewired by an American serviceman on a nearby US airbase. It came with an eighty-year-old bidet. It was adjacent to a disused stone windmill with four-foot walls, the base of which had been turned into the sturdiest single-car garage the world had ever known. We were starting to suffer from too much hotel food and lack of somewhere to root, but we couldn't take the chance of random electrocution.

Freedom came in the form of a 1980s palace in a Peterborough neighborhood called Orton Wistow, on a lane called The Rookery. It was adjacent to a country park and had comparatively large rooms. The earth-tone curtains depicted small natives in yurts and emitted a menacing cloud of dust at the slightest touch. The kitchen's faux wicker cabinetry was permanently sticky from years of vaporized chip (french fry) fat. The kitchen floor was a tessellation of Grecian pool shapes, originally the color of flesh before the dirt of three decades permanently impregnated the linoleum. Ben wondered aloud if the house had been featured on an imaginary home decorating show called *Nan or Man*. Sure enough, the bungalow belonged to an old woman who was recently relegated to a rest home. The funk of 40,000 years hung heavy in the air, but the private garden was beautiful, if overgrown. Ben puzzled at a weathered little plastic goose that sat next to a miniature bird bath. I thought it might have held bubble bath at some point during the Thatcher administration. We hopped on letting it based on our experience with the madman's lair, and rang the removals firm with the wonderful news that we had somewhere to unload all our stuff.

The movers arrived in tandem. First, there was the well-paid driver who arrived from the seaport Felixstowe with our cargo container on a large, flat-bed truck. It was impossible for the truck to get closer than a hundred feet from our front door, thanks to a quintessentially British, narrow cul-de-sac. The firm would first need to offload all our things to their own van. The expensive container and its driver were paid by the hour.

Many of the removals staff were downright petite, save one elderly, burly gentleman from Yorkshire. (Thanks to Ben, I knew to pronounce it YORK-shur, as opposed to the Shire in *The Hobbit*.) The men got along just fine, but they clearly expected me to supply them with tea on demand. To me, that felt like an unreasonable request. I was not stopping to make myself a tea, nor was I sure I could lay hands on enough mugs and fresh milk to meet their needs. But even I could see that resistance was dangerous to the health of our belongings. Thankfully, Ben had acquired a kettle before we had a house to put it in, so I promptly unpacked it from the boot of our car and boiled water for the good of morale.

We saw an older, blonde woman marching toward us with a seriously senior citizen shuffling behind her. It was the daughter of our ninety-year-old new neighbor. She offered a cursory introduction, then told us that our movers would have to carry all our possessions an extra hundred feet because she knew the van would structurally undermine our one-year-old asphalt common drive.

" 'Twould greatly worry Mummy." Mummy was staring into space. She was yellow with age and nicotine. She didn't look worried about anything except where her next smoke was coming from. Her daughter claimed Mummy fretted about phantom Styrofoam stuffed in her bins or cosmetically irksome Sky TV satellites. I wasn't buying it—I could see Mummy's cataracts from twenty paces.

I tried chatting with Mummy shortly after we moved in. She had the lung capacity and ongoing resentment of an old French man.

"Far div ye bide?" She stared at me for an answer. Hell if I knew. She pointed to our new home next door.

"Wee broon hoose?"

"Yes!" She saw the lightbulb in my eyes after so much effort.

"Och...I shid niver hae moved fae Aiberdeen!"

She waved me into her house, and I stepped one foot over her threshold into the front hall. It was originally cream, but after so much pollution, the color was closer to *cafe au lait*. I'd been in fresher-smelling billiard parlors.

I learned later that her Doric dialect was one of the most unintelligible of all the Scottish accents, but she'd been in England around seventy years. The smoldering cigarette in her hand trembled as wafts of blue smoke billowed past me and out her front door. My eyes teared.

"Ma quine said am tae cam roon fur Christmas denner wi the geets..." She trailed off and stared. Her voice had the gusto people reserve for describing their next colonoscopy.

"That's nice," I said. I understood the word "Christmas." I was desperate for subtitles.

"Och, noooo... Aiberdeen..."

Clearly, Mummy was being menaced by a retired child who relished inventing little gripes on her behalf. She might enjoy some company, so I risked it. "Would you like to have a cup of tea?"

"Nae, dinna fash yersel. [No, don't trouble yourself.] Ma tea'sn the oven." It was 4:30 in the afternoon. I had no idea what to do with this comment. Did Brits store their tea mugs in the oven to keep their drinks warm? She stared me down for a few seconds through the fog.

"Canna stand aboot en. Ah need tae eat ma tea th'noo!" Her petite body lurched toward me, and I stumbled backward. Once I'd cleared the frame, she shut the door in my face.

I pictured both the air and her milky tea so thick she could cut them with a fork and knife. After a few minutes of confusion, I figured out she was using "tea" to mean dinner. So much for neighborly friendship. At this stage of her life, she had been smoked like Scottish salmon, and she was best left to waft in peace.

I also took some pity on the removals men, whose pet topic was how poorly their American counterparts had packed our belongings into the cargo container. This was clearly a well-rehearsed routine performed for our benefit, meant to soundly deflect any damage accusations at their hands. I was ready to accept their opinion, based on our newly broken sofa frame, lots of surface marring of antique furniture, and one small antique chest that looked like an unattended piece of airport luggage after a visit from the bomb squad. We were grateful our stuff hadn't met the same fate as one cargo container of corporate legend that Ben saw on an email chain—a container diagonally wedged between a cargo ship and the concrete dock after being dropped by a crane at port. The story ended with all of the container's contents in toothpicks and a giant settlement check cut to its unlucky owners.

To allay the guilt I felt at such diminutive people carrying such heavy loads, I thought I would offer them a sandwich on their lunch break. I walked a large plate of peanut butter and strawberry jam sandwiches out to the back of the lorry (truck), where they had all congregated for their cigarettes and tea. I saw nothing but distorted faces and not a single taker. I didn't realize that the American standby of peanut butter and jelly is an unholy combination for the British, only explored by the very young who have been exposed to its controversy by watching too much American television. After I told him what happened, Ben said this was the best move I could have ever made to ensure the crew never approached us for anything ever again.

We were given the number of a reputable antiques restoration firm outside London for all our cracked, scratched, and exploded furniture needs. I knew that many English people lived, worked, and socialized in properties several hundred years old or more. Surely restoring our comparatively juvenile 1930s sideboard would be a mere trifle. And now that we actually had a kitchen, I could ditch the *Rime of the Ancient Mariner* thoughts and move my saucepans from around my neck into my cabinets. Ben went straight to John Lewis department store and bought "The Animal"—a Dyson meant for the worst dirt and fluff. He snapped the attachments together with precision, ready to assassinate any remaining dirt on the yurt curtains. We were home.

## Caution: Contents May Settle

I KNEW IN MY head I should explore my new surroundings. How was I ever going to know enough about "Life in the UK" if all I did was watch excellent British television and stare at the giant wood pigeons in the miniature birdbath? But arriving in a new place with no friends, no job, and no sense of direction conspired to keep me at home. I missed having somewhere to go every day, especially somewhere that paid me money to show up and be useful. For long and boring reasons, my American law degree—seven years of higher education—didn't translate into an English credential, so I was just like any other joe looking for work in the 2009 recession. I had heaps of instantly irrelevant work experience and a language gap. Some days, I even missed the felons. I desperately wanted company, but at the time, I didn't grasp that in order to meet friends, I needed to leave the house. Most people my age either worked, or if they were home, had children to look after. I had no kids, and frankly, found their debris fields scary. After so many weeks on end feeling homeless, all I wanted was to cocoon. I was frustrated with myself because the English summer was passing me by.

Instead of spending those initial days getting the lay of the hedgerows in our new neighborhood after Ben had gone to work, I developed an unhealthy relationship with a Facebook-based game called *FarmVille*. A player had a bit of money and a small plot to sow with purchased seeds. By returning after a certain amount of time, she could harvest and sell her crops for more money, allowing her to progress through the levels of flashier farm implements and expand her plot into more exotic produce. I never have been much into games, but I felt profound gratitude when I logged in after breakfast to find my *FarmVille* friends back in the States had gifted me chickens and apple trees overnight. Of course, I needed to reciprocate with a sheep and a lemon tree. My crops became more sophisticated as my fortunes grew—I had worked my way up from boring corn to pomegranates and avocados. I knew it was time to reexamine my choice of recreational activities when I insisted on returning home from dinner out to pick my cotton before it withered on the bushes and I wouldn't have the money to buy the pink tractor I wanted. Ben didn't say much, but his look helped me grasp my own ridiculousness. A therapist would have said I "gained insight."

I was lucky that my cultural insight was progressing at a faster pace than fellow Americans who hung out with only Americans. I had a British spouse to keep me grounded—he'd remind me that it was possible to exist in a universe with different ways of doing the same things. I was warned against spending too much time with Americans who were short timers, especially female "trailing spouses" who followed their husbands all over the globe on international work assignments. I understood—back in the States, I'd witnessed a group of UK expats fall into massive gripe sessions about "cowboy" Americans' love of huge portions, iced tea, and inferior cheese. After a while, it was exhausting. It also struck me as ungrateful because I knew first-hand how few expenses these houseguests paid in the country they seemed to hate.

When I became a stranger in a strange land, I suspended my disbelief and met with a few Americans who embraced their new surroundings. But like déjà vu, I saw groups of American expats take joy in reciting a litany of complaints about all that was wrong with the UK. They ranged from underpowered clothes driers to mandatory MOT inspections. (Unlike the

US, the UK's Ministry of Transport requires vehicle owners to prove their cars are roadworthy once a year.) I didn't want to get trapped at a surprise pity party, so I chose my American company carefully.

British daytime television added to my social inertia. It was all so new and interesting, and I rationalized that I was improving my cultural knowledge. We had to pay for a TV license, about £150 per year (but only £50 if our television was black and white). There was only a 50 percent discount if you were blind, which I found a bit ungenerous given the circumstances. TV license funds paid for the British Broadcasting Corporation (BBC): commercial-free television, radio, and all of the related web sites. At first I found the cost appalling, but living in a world without so many commercials was worth it. I discovered British television networks routinely air adult content after 9 p.m., still in the danger zone for older children. A medical series showed absolutely every angle of the human body, which I was unprepared for watching in my living room at age thirty-three. The history and culture programming was infinitely more interesting that what my beloved PBS offered back in the US.

I grew particularly fond of antiques game shows, particularly one called *Bargain Hunt*. Contestants were given money to purchase their choice of three mostly hideous bric-a-brac items at various antique fairs around the country with the object to make money once their items were auctioned later in the show. There was also a show called *Dickinson's Real Deal* where contestants took their chances weighing an antique dealer's offer for their old crap versus what auction might bring them. This show was hosted by a goofy older man who had tanned himself into an alarming shade of quarry tile terra cotta. Thankfully, I was put off enough by him to shut off the TV and try out the local municipal pool.

It was still summertime, and the living in a foreign place wasn't exactly easy. Despite my inertia, I located what looked like a splendid outdoor pool in Peterborough called the Lido. As I learned, lidos, or large outdoor pools, used to be common and many were built in the art deco era. It was increasingly rare to have one still open and functioning because of their maintenance costs. As an avid swimmer I rejoiced—the Lido's website said it was both Olympic-size and heated. The water looked relatively clean and the building next to it was doing well for its age. I arrived just after nine in the morning to avoid the kids on summer holidays from school, which usually starts mid-July.

The pool was empty, except for two men swimming laps. One had just done a flip turn in his Speedo and was clearly powering through his English Channel training. The other swimmer was approaching from the far end of the pool, but his body did not match the color of his pinkish face as he drew nearer. This older man was wearing a wetsuit, which gave me a shiver in itself. By the middle of July, there had been perhaps two days all summer where the temperature broke 80°F. I should have turned on my flip flop and tried an indoor pool, but I was too committed to flee. I was standing there in my swim cap and goggles, and had already chatted to the lifeguard in his Ray-Bans. Besides, the pool was heated. I strode to the deep end and jumped in.

The frigid water hit me like a million tiny needles at once. I could feel my breath leaving me and my limbs growing rubbery. I sputtered to the surface and waved to the lifeguard to assure him I wasn't drowning. I scuttled to the side of the pool and tried to move every part of my body that would cooperate in a desperate attempt to keep warm. We had an in-ground pool growing up that might get up to eighty degrees in a run of baking summer days. Surely this water temperature was fifty-something. My toes felt blue, but my legs were flailing so fast that I couldn't actually see them. The man in the wetsuit gave me a smug grin as he glided past. I did ultimately attempt a swim.

After losing feeling in my face, I got out and felt compelled to interrogate the lifeguard. "I thought this pool was supposed to be heated!" My teeth were chattering.

"It is, love. But we don't turn it on much. If we did, you wouldn't appreciate the warm day," he beamed, as he held out his hand and caught a bit of rare British sunshine, superior in his dry lifeguard uniform and Ray-Bans. What a warm bastard.

I sighed and pictured large, steaming mugs of cocoa as I fashioned my beach towel into a burqa. His words were vaguely familiar. I got a flashback to Ben in the States, objecting to me turning up the heat in his car to full blast on a sub-zero night. To me, the heat in such cold weather was one of the most pleasant experiences I could have, but Ben switched the fan down. "You won't appreciate the warmth once we're home," he warned. Appreciating warmth? What was this British penchant for self-torture? Why couldn't we appreciate warmth in a number of locations? It must have been a warped bit of leftover wartime make-do. It reminded me of the groups of "ramblers" who marched over countless miles of wild countryside on the weekends, yet described their activities as "going for a little walk." I was finding that the English were fond of rationalizing deprivation as a tool for feeling gratitude. Had they not been introduced to the ubiquitous "Grateful" porch signs that pop up around the States at Thanksgiving time? Surely they could express appreciation via their décor choices and spare the nation vast amounts of collective misery.

Eventually I stumbled upon a bargain-basement wet suit at the marvelous jumble sale grocer/retailer, Aldi. Wrapped in cheap neoprene, I braved a return trip to the Lido. The man in the wetsuit gave me a knowing nod of approval while the lifeguard flirted with bikini-clad young women. I heard their screams as they ventured in the water to their ankles and rushed back out again. Amateurs.

I moved into the indoor public pool for a warmer experience. I enjoyed water aerobics, and as I was fiddling with my floatie belt in a somewhat geriatric-populated class, I spied a large, dark pink splotch on the shoulder blade of a woman who had acquired a certain patina. She looked the wrong side of seventy if she was a day and I pitied the poor soul. She had probably undergone an unpleasant laser treatment or skin biopsy for a condition ending in "oma." The instructor called out to paddle into a circle formation during the last minute of "Disco Inferno," and I found myself bobbing behind the "oma." I tried not to stare, but the temptation was overpowering. Upon closer scrutiny, her skin affliction was actually a freshly inked pink elephant that loafed across her entire left shoulder blade. I felt a pang of guilt and looked away, but not in time. She splashed me in the face with her floaty water dumbbell. At least I was blinded and spared from further visual assault.

Tattoos were everywhere in the UK, and they didn't carry quite the stigma as they did in the US. Of the two schools of thought on tattoos, I am firmly enrolled in Anti-Tramp Stamp U. Not only are they permanent signs of a temporary fancy, but what sounds like a fine idea after a few drinks in youth turns into a shapeless blob with age. (I mean the tattoo, not its wearer.) I spied a manly, professional gentleman who looked perilously close to retirement, but the tattoos all up and down his forearms retired years ago. One blob looked like a ladies' handbag. Could he have foreseen that effect?

I knew a girl in college who was particularly proud of flashing everyone a small Kermit the Frog she had tattooed in her underwear zone. Some women with tattoos were obsessed with showing the world their poor judgment. A girl pouring drinks at a pub turned to get a bottle, and I noticed the bigger-than-life bat wings tattooed on her back. Weren't there easier and cheaper ways to look like one of Satan's minions?

I cheered up when Ben and I found a newly refurbished indoor pool for me to swim in at a local health club. The changing room didn't smell of wee and there were fewer tattoo-ligans than at the municipal pool. A group of women I called the gray-haired mafia completely booked up a large number of the daytime land exercise classes, but there was a rare opening left in one morning's aqua aerobics. I hopped on the last slot. Another term for a retiree in the UK is "OAP," island lingo for old age pensioner. If I saw them having tea and cake en masse in a particular venue, it generally boded well for quality. I applied the same rule to aqua aerobics.

I was no stranger to aqua aerobics, Stateside or in the UK. Apart from the smell and tattoos, the class at the municipal pool had been very good. Just because aqua aerobics was frequented by older women did not mean the classes had to be feeble. My favorite water aerobics class at a YWCA back in the States left me gasping and struggling not to gulp pool water.

The health club instructor was a white-haired woman in reasonable shape. Upon arrival, average age looked to be sixty, but far worse was the sight of every one but me wearing a headband with little yellow spring-mounted bear ears attached. I had forgotten that day was a na-tionwide fundraiser called Children in Need, which benefited the Great Ormond Street Children's Hospital in London. Their mascot was Pudsey the bear, and this group had taken the philanthropic spirit to a new and cheesy level. I wasn't much of a joiner when it came to wearing hokey things—I used to object to my ID badge at work, but it was useful for opening locked doors. I also loathed hats, or anything on my head, for that matter. I was, however, feeling strong urges to belong in my new country, so I succumbed to the groupthink and donned a pair of ears.

The musical selection was a combination of remixed ABBA and every Beatles song ever written. I didn't know it was possible to work "Eleanor Rigby" into an exercise mix. I reluctantly participated, in half-gestures, when the entire class danced the YMCA. All in all, the class was lame. It was hard to justify changing into a swimsuit and showering when I could have stayed home and learned to knit for the same caloric expenditure. Regardless, I tried to make it as challenging as possible for myself without getting too carried away and being branded a rabble rouser. When the kegel exercises started, I knew for sure this was a waterborne waste of time.

After class, I was keen to jettison my stupid sponge bear ears and flee when the instructor spoke to me, still wearing her microphone.

"Is this your first aqua aerobics class?" I immediately expected her to compliment my apparent aqua savant-ness, my perfect form, or suggest a higher intensity class.

"Oh, no."

"Well, the first rule of aqua aerobics is no gum. *Lose it!*"

I was stunned and mentally transported back to my primary school library, where Mrs. Howsell magically divined the presence of bubble gum amongst eight-year-olds and issued its chewers ugly two-cent fines.

I stammered an apology and an excuse—that I had forgotten I was chewing gum. I resisted the urge to swallow it on the spot. As an act of rebellion, I seethed in my soaking wet swimsuit and chomped even harder as I stared in her direction. To think I had put on those stupid ears for this.

In hindsight, I don't regret my gum chewing. I'm sure it produced my highest calorie burn of the hour.

—eee—

NOT LONG AFTER OUR arrival, Ben's mother and her husband visited from Cornwall. Ben had to work one day of their stay, so just the three of us set out in search of a culture segment. I was accustomed to this as Ben had adopted his father's habit of incorporating cultural appreciation into family outings wherever possible to improve their overall tone and educational value. It was a bit more highbrow than American parents fixated on driving a couple hundred miles out of their way to see the world's largest ball of rubber bands.

We decided on a place called Flag Fen. Flag referred to the flag iris, which was a wetland plant native to the area. In the 1700s the Fens had been drained and converted to extremely fertile farmland by Dutch experts in dewatering low-lying areas. This was excellent news because I wasn't up for donning rental hip waders or whipping out my new wetsuit. I got cranky during rain showers in those early days. I was surprised and disappointed about how often they descended out of oatmeal-colored skies without warning, unlike the alien spaceship storm clouds that stretched for hundreds of miles in the Midwest.

Flag Fen was an archaeological site dating to the Bronze Age, which made it around 3,500 years old. Our tour guide was a pleasant older gentleman in a windbreaker who kept reminding us that while there were Celtic people there in the Bronze Age, there were a lot of unknowns because no one was taking notes, unlike those clever Egyptians who wrote everything down. My cultural companions, stalwarts of the wild Cornish coast, came equipped with completely waterproof, hooded windbreakers. In contrast, I was trying to make do with a shabby jacket, left over from my days of walking everywhere in college. I used this learning opportunity to realize that, in England, my umbrella should be omnipresent, extendible, and an extension of my personality. I especially admired one decorated with pictures of frosted donuts.

The builders found Flag Fen after World War II when the city of Peterborough began excavations for a new power plant. They unearthed a giant wooden platform the size of London's Wembley Stadium, supported by 60,000 upright timbers that had been sunk into the peaty, watery fen for thousands of years. As a result, they were perfectly preserved, without exposure to the oxygen that causes rot. Some ancient finds were exposed to air in a viewing pit, but sprinkled on the minute with water to keep them from turning to dust. The display's corporate sponsor was, naturally, the local water company.

I used to be an avid viewer of the PBS home improvement show *This Old House*. I was a groupie of Norm Abram, the show's humble, flannel-clad master carpenter. I couldn't help thinking that splintering and threatened wood rot on this scale would be his worst nightmare.

Not only did archaeologists find a giant promenade deck, but all manner of well-preserved cast-offs tossed into the surrounding peaty bog. In fact, some artifacts weren't thrown away at all. There were pieces of clothing, rare gold jewelry, pots, bones from joints of meat, dog skeletons, human skeletons, metal shears, glass beads, rare wooden handles from axes, and what's believed to be oldest wheel in England. If only the monks of the dark ages had taken up the actual sport of bog snorkeling, they wouldn't have had to reinvent the wheel.

Ben happened to call me from work on my mobile phone to check our guests' status while they were in my sole custody. My jazzy Nokia tune disrupted the ambiance of furiously itchy burlap clothing and stinky hanging animal carcasses that surrounded me. These turfy homes would never work nowadays. All that grass growing on the roof led to terrible mobile reception. And who would want to get up there and weed it?

He skipped his usual pleasantries. "Where are you now?

"I've just stepped out of a model roundhouse," I said, choking from the smoke of the roasted jerky demonstration going on inside. "I'm staring at the turf roof."

"Good. When's the last time they had tea?"

*Ahh.* Ben knew my ideas on the appropriate interval for tea administration were inadequate by his standards (and the rest of the island's). I checked my watch.

"About three hours ago."

"Oh dear." His tone was serious. "Oh dear" was the most popular, all-purpose British lamentation. To my ears, it sounded like something Ancient Aunt Bea might say upon discovering the village of Mayberry was out of headache powder.

"Best find a tea shop straight away." He hung up.

After giving the phone a dismal look, I took a survey of my guests.

"Is anyone up for a cup of tea?"

"Yes, please!" they said in stereo, with the enthusiasm the foreign legion had for taking a water break in the Sahara. We managed to avoid being headbutted by the menacing rare-breed sheep as we beat a hasty retreat. In a moment of déjà vu while settling in for refreshments at the nearest Sainsbury's grocery store cafe, I realized that PG Tips, without milk, is exactly the color of the peaty water preserving the wooden spikes at Flag Fen. I decided to monitor Ben and his six-cuppa-day habit to see if the beverage had the same preservative power.

As I'd learned the hard way, tea was a sensitive subject in the UK, provoking emotional responses regarding what was proper and what was just wrong. Contrary to what most Americans thought, "high tea" wasn't a ritzy, pinkies-out affair, decorated with cucumber sandwiches and scones with jam and clotted cream. That would be afternoon tea. High tea was usually shortened to just "tea." It meant the big meal of the day, the only thing I'd learned from Mummy next door. "What are we having for tea tonight?" was a very British way of asking, "What's for dinner?" The names for meals in the UK vary widely by region and class. It was a minefield for residents, let alone visitors.

Ben and I could not agree on fruit tea. He was so convinced that fruit tea is tea blasphemy, in fact, that he referred to it as "so-called fruit tea." I couldn't imagine myself having this conversation anywhere else in the world but England. As with all fruity beverages other than a vile, fizzy and unsweetened quaff called Vimto, I was a fruit-tea addict with no desire to go to rehab. Despite Ben's violently held opinion, fruit tea abounded in the UK and was completely legitimate. My favorites were blackcurrant, blood orange, and rhubarb. It was sold the country over, in the shops and in tearooms, at the national grocery store chain, Tesco, and even the occasional quick mart for those who couldn't bear to be away from fruit for any significant length of time.

I did drink the occasional cup of "real" strong black tea with sweetener and milk, though I couldn't fathom the caffeine tolerance that the British have evolved over hundreds of years. Tea was a bedrock of international trade for five centuries, with the Portuguese princess Catherine of Braganza to blame for introducing the stuff to the English court and creating hundreds of years of addiction. I wasn't a tea-seeking missile like some Brits, but I didn't agree with the American television character Ted Lasso when he called British tea "hot garbage water."

On the first occasions I'd had afternoon tea in a tearoom, I hoped no one was rolling video for one of those hit parades of embarrassing moments online. The tea came in its own pot, not to be confused with an electric kettle. In the homelier (that is, ordinary and pleasant, not ugly) tearooms, the pot was nestled into a granny-quilted or knitted tea cozy. I poured it from the pot straight into my cup, realizing too late I had a strainer to filter out the detritus of whole leaves, twigs, and branches now swirling in my drink. I'd dump the cup contents back in the pot and try again, but inevitably, I left stains on the tablecloth. Once I had successfully filtered my tea over the small, hot puddle of my first attempt, I plopped the strainer's weepy contents on my tray without a further thought. I did not realize that I had a stainless steel receptacle to hold the filter and strainings with decorum. Ben looked like he would rather pull a tea cozy over his head than be seen with such a rank tea amateur faffing (messing) around.

In a rare moment, he lost his patience with me. His words stuck like a used teabag to the empty cup of my memory. He wanted a tea before we set off on an errand, and I was a bit too dismissive.

"Claire! Tea is important!"

## Lost in Translation

As I LEARNED JUST after arrival, the locals didn't assume I knew how to speak English. In sharp contrast, I spoke American. The difference between the two could be extreme, if not extremely funny. Strangely enough, some American pronunciations are far clearer than their British counterparts, giving me the impression that I spoke better English than the natives. I could never let that secret out—uttering it aloud in British company would be an act of war. I might as well throw a thousand "decent" teabags into the nearest body of water. And none of that Lipton business, we're talking Yorkshire Gold.

Outside of wartime, tea was vital to my domestic tranquility. Personally, I could quit hot tea anytime. One of my dad's ancestors was a Revolutionary War flag bearer for the patriots, or traitors, depending on your perspective. Tea ambivalence was hard-wired into my genes. But when our brand-new tea kettle died during breakfast, I knew Ben would churn until his reliable hot-water source returned. I didn't know my pronunciation could stand in the way of happiness restored. I spent a particularly confusing hour in a department store called John Lewis in the early days when I was still asking for a new "keddle." John Lewis is known for great customer service. Once the assistant understood me, she internalized that a faulty kettle meant a halt to all tea production. This constituted an emergency in the UK and I waited less than five minutes for a replacement.

A few years before we moved to the UK, I asked Ben how things were going at work.

"It's all gone pear-shaped, Claire."

My imagination took over as usual, and I pictured all the people in his office rushing to one side of the building. My second guess was that all his male co-workers had hourglass figures.

"Huh?"

Ben sighed and explained that if something went pear-shaped, that meant it went horribly wrong.

You can imagine my horror when I heard someone announce with pride that she had just "knocked up a model at work." The speaker was female, so that task was biologically impossible unless she was moonlighting at a fertility clinic. She showed me a picture of herself next to a small computer kiosk. After several minutes of linguistic lag and confirming she hadn't switched jobs into reproductive medicine, I figured out she had put together a demonstration model with little effort.

Delving deeper into British vocabulary, I came to the interesting but fairly derogatory term "chav." I first heard it on television and had to consult Ben, my personal urban dictionary. A chav was shorthand for a young, ill-regarded member of the underclass, generally wearing designer knock-offs and sporting car hood ornaments as jewelry. I read the term was an acronym for "Council House and Vauxhall," which referred to the social housing they lived in and the lackluster make of car they liked to drive. I thought I'd met some chavs walking in the city center. It was hard to quit using "downtown," but I found that term got me laughed at and labeled as that charmingly bumpkin American who probably owned a gun.

The opposite of a chav was a toff with a cut-glass accent. That had nothing to do with home décor. It was a way of pronouncing language purposefully and clearly, as in the peculiar, stilted way the Queen spoke. I noticed it was harder to break free from the constraints of social class in British society, that more people were consigned to their lot in life. Ben came from a working-class family, and I always felt sad to hear him say he never aspired to be anything when he grew up. Telling children they had unlimited potential was a very American thing to do.

Some Brits internalized their social status, and unfortunately, many at the top were interested in knowing a person's pedigree before they stooped to mingle. The same class transcendence problems existed in the UK as in America—if someone were to drop the regional accent that betrayed their working-class roots, that would be called "going posh." I had a fairly unremarkable Midwest accent at home, but the British ear wasn't usually fine-tuned enough to hear it as anything other than "American." That carried enough baggage, good and bad.

My best guess for why social status was more impermeable related to local accents. They carried a lot of class stereotypes. I'd read there were as many as sixty-two different regional accents and dialects in the UK, as opposed to less than half that in the US, a country forty times as big.

The social classes spoke their own languages. Chavs were likely to use the word "innit." Innit is a slang shortened form of "isn't it," but grew far beyond its original meaning. I consulted an online urban dictionary which gave a helpful example of modern use amongst chavs: *"Me was meeting up with me mates, innit, and we was going down the pub, innit, when this bloke, yeah, comes over and said like, 'Gimme your wallets before I slice you like a tin of beans,' and we was like, 'Innit.'"* Perfectly clear. It wasn't a word I should put in my vocabulary.

The best backfire of innit appeared in a number of newspapers: the teenage girl who used Cockney rhyming slang to order a taxi for a trip to the airport the next morning. She dialed directory assistance, but when the operator didn't understand her use of "Joe Baxi" as Cockney rhyming slang for a "taxi," the girl said, "It's a cab, innit?" The operator transferred her to the number she needed, and the girl told the person who answered,

"All I want is your cheapest cab innit." She paid £180 by credit card, and discovered a versatile piece of storage furniture arrived at her South London home before ten the next morning.

"Innit" and its fuller relatives, such as "doesn't it?" were added to the end of sentences when someone dared have an opinion that might be against the grain. I viewed it as a patronizing, passive-aggressive way of steamrolling over me without raising their voice. But I am willful, and I'm not afraid to disagree with the right evidence. My most vivid example was an owner of a commercial laundromat who used up nearly an entire tub of my expensive washing powder on the duvet I had left in his custody.

"Did you need to use all of it?"

"Well, these are bigger machines than the one you've got at home, aren't they, love?"

"I don't think you know what kind of washing machine I have at home, and I certainly can't comment on how much detergent your machine typically takes," I replied as I swept up my over-soaped duvet and left in a huff.

For better or worse, I'd been under Ben's British English tutelage since we met, but being in-country brought out an entirely new level of vocabulary. For example, he announced that he expected a fair amount of "bun tossing" at his next work meeting.

"Bun tossing?"

I wondered if it related to some sort of lewd Sumo wrestling event. He explained it meant a weenie fight, common to public (private in American) schoolboys. It was probably directed by the same people who were prone to "throw their toys out of the pram" (Britspeak for baby carriage). They also enjoyed old-ladylike, sissy fights called "handbags."

One of the delights of living in a country that developed the language I spoke was discovering the origins of words I only thought I knew. Take, for instance, windfall, an unexpected bout of good luck. I happened to be watching a show on Victorian farming when the lads dressed in puffy Victorian farming shirts and tweedy farming trousers remarked that cider-making that year would be productive thanks to a great windfall. I consulted my friend Merriam-Webster, the controversial American dictionary that is not Oxford:

*wind·fall:*

*1: something (as a tree or fruit) blown down by the wind*

*2: an unexpected, unearned, or sudden gain or advantage*

The first definition dated from the 15<sup>th</sup> century. Just when I thought I spoke English, I felt a bit inferior. It was depressing when the Portuguese immigrant in line ahead of me at a shop clearly understood a shopkeeper's heavy regional accent far better than I did. I struggled with identifying the various accents because my ear didn't have a lifetime of learning their frequencies. I remember having this uncertain feeling in first year high school Spanish when Señorita Sponsler got after a dullard who kept calling his hand ("mano") his monkey ("mono").

I found a few new terms that didn't play well, despite their similarities.

Exhibit one: A scrum was the name given to a huddle formation in rugby—so Ben told me, although I couldn't claim I ever intentionally watched a match for more than thirty seconds. I remembered it this way: scrums display bums.

Exhibit two: Scrumpy is a type of hard cider, perhaps made from a windfall, that has a particularly high alcohol content. Scaled-down versions were available in pubs, but the real thing from farms would leave you legless (drunk, so I am told). I was trying to connect the mental dots—perhaps people willing to get in the scrum drank a lot of scrumpy. So far, so good.

Exhibit three: A contraction of "scrumptious" and "yummy" was "scrummy." I heard the linguistic needle scratch the Britpop record in my head. My first guess at the meaning of "scrummy" would have been "of or like the rugby scrum; displaying a predisposition to mob action in a rugby-like manner." But no. Scrummy also described men who were easy on the eye. My research led to a quick Google of "scrummy," which linked to a "UK's Scrummiest Torso" contest. Case closed.

I HAD LEARNED AN important cultural lesson fairly early in my marriage: never underestimate the influence of Monty Python on the English language. I did ask myself how a comedy troupe could be so powerful, especially knowing I had fallen asleep during *The Life of Brian* both times I had tried to watch it with Ben. The Pythons' influence came to roost while I was making an especially tasty cheese dip. The recipe called for green bell pepper diced into minute pieces. After a random rummage through the kitchen cupboards, I rejoiced at the sight of a long-lost Handichopper.

"Ben, I've found a whole new way of mincing!"

A cloud of confusion rolled across his face.

"Can you demonstrate?"

I protested. There was nowhere to plug in the chopper near the television. Cooking demonstrations were best done in the kitchen. I was in familiar territory—something was lost in translation.

Instead, I asked him for a demonstration. He explained that, to him, mincing meant short, effeminate strides with a bit of hip wiggle. Ben would describe the motion, but I couldn't get him to show me what he meant, despite clearing a runway for him in the dining room.

"Come on," I urged. "You're just being silly."

"No, silly walks are something entirely different." He went on to describe the oddly disjointed and impressively limber strides John Cleese made famous in his "Ministry of Silly Walks" Monty Python sketch. He offered up his Pythons on DVD collection for further cultural enlightenment. Sometime before I wrenched my knee ligament trying to duplicate John Cleese's high kicks, it dawned on me that just as I was ignorant of mincing and silly walks, I shouldn't take the things I thought "everyone" knew for granted in another country. It was time to let go of cold drinks with extra ice and go with the flow.

# Motoring Mayhem

I ASSUMED THAT TEA would not figure into other pressing topics, such as passing the UK driving test. Yet again, I had underestimated both matters' significance. The Driving and Vehicle Licensing Agency (DVLA) gave me a year from arrival to pass both the theory and practical portions of the test, so I spent many rainy days communing with the Highway Code. If we believed the old paperwork in the glovebox, we owned a used Mercedes A170 that had once belonged to Rowan Atkinson. Mr. Bean's former ride was a clown car compared to the Jeep Grand Cherokee I used to drive. I missed my Jeep for the comfy leather seats, the radio controls on the steering wheel, the moonroof, and most of all, for its ability to transport half the contents of my formerly cavernous closet at once.

Despite its resemblance to a mobile Dustbuster, the Mercedes A170 was a small, but surprisingly spacious, diesel automatic that got about fifty miles to the gallon—once Ben had done his mental conversion from liters. Mr. Bean drove it lightly without any stuntwork. Depressing the accelerator with gusto produced a lovely swamp cloud of charcoal diesel fumes, perfect for smoking out annoying drivers crawling up my tailpipe or Ben's particularly bothersome work colleagues we happened to randomly spy in the rear-view mirror. "It's a bit of a Tardis!" my English passengers remarked. At first, I thought this was some sort of slight related to its feeble, smoky acceleration or resemblance to home cleaning appliances. I learned that referring to something as a Tardis was a reference from the British television sci-fi cult classic, *Dr. Who*. The Tardis was a small phone booth that the Doctor traveled in, but it was a deceptively expansive cavern of a ship on the inside. On a good day, we could wedge in three adults, two Ikea Billy bookcases, a Poang chair, a complete bath towel set, several drinks, curtains, an area rug, and a bag of hard candy for the road. In an extreme test of its cargo capacity, we also managed to crowbar in a cast iron fireplace and surround, but that felt like driving home with a chainsaw motor under the hood.

Our rental Volvo wagon days had taught me there was no way my monstrous Jeep could have maneuvered into what passed for UK parking spaces. In fact, I thought lawnmowers would have serious difficulty fitting into some of these slots. I opted to pay a bit more for an automatic because the vast majority of cars sold in the UK are manual transmissions. I had also learned that if I did not take the practical (driving) portion of my exam in a car with a manual transmission, my license would be permanently blighted as valid for automatics only. It was the DVLA's version of *The Scarlet Letter*. As Ben's used Alfa Romeo was a manual and I technically was its part-owner, being deemed unfit to drive one of my own vehicles was unacceptable. I resolved I would not only learn to drive on the wrong side of the road from the wrong side of the car, but do it while shifting with the wrong hand. Thankfully, the British driving gods had kept the pedals in the same order as America or else my brain would have spontaneously combusted. We only needed to acquire a Japanese vehicle to represent all of the Axis powers.

Getting a US license was a cakewalk compared to the rigors of UK licensure. In theory, I didn't object to intense vetting in light of keeping the roads safe. It only became an issue when I was the subject of this vetting. First, I had to take a theory test, which contained an accompanying "spot the emerging hazard" video. I was expected to sit at a computer screen and watch a pre-recorded scene, clicking on all the potential hazards as I saw them unfold. I had a practice DVD I could use at home, and I was surprised how often the "emerging hazards" involved sheep in the road. If I didn't click on a distant wool ball fast enough, she'd inevitably stray into my lane and scupper my pass rate. If I passed this hurdle, I could proceed to the practical driving test. My new UK friends, mostly friends of Ben, told me people take driving lessons not to learn how to drive particularly well, but how to pass this test.

I contrasted my experience with tales of Ben's Illinois driving test, as well as the stories of his fellow Brits who sat around dinner parties and laughed heartily at the thought of how stupidly simple it was for them to get their US driver's license. In Ben's case, he had splashed out on a small, used Jaguar upon arrival in the US because his pound paycheck was suddenly twice as valuable, most of his living expenses were paid, and his grandfather used to work for Jaguar in Coventry. It was indeed a lovely car. He took it to his driving test and a woman examiner climbed into the passenger's seat. He looked over and deemed his chances of passing to be 100 percent when he caught her stroking the burled walnut trim. Another British acquaintance had a bout of road rage during his test and actually honked and yelled at the driver in front without any detrimental effects on his test score. Worst of all, one English woman showed up for the test seriously hung over, managed to hit the curb, and still walked out with a shiny, new license. Any of these activities would be duly noted and clucked over by a British driving examiner during his or her "You have failed" speech—well-rehearsed given the 47 percent pass rate at our local DVLA. In fact, the English road rager remarked how he always used a small-town DMV nearby, simply because it was populated with female staff who swooned over his accent. I weighed this sort of treatment against a British male driving examiner hearing my American accent and asking if

I had a handgun in my bag. On second thought, maybe that could work to my advantage.

I sat on my repaired sofa and filled out the health section of the DVLA paper application. It was going well. I was denying I had all sorts of maladies and syndromes and feeling unusually healthy when question nine stopped me and my mandatory black ink pen in its tracks:

*Had I ever had, or did I currently suffer from,* **repeated** *attacks of sudden disabling giddiness?*

This was a real question? Using the only definition my American brain knew, the answer would have to be yes.

I took mental inventory. There was the time when Ben and I went wedding cake testing back in Peoria. The shop was so generous, they gave us six pieces of cake, all slathered in different flavors of Italian buttercream icing, a refined type of crack. When I expressed interest in the ganache, the cake lady used a trowel to spade a massive portion of its dark chocolate nirvana into a carry-out container. She helpfully suggested we take it home. Of course, I ate the most of the cake *and* all the ganache with the helpful spork she included. Next thing I know, Ben claimed I was levitating off the couch. I think I was flapping my wrists for some reason, but I really have no recollection of events before what is now known as the Massive Sugar Crash of 2008.

There was also the ugly Mountain Dew incident of 2007, where I ignored my heightened sensitivity to caffeine and drank a 22-oz bottle of the extra high-wattage Code Red on an American road trip. Ben insisted on listening to a CD by the Arctic Monkeys while he drove, and I insisted on percussing him in time to the music with the empty soda bottle during a drum solo. Although my memory of this incident is sketchy as well, I do remember the satisfying, hollow thwack the bottle made when it hit his arm, so much more so when I got lucky and hit his elbow joint. I am grateful he didn't screech to a halt and force me to do a ninja roll onto the side of the highway, my impact cushioned by Illinois farmland roadkill.

Perhaps I was being too broad in my definition of "giddy." I asked rational, emotionally controlled Ben if he thought I "suffered from repeated attacks of sudden disabling giddiness."

"Only when you come across a roadside fruit stand," he replied.

Was this the British sense of humor talking? He did have a point. He had not forgotten yet another incident, shortly after our move to England, where I burned up Mr. Bean's former brakes at the prospect of patronizing a massive pick-your-own fruit farm.

"It's not as if I left tire marks on the road. I mean, they had tayberries!"

"I know. Don't worry, the whiplash only lasted a day."

It wasn't looking good. I feared I would be barred from driving purely on the basis of experiencing intense *joie de vivre*. No wonder the UK motorways were filled with such grumps.

When in doubt, Ben consulted the atlas, regardless of the matter's relevance to geography. In moral quandaries, I consulted the dictionary. To my delight, Merriam-Webster came to my rescue once again:

*gid·dy:*

*1a. dizzy; 1b. causing dizziness; 1c. whirling rapidly*

*2a. lightheartedly silly; 2b. joyfully elated*

I was only familiar with definition two. I may have whirled rapidly after the cake incident, but the rapid movement was restricted to flapping hands. If I did dervish even a bit, it was in the living room and I posed no danger to anyone but Ben.

What a relief. I wouldn't have to file an emotional discrimination claim. I was elated, but not enough to be giddy.

_ele_

M Y SELF-STUDY DVD INCLUDED a bank of actual exam questions. After reading a few, I began to spot an alarming trend:

*You arrive at the scene of a crash. Someone is bleeding badly from an arm wound. There is nothing embedded in it. What should you do?*

*1. Apply pressure over the wound and raise the arm.*

*2. Apply pressure over the wound and keep the arm down.*

*3. Dab the wound.*

*4. Get them a drink.*

Next, I considered this question:

*You arrive at the scene of an accident. It just happened and someone is injured. Which three of the following should be given urgent priority?*

*1. Check their breathing is okay.*

*2. Clear their airway and keep it open.*

*3. Stop any severe bleeding.*

*4. Get them a warm drink.*

*5. Look for witnesses.*

*6. Take numbers of vehicles involved.*

I supposed the first question's drink option could be interpreted as alcoholic and therefore appropriate for a Brit in distress. But in the second question, this mystery drink of choice was thinly veiled as tea. The examiners had dreamed up plausible and appealing British answers for the multiple-choice section. An American version might include, "Call their personal injury attorney right away," so I was not at all offended by this more genteel option. In fact, I could easily see an older injured person ignoring their own blood loss and asking for a cuppa and a biscuit (cookie). Better yet, a piece of cake. And could I blame them?

I mentioned my amusement at the recurrent "tea option" to Ben, who expressed no surprise whatsoever.

"Have we not had this conversation, Claire? Tea is important!"

I felt like a doofus not to have gotten it by now. Just in case, I started keeping a travel mug of tea at the ready when out motoring.

The theory exam was fifty multiple choice questions, some totally trippy, and those dreaded fourteen video clips where I had to spot and click on developing traffic hazards. Sure enough, I spotted my favorite hazard, a small flock of confused-looking sheep. (To be fair, confusion is a sheep's default mode.) Thanks to several hours of rigorous study, I became the proud owner of a letter that said I'd passed the theory portion of my driving test. It was the golden ticket that I had to use to book the driving portion.

Looking at the government's historical pass rate data, Peterborough's 47 percent pass rate was one of the higher figures among nationwide test locations. Women fared worse—sometimes, up to 10 percent lower pass rates than men at the same location. Were we really that terrible at driving, or did the examiner just think we stunk? *Good Lord.* It was far easier to pass the Illinois bar exam. I was lucky that I had a native driver to help coach me, but spouse criticism was tricky. I had been driving for the better part of twenty years, and my "bad habits" were hard to break. My eyes kept flitting to where I'd expect oncoming traffic back in the US, which was the polar opposite of where it would come from in the UK.

For most Americans, navigating by car in the UK is a shock to the system—a small island with mini-cars, all driving at once. The US is the land of wide-open spaces, which gave birth to my father's favorite motoring defenses: "Could have backed up and done it again!" and "Could have fit a Mack truck through there!" I lived by another of his motoring mantras that was perilously close to coming true nowadays: "Doesn't count unless you hit 'em!" In the States, I used to navigate by gas station, restaurant, or heaven forbid, street name. Frequently, their British counterparts were either hidden behind hedgerows or on a sign halfway up a building. UK lane use was its own dark art because lanes end and continue at what seemed to me like random spots. Car parks were downright lawless. And, of course, all this was happening on the left. The Highways Agency had also seen fit to write helpful little messages on the pavement, usually about which lane to use for any of the seven or so roads convening on a single intersection. It gave reading the road a whole new meaning, and it was easy to miss if I was too busy trying to remember which mulberry bush to turn left at. There were other major navigational landmarks too: blackberries, hazelnuts, stinging nettles, sloes, or even wild plums.

I had some experience with written messages on the road. While traveling a country lane in Cornwall as a passenger several years before, I wondered aloud, "What does *mois* mean? And why are the words on the road in French?" After some follow-up questioning about where exactly I had read this mysterious French missive, every occupant of the car burst out in laughter. I was hit by the comedy grenade about five seconds later when I realized that any messages the Highways Agency gods had for us would be printed on the left-hand side of the road, and they certainly wouldn't be in French. My eyes were so trained to look at the right lane, I read the word "slow" upside down as we drove by. I did not dare ask any more insightful motoring questions on that trip.

MY AMERICAN DRIVING STYLE was another problem. I gripped the wheel at the bottom, which Ben likened to driving a big rig truck. I steered by nudging the center portion of the wheel whichever way I wanted to go, as opposed to actually gripping the thing. I didn't find my truck-stop method problematic, especially when I was driving my Jeep on wide-open US roads, but Ben assured me such a relaxed approach would get me not only laughed at, but failed by any UK driving examiner.

It was time for a change. I didn't need to reach anything inside the car anymore—there was nowhere in my little A170 where I could stow my favorite 32-oz Big Gulps of fruity diet soda. In light of shedding my trucker ways, I channeled the ten-two hand position when steering, got rid of the kiddie-pool sized drinks, and continued to practice.

Driving on the left was easier than I thought. Shifting on the left was more harrowing. It took me a while to reprogram my brain to judge distance from the center of the road while sitting on the opposite (aka wrong) side of the car.

It wasn't all daffodils and tulips, though. I didn't have fond memories of our early exchanges in Ben's School of Driving.

Me, driving around a roundabout: "Look kids, Big Ben!"

*I hear the sound of crickets chirping. Apparently, he had never seen the fine feature film,* National Lampoon's European Vacation, *where the notoriously goofy Clark Griswold urges his kids to admire the scenery because he can't figure out how to drive the family car out of a roundabout in London.*

Ben: "Pay attention!"

Me: "How do I get off this thing?"

Ben: "Turn right."

Me, panicked: "Right?! How do you expect me to do that? It's a series of lefts!"

Ben: "I want you to go straight over the next roundabout."

Me: "How? This car doesn't have four-wheel drive like my old Jeep did."

Ben: "What are you talking about?"

Me: "You don't want me to drive through the grass, do you?" (I edged straight forward toward the impatiens in the middle of the circle, artfully planted by the local Women's Institute.)

Ben: "NO! (He frantically stomped an invisible brake pedal.) "Go around, AROUND! Take the opposite exit!"

I had no idea in so many ways. Nothing I could do was right because it was all left. In a roundabout, "turn right" meant take the exit at 3 o'clock. "Go straight over" meant take the exit exactly opposite you. Most importantly, the quickest way to change Ben's usually pleasant demeanor was to put him in fear for his life. My lessons on how to pass the driving test would start the next week. It was cheaper than marriage therapy.

I found my instructor through an American acquaintance and she came heartily recommended. I knew she had some experience in working with American expats and I projected I would need just a few refreshers to learn what the examiner was looking for.

Valerie was a petite woman with a direct but calm manner I found completely unnerving. She was reminiscent of the *Terminator*-esque Dominican nuns who taught me in high school. When she spoke, the fear of the Lord was not far behind. We met at a giant car park frequented by other learner drivers and their instructors. A young blonde girl sitting next to a bored old man in a Nissan Micra (as small as it sounds) was busy furrowing her brow and driving thoughtful figure eights with mind-numbing frequency around one empty section. I hoped we would not join her in some sort of warped student driver *pas de deux.*

One of the hallmarks of the truly incompetent is that not only are they incompetent, they are unaware of it. Valerie asked me to drive through a neighborhood, clearly to see if she was dealing with a hopeless case and should resign on the spot. I would have felt less nervous driving through a West Bank demilitarized zone without a flak jacket. I thought I was doing fine until she interrupted my delusions—accelerating past a pedestrian crossing named after some species of animal, while not speeding, could constitute a serious driving fault, failure, and possible death by dangerous driving. She called it a zebra (short e sound) crossing and her tone was ominous. Pedestrian crossings went by strange names. I could remember zebra without a problem, but when they went into animal species like pelican, puffin, and pegasus (for equestrians), it was a hopeless mental menagerie. I was channeling my inner cowboy—why didn't the Highways Agency just call them dodo crossings and let natural selection dictate who survived stepping out into traffic?

I also got heavy criticism for my lane position, oblivion to life-threatening peril and related jail sentences, lack of mirror usage, long-haul trucker steering tendencies, and the bizarre salsa steps I made with my feet while driving a manual transmission under scrutiny. This was ridiculous. I had spotted every single sheep on the theory test. Surely I was not this bad? I had never paid so much money for the privilege of feeling like a loser.

I was overjoyed to head home, but Valerie rattled me enough to stall the car right in front of our neighbor's house. I saw them staring out their front window, so I slinked down my seat and tried to retrieve my pride off the floorboards. As a peace offering, I said that I'd try to break my long-haul trucker steering habits.

"Don't worry about your hands just yet. Work on sorting those feet of yours out!" The nun piano teacher of my youth used the same tone, complemented by a retractable metal pointer she banged on the music rack to highlight how I was killing Mozart all over again.

I threw cash her way and fled her tiny clown vehicle, wondering if I should start pricing bus passes. This must have been how teenagers felt when threatened with the loss of their driving privileges. As a child of the late eighties and early nineties, I wanted to shut myself in a dark room and listen to Duran Duran while organizing my hair scrunchie collection.

With a bit of practice, I began displaying the behavior Sister Shift was looking for. We only had one incident where I motored into a roundabout and cut off a large Volvo wagon. It was probably the hire car I'd smacked the side of the country barn with months before.

After my third and final lesson, I became obsessed with the practical driving exam. Although Valerie had assured me passing would not be a problem, she did it in such a non-committal way that I couldn't be sure whether she was serious or just trying to calm me out of professional courtesy. She told me the story of her recent student who flunked for failing to see a large lorry when trying to change lanes in a roundabout. With that comforting anecdote, I discounted professional courtesy.

My test was scheduled for two days before my year of free driving expired. If I failed, I would be effectively grounded. I wondered if driving license standards applied to mobility scooters. Some of those could get up to twenty miles per hour or so, and you could buy festive enclosures to keep the rain out and advertise the football (soccer) team you supported at the same time. It wouldn't be so bad until I forgot and walked away from the scooter without a limp.

Because my coping mechanism is knowledge acquisition, I was a practice exam maniac. I rehearsed how to check the tire pressure, among other car maintenance issues that could appear on the test, for hours on end. There was one puffball among the "show me" questions that examiners asked, and that was demonstrating how to use the horn. No examiner in their right mind would use that gift on a silver platter, a nut-coated cheese ball on the question buffet. I prepared for the worst and rehearsed how to check the oil instead.

The surest route to disaster was being caught out by unholy junctions in places I had never driven before. The local testing authority had to publish all the test course routes it used through the city, which stood at thirty-nine in Peterborough. I grabbed my A–Z map of the city and painstakingly plotted each one with pencil, trying to imagine if I had been there before and whether I needed to watch out for a particularly nasty puffin crossing or any wayward sheep.

Test day arrived. I was scheduled right after lunch. In particularly Dominican nun tones, Valerie had solemnly approved of my time choice as "relaxed" and least likely to be full of traffic. There were three examiners taking turns escorting victims to their vehicles, and I drew the lot of a particularly rotund, middle-aged man. I was unsure if he could wedge himself into Ben's small Alfa. I'd eschewed my A170 automatic because I wouldn't be legal to drive a car with a manual transmission unless the car I presented for the test had one.

He greeted me politely as we walked to the car and I lost all shame.

"I've been driving for eighteen years, just in the wrong country!" I tried to embody exuberance and charm. Had I thought to bake, I would have produced a chocolate chip cookie from my purse and handed it over. He didn't flinch.

"American?"

"Yes!"

My tone was too congratulatory, as if he'd won the showcase on *The Price is Right*. He asked me to recite a random license plate at a distance of fifty meters to check my vision, then he crammed himself into the Alfa. I was afraid he would permanently injure himself on the shifter. He managed to find the seat adjustment using an impressive between-the-legs pretzel contortion. He sighed aloud with relief with another foot of room for his girth, and before I could flinch, got on with his business.

"Show me how you would use the horn." I know my face betrayed my relief, but I stared straight ahead. *Hello, cheese ball.* Surely his plan was to lull me into a false sense of security before we had even left the car park, then ask me to back into a three-foot parking space later on. I honked the horn. I knew it was coming, yet I levitated out of my seat. The petrified young trainee driver beside us hit the ceiling of her tiny Peugeot.

"Very good." I felt grateful and patronized at the same time. We set off through a part of town I knew from my many training runs, and as the time wore on without calamity, he started to make conversation.

"So, what do you do when you're not taking driving exams?" he asked. I decided to play the part of the good student.

"I plot out all the test routes in my A–Z map," I replied while correctly going straight over a small roundabout. The examiner let out a hearty laugh as if I were joking, so I joined him with a few manufactured guffaws before he gave his next instruction. His posture loosened and I caught him looking all around the neighborhood, pausing to admire a small settlement of garden gnomes. My information strategy had worked. He was phoning it in, and I was going to pass.

But then I hesitated. I waited for an approaching car to pass, although I was reasonably sure I could have pulled out without an incident. According to Sister Shift, hesitation was a sin.

"Oops!" I said. One hand flew up to cover my mouth, leaving the sacred ten/two position. Double whammy.

I couldn't stifle the need to be a chronic broadcaster when moments of silence cried out to be filled. I was doing his job for him.

Sure enough, I passed with flying colors. My only fault was my "oops" announcement, logged as "hesitation." I got my license in the post a couple weeks later. Armed with my new credentials, I felt prepared to explore England in a small vehicle, far away from the broad sides of barns.

—*ele*—

U NLIKE US CAR INSURANCE, UK car insurance followed an owner, not a vehicle. Only Ben and I were insured to drive my car, and even that was a miracle. Instead of using agents, there are myriad insurers that operate by phone and website, as well as comparison websites that help shoppers find the best deals. One website began by asking me my age, how long I'd had a license, what kind of car I drove, and other standard fare.

I was stopped short when it asked me what Ben and I did for a living. It wanted me to select our job titles from a list of thousands of occupations it officially recognized. Just the day before, I noted a black CCTV camera staring down at me while I waited to cross a street. Another camera surveilled me from a hundred feet away. CCTV abounded in the UK. The council (local government) knew every move I made already, so this website riled up my libertarian streak. American insurance didn't care what I did for a living. In the words of the locals, sod them—would they want to know my bra size, too? I selected the letter "c" and clicked the first job title that appealed to me. Our quote was horrendously expensive. Surely something had gone wrong. I gave up in disgust. That evening after work, I told Ben how invasive I found the line of vocational questioning.

"But, Claire, that's a standard question here. So what did you put?"

I paused, knowing I was giving him material for the next decade.

"Clown."

His cheeks puffed out.

"You're joking?"

"I said you were one, too."

"No! At least you didn't give them our address."

"I did. It was a required field to get a quote. It was really expensive."

His face fell.

"Of course it was! Clowns are high risk! Now we're going to start getting junk mail from every clown vocational group known to man. I can't believe you did that."

He stalked off, probably to look for tape to seal the mail slot shut. I was unaware that clown vocational groups were prospecting via Royal Mail. I suppose stuffing as many co-workers as possible in a car *was* a high-risk way to drive.

One day, Ben and I found ourselves in the old industrial town of Swindon, but despite the name, we didn't happen upon many swine. We did see the most infamous traffic feature in Britain, the Magic Roundabout. It's a series of five roundabouts arranged together in a pentagram. Despite my freshly-minted driving license, any attempt of mine to run its gauntlet would have led to a significant insurance claim, regardless of whether clowning was my vocation. I closed my eyes as Ben drove through, pausing and advancing to each mini roundabout circle in a confounding automotive ballet.

I couldn't imagine ever knowing exactly what was going on at the Magic Roundabout unless Valerie sat me down with a pointer and a schematic diagram. I saw the ideal diagram for how the Magic Roundabout was supposed to flow—it looked like five automotive pinwheels blowing counterclockwise at the same time. How whimsical. This would take years of study to even attempt, never mind master. If this was where the clowns drove, no wonder their insurance rates were so high.

# Part Three:

## You May Now Move Freely About the Country

*The stately homes of England, How beautiful they stand!*
*Amidst their tall ancestral trees, O'er all the pleasant land.*

– Felicia Dorothea Hemans, English poet

## The Stinkiest Tourist Attraction of All Time

PRESENTED WITH A LONG bank holiday weekend, Ben and I went into touring mode and drove a few hours north to York, a city on both of our sightseeing wish lists. Despite living most of his life on a small island, he hadn't seen some of the best historical sights. I related—I grew up in Springfield, Illinois, and had never made it to Lincoln's Tomb.

Yorkshire was the home of Yorkshire pudding, an unsweetened, puffy pancake, usually the size of a large dinner roll. A jumbo size Yorkshire was the size of a small dinner plate, filled with meat, gravy, and vegetables. Mini-Yorkshires are readily found in every freezer case in the country. I attempted a homemade version that could equally have held pride of place in our rock garden. The prospect of getting a decent Yorkshire pudding is probably why visiting York was near the top of Ben's travel wish list. Apart from the food, we'd read that York was a cultural treasure, one of England's greatest sightseeing hits.

I happened to mention we were going to York to my dad back in the US.

"Is that where the little dogs come from?"

"What little dogs?"

"You know, Yorkies. The little yappy ones."

As someone afraid of dogs, especially small ones, the thought hadn't crossed my mind. "Probably," I answered, although I had seen no mention of Yorkies in any of the York tourist board materials. So far as I knew, there was no Museum of Yorkie Culture or towers of Bonio dog biscuits built in tribute.

I didn't know how subliminally the question had roosted in my brain until the next morning. I had dreamed I was being chased by a dirty, feral pack of wild Yorkies, all nipping at me as they gnashed madly at my ankles. I woke up in a cold sweat I mistook for doggie drool. I'd had the occasional prescient dream before, so I kept an eye out for little dogs once we arrived on the narrow, medieval streets of York. One small gnasher in particular looked a bit menacing, but he was a dachshund on a leash. He didn't fit the profile.

York was home to a massive Nestlé Rowntree chocolate factory not open for public tours. I was crushed. Historically, the plant had manufactured the infamous Yorkie chocolate bar, with a slogan that has led to many testy exchanges between Ben and me. I thought "It's not for girls!" was just another of Ben's attempts to prevent my death by chocolate. It was early days in our dating life when he first drew my attention to a Yorkie bar in the English food section of our local supermarket. His misogynistic put down was filed in my mind's dossier of slights and wrongs until he pointed to its wrapper. "It's NOT for girls!" shouted at me in shiny blue and gold letters. The slogan was bad enough, but I found the wrapper's anti-girl logo even more injurious—it was a basic silhouette of a woman in a red circle with a menacing "anti" diagonal bar drawn across her. How could the makers of a whopping, chunky candy bar expect to keep estrogen-fueled chocolate seekers away? Moreover, why would they want to?

Apparently, the company developed Yorkie bars to fill a hole in the "manly" chocolate bar market. Or was it a reverse psychology ploy designed to make me want one even more? It worked. I found Yorkie bars were disappointingly delicious, despite being an affront to women. Thankfully, the company laid this misguided ad campaign to rest in 2011.

Long before it began banning women from its chocolate bars, York was established in 71 A.D. as a Roman outpost named Eboracum. Roman legions used Eboracum as a mustering point to defend the northwest reaches of the empire, marked by Hadrian's Wall. Ben picked up a silver denarius he seemed chuffed (Britspeak for pleased) with at Spink's rare coin shop. One denarius was about what a common laborer or soldier would get paid *per diem* in the time of Christ. It dated from 202 A.D. and showed the head of the boy Emperor Caracalla, who assumed the throne at age ten and was dead thanks to warmongering by age twenty-nine. It beat out the "York is for Dorks" ruler that I was considering as a souvenir.

Spink's street address was 47 Shambles. The Shambles was a collection of well-preserved medieval buildings on a cobbled street barely wide enough for a single, tiny English car to navigate. The street name made me smile until a tour guide revealed its history. The term "shambles" didn't used to mean a place in a state of utter chaos or disrepair—in medieval times, it was a word for open-air meat markets and slaughterhouses.

The old Roman fortress was built on the current site of York Minster, the city's whopper of a cathedral. We toured the undercroft to see what remained of the fortress walls and Roman artifacts unearthed when cathedral construction began in 1230. One of York's most infamous ghost stories involved Treasurer's House, next door to the cathedral and built over an old Roman road. In 1953, a young heating apprentice named Henry Martindale was in its basement working when he saw a disheveled Roman legion returning from battle. They were visible from the knees up, as the level of the Roman road that led back to their garrison was about fifteen inches lower than the floor of the basement. I was faint of heart, so I swore off indoor tours with nowhere to run.

York had a magnificent medieval city wall still standing, mostly intact, which was a rarity. Some parts of the wall are Roman, some are Norman (post 1066), but the newest additions are medieval. If Roman Britain was anything like modern-day Britain, those latest additions wouldn't exist today because the people of York would still be waiting on their local council to grant planning permission for some newfangled renovations.

Boiling oil, longbows, crossbows—they all got fired off the top of the wall at invaders below. I got nervous walking under a piece of the city wall that contained a portcullis, a massive, waffle-like gate with spiky ends that secured the city on demand. I thought of it as a rusty piece of sinister Shreddies (Chex), ready to drop at any moment. So far as maintenance went, I was sure the warranty had long since expired.

After a busy first day of sightseeing, a work colleague visiting York with his wife called Ben's mobile and suggested we meet up for a drink somewhere. The problem was that we were already out and about in the city, without daylight or a map. I dismissed any practical hope of finding them.

Restricting a missing persons search to pubs in a major city center doesn't really narrow things down much in the UK. I started peering in the lit pub windows, pretending that I might actually see them, when a couple in a front window started frantically waving at us. Ben was still on the phone, and by pure chance, we had stumbled onto them. I looked up at the sign that hung high above us. The pub was called "The Yorkshire Terrier." The sign showed a small dog snarling, drool dripping from his furry little gob.

I forced myself over the Yorkshire Terrier's threshold, and thankfully, there was not a dog to be found. Perhaps the nickname "Claire-voyant" didn't fit. I found that a pint of cider took the edge off my heebie-jeebies.

The next day, we visited the York Castle Museum, which was really a series of buildings that included the former jail. It was among the most interesting museums I'd ever been in. The ticket counter guide told us to expect our trip to take one and a half hours, but Ben and I were there for three and a half. It was like some Victorian gran's attic on steroids.

The featured exhibit at the time included an expansive display on the Victorian fascination with cleaning. While academically interesting, it wasn't a theme I could personally relate to. It contained a complete Victorian high (main) street, including dim gas lighting and cobbles. All the shops were fully stocked with haberdashery, pawn items, jewelry, and glass, including a chemist (drug store)—the sheer quantity in the shop windows was mind boggling. The sweet shop offered sugar mice on sale for fifty pence in modern money, but more likely a farthing in Victorian times, a quarter of an old penny. The prospect of sugar vermin made me wonder if the Victorians ever splashed out and upgraded to sugar rats or sugar pigeons on special occasions.

One area contained time-warpy kitchens through the years. The model 1980s kitchen looked exactly like our own. If only the old lady had thrown a microwave as big as Sputnik into our rental package, we'd be completely authentic. Even our linoleum wasn't far off—it was a vision in mushroom by the proper color name of the era, but was closer to the color of pink flesh. Embarrassed that another visitor might sense our familiarity with this exhibit, we moved on to York Castle Prison.

York is allegedly the most haunted city in England, but I'm not sure which creep committee gave that award. Regardless, it had plenty of gloomy spots and tales of woe. At one point, there were 220 separate offenses that incurred the death penalty in England, which meant the same end for convicted traitors, cattle thieves, and hungry people who vandalized a fish pond. The museum had a database of prisoners and their fates for visitors to search for wayward relatives. My family names came up spotless, but Ben's surname produced some rogues. We would know for sure that the executed were his relations if their crimes had been chronic carriage cleanliness, but it was just highway robbery.

I debated taking a ghost tour that left from The Shambles every evening. Various travel guides heartily recommended these tours for entertainment value, although my cowardly nature made me wonder if I could handle it. I read a review that said someone's twelve-year-old had really enjoyed the tour. But were they into video games that had left them with the gore tolerance of a coroner? I decided to risk it.

We stood at the appointed corner and watched people we thought might also be on the tour with suspicion. A woman arrived—dressed head-to-toe in black, powdered into anemic tones, and accompanied by a goth male companion. My mind was busy spinning out a picture of her as a plus-size Stevie Nicks when I saw a young Asian couple toddling through my line of sight. The female half was wearing silver, spike heels that could have been used to grill some very generous kebabs. Her companion was hopelessly hip in his grungy denim, punctuated by a jaunty scarf. She teetered over to witchy woman and tried to pay her the cost of the tour. As I watched witchy woman try to explain that she was not the tour guide, I wished for a life remote control.

The tour was fun and interesting, especially watching the Asian woman walk through medieval cobbled streets wearing the most spectacularly inappropriate footwear on the planet. At least we could have used her to defend against a surprise pair of vampires.

It came as no surprise that Ben was interested in visiting the Jorvik Viking Centre. He had a soft spot for Vikings. It took me the longest time to learn the difference between the Viking ship called a longboat, and a narrowboat, a colorful houseboat that trolls English rivers and canals at a pontoon's pace. Whenever I'd slip and say, "Look, a longboat!" he'd reply, "Really? AARRRGH!"

York used to be called Jorvik when the Vikings arrived, pillaged, plundered, and generally made themselves comfortable between 800 and 900 A.D. William the Conqueror finally gave the Vikings the boot when he took over in 1066.

When excavating the center of the city in the 1970s, archaeologists started finding a treasure trove of dead Vikings and their well-preserved stuff, so much so that it warranted a museum to display it all. Someone took a cue from Walt Disney and designed Jorvik as a ride, where visitors get in a car that transports them through time to a recreated Viking settlement with animatronic people and replica relics.

The first thing I noticed after hopping in the car was a certain funk. After Ben and I confirmed that both of us had remembered deodorant that morning and refrained from recent cruciferous vegetable consumption, we figured out that the manky, smoky smell was being piped in for our olfactory entertainment. It was a nice touch, until the ride literally took a turn for the worse. As our car rounded a corner, an animatronic man squatted behind a small wicker fence rocking, grimacing, and grunting. It took a moment to sink in, but to our horror, he was reenacting taking a giant poo. The unmistakable smell of sewer wafted over us.

Two things occurred to me. I had no doubt that poo was historically accurate. However, was it that enlightening to demonstrate to the masses? Secondly, where on earth do they source a synthetic, aerosol sewer smell? (At least I hope it was synthetic.)

We disembarked our cars and took in some of the relics displayed in glass cases. A young woman dressed in Viking regalia dared the children in our group to guess what a large, oblong stone was, laid out in its own case next to her. Compounding our horror, she identified it as a rare piece of coprolite, the largest mineralized human turd ever discovered. One pale-oscatologist, a scientist who studies fossilized poop, claimed it was more valuable than the crown jewels. It was found under the site of what was to be a new bank, so the locals took to calling it "the Lloyds Bank turd."

Much like the pack of rabid Yorkshire terriers, the giant fossilized turd haunted me for a long time after our visit. Even years later, it was impossible to unsmell. The British were sticklers for historical accuracy.

—ℓℓℓ—

# Lifetime Learning in Cambridge

B EN AND I TOOK a jaunt to Cambridge, not terribly far from us given that we lived in Cambridgeshire. Unlike the universities I was used to, Cambridge is an association of thirty-one different colleges under different names, of which King's is probably the most famous. The city surfaces scream university town—full of notices on plays, concerts, and protests. By 1200, Cambridge was an established scholar's hangout made up of brainy sorts who found the townsfolk in Oxford to be a little too conservative for their tastes.

Some things never change. Right from the start, Cambridge had problems with young students making a ruckus and disturbing the locals. There were also landlords who extorted unfair prices for food and housing from the poor students at their mercy. This seems like the medieval equivalent of moving into a US fraternity house mixed with some slumlord action.

Flags posted all over the city celebrated the university's 800th anniversary. I wondered who would come to party down with the class of 1209? I didn't see a class picture chiseled into any of the buildings' walls. Maybe they'd be lured back with the promise that the Troubadours were getting back together for a one-night-only concert with some funky Morris dancing, a terribly English pastime where dancers dress in ribbon shards and tap sticks in unison. Be there or be square.

Cambridge was full of tourists, but not to the point of overflowing. We saw young people with student vibes shopping in the high-end stores within the city center. I figured that only the children of the wealthy could afford to attend, but tuition and fees were only £9,000 per year ($12,000 US) for UK residents in 2012. This was an outrage to students, who used to pay only board, not tuition, before fees changed nationwide. Of course, getting in was a long shot, and there had always been debate about whether it improved a student's prospects to be privileged. After government tuition funding was slashed, most other universities in England (but not Scotland, which remains free to Scottish students) would be charging the same amount.

Cambridge was full of beautiful, ancient buildings. It was possible to walk into the outdoor spaces of some colleges, most of which were built around a central courtyard. Dining and living quarters were inside, as well as each college's porter. Porters didn't necessarily help with luggage, but they maintained the health and safety of the students besides looking after all things building-related.

It was nicely multicultural as well. I could send a postcard to the States at a town center post office and get a takeaway saag paneer with a couple samosas at the halal deli in the back. A majority of the shops downtown were owned by the various colleges, which ensured a perpetual income. Astronomical rents barred shopkeepers of average means. The university has one of the largest private collections of wine in the country at about 50,000 bottles, worth millions of pounds and larger than the government's own cellar of around 40,000. Cambridge rents were about 50 percent higher than where we lived, just forty miles to the northwest.

People who tried to drive through the center of Cambridge probably wished for a rescue helicopter. It was a very cycle-y city, and with medieval, winding streets, cars were a nightmare. We were wise and ditched ours at a car park that also served the YMCA (and as an outdoor urinal for the village people, by the smell of things). Some of the colleges posted signs that bike parking was for fellows only, post-graduate assistants who got monetary support from their college.

I happened to go to a ladies' public toilet in Cambridge. (Brits chuckle at the American term "restroom," as if we go there to relax on a *chaise longue* and sip a refreshing beverage.) Some public toilets charged 20p for the privilege of answering nature's call, but others were free. Given the highbrow academic atmosphere, I expected to see advertising for the latest production of *Rosencrantz and Guildenstern are Dead* or a lute jam session. Instead, I saw a thoughtful plaque stating that the "loo" I was currently using was twinned with one in Burundi, and its owners were "helping to flush away poverty." This was the latest in a wide array of charity appeals, starting from the Donkey Sanctuary, via Cancer Research UK, to WaterAid. Despite their general reserve, WaterAid used a plastic, remote control turd to chase unsuspecting people around London's Hyde Park, with the point that it was impossible for some people in the world to escape their own sewage. I flushed and thought of Burundi.

At Cambridge, individual colleges taught by using small sessions of three to four people studying under the supervision of their director of studies, in addition to attending lectures. I finally understood Sting's reference to his 'college tutor' in one hit song by The Police. Some students made a bit of extra cash as punt chauffeurs, tour guides on flat-bottomed boats with square-shaped boughs. The chauffeurs used a long stick to propel punts full of tourists down the River Cam, which wound through many of Cambridge's most scenic and famous colleges.

We roamed on foot around St. John's College and crossed the Bridge of Sighs over the river, allegedly Queen Victoria's favorite spot in Cambridge. It was a marvelous white stone bridge with ornate windows that bore no resemblance to the original Bridge of Sighs in Venice. The Italian version got its name from the prisoners held at the Doge's Palace crossing the bridge on their way to be executed. I hoped the pressure of exams didn't leave St. John's students feeling the same way. Much like the Venetian gondoliers, punts full of tourists played bumper boats below. After all, the Cam was the punting capital of England and the best views of the colleges' architecture were from the water. The river could be teeming in good weather—maybe that was where the UK slang "punters" came from. It means customers, a relief for American football fans who might expect a swift kick instead. Punters could pay an experienced chauffeur to propel the punt for them. The riskier option was to rent a punt and propel themselves, but there were countless stories of tourists with shaky balance taking an unexpected dive into the river, or dislodging themselves as they tried to get their poles unstuck from the muddy river bottom. One unlucky tourist was knocked unconscious and hospitalized by a wayward pole that fell on her head during a mid-Cam collision.

Punting was serious business in Cambridge. The city council had a history of complaints against salespeople using aggressive tactics to sell punt tours. The council threatened the worst offenders with ASBOs (pronounced AZ-bows), short for anti-social behavior orders, the American equivalent of being criminally charged with disorderly conduct. ASBOs matched the vibe of council estates, UK for public housing, not the genteel, academic towers of one of the world's most renowned universities. We took a pass on punting and enjoyed the sights from land.

I knew the area around the Cambridge train station fairly well—it was the location of my first paying job. Shortly before my arrival, the Solicitors Regulation Authority branch of the Law Society of England and Wales cracked down on the methods foreign-trained solicitors (lawyers who generally don't appear in court) could use to gain legal accreditation in the UK. Lawyers who routinely argued cases before a court were called barristers. In the best of times, finding a job in the exclusive club of barristers' chambers was difficult. About 20 percent of the country's solicitors were trained elsewhere and there were fears that these people weren't as well acquainted with UK law as those trained domestically. It used to be an application process, where I merely had to show my equivalent credential in any number of approved jurisdictions. Now, there was a practical training requirement. In theory, if I could find a contract working as a trainee solicitor under the supervision of someone already in the Law Society, I could apply for membership. But I felt like a unicorn—I didn't practice corporate law or intellectual property, or another field that translated better across countries. I didn't work for a multinational corporation where I could transfer to the supervision of a qualified solicitor in a UK office. My knowledge was particular not just to the US, but to Illinois specifically. Even though the British and American legal systems evolved in similar ways, the devil was in the details. It would make no sense for a firm of solicitors specializing in criminal law to hire me as a trainee when people fresh out of a Legal Practice Course came with more relevant knowledge. It would have been better for my ego if the rules completely shut down any possibility of me continuing my career.

As a way of making the best of the legal training I already had without having to worry about jumping through the practically impossible hoops to gain a UK credential, I finally started digging around for ways to keep gainfully occupied. I was miserable sitting at home. I felt guilty not working for income. My spouse visa entitled me to work, but paid employment wasn't terribly likely. We had moved to the UK in the throes of a recession, and jobs were being slashed by government and private business every day. On a whim, I applied for a part-time library clerk position in my first weeks of living in the UK, along with 125 others. I spent a lonely first summer feeling stuck in neutral. My personality was naturally introverted, yet I fed off the energy of interacting with other people. Sometimes Ben would return home to find I hadn't left the house that day. I was desperate to fill my time with a bit more social interaction than avoiding Mummy next door, relapsing into my *FarmVille* addiction, and breaking up yet another wood pigeon brawl in our backyard birdbath. My mother-in-law suggested volunteering would help.

At first it rankled me to work for free because I wasn't helping our bottom line, but the cost of sitting at home was taking a toll on my mental health. In scanning for volunteer opportunities, I stumbled across Citizens Advice Bureau (CAB), a national legal charity with a network of local offices. It offered the public advice free of charge, regardless of income. CAB was an institution born out of World War II, when thousands of people were in dire need after their homes and livelihoods were destroyed. I got over my misgivings and joined an intake of trainee advisors in the Peterborough Bureau.

The wife of a Brit who worked with Ben in the US was a long-time CAB volunteer, and I called her to get the scoop. Back home, I volunteered as a legal aid attorney, and the working poor were the hardest to help. They had jobs and income, but were just a bit too well-off to qualify for free services, despite finding it hard to pay their bills and make their rent.

Citizens Advice relied on rigorous training and an expansive proprietary database to dose out advice to the public. In the States, I wondered if their business model would fall under the heading "unauthorized practice of law." But it was a very British sentiment to pull oneself up by the bootstraps over a cuppa and a nice chat. Thankfully, the more complex issues got referred to legal specialists.

My trainer was a large, gregarious woman named Ann whose wardrobe skewed bohemian. She was one of the rare people in life who had access to an inner wellspring of joy, and I looked forward to seeing her, as well as just having somewhere to be. She was enthusiastic, welcoming, and the least judgmental person I had ever met.

Not only did I get happier, but CAB was a goldmine for learning about real "life in the UK." The thing I found most difficult to wrap my head around was the benefits system. It was expansive, and from an American's perspective, rife with potential for needless spending. At the time, the biggest waste I saw was called child benefit. It amounted to £20 per week paid for each child universally, regardless of income. Tweedy people living in a manor house were just as entitled to this benefit as people who lived on council estates. No one asked for my opinion on child benefit, so I kept my mouth shut. In 2013, the government would finally restrict eligibility.

Winter Fuel Allowance also caused my scalp to itch. That was a one-time payment to people over the UK pension age each winter, meant to help defray heating costs. Again, it wasn't limited to those with low income. There were always cheery charitable campaigns encouraging affluent seniors to donate their Winter Fuel Allowance to the cause *du jour*.

On the other hand, fewer people fell into grinding poverty in the UK compared to the US, thanks to the smorgasbord of various benefits and the National Health Service (NHS), free healthcare funded by tax proceeds. There were Brits who criticized the generosity of their government, and I occasionally heard the term "nanny state" tossed around. For this system, we paid 40 percent of our income in taxes, as opposed to 24 percent in the United States. But a pound of parsnips from the city centre vegetable market was about 75 cents, compared with $3.50 for the same amount in the US. I couldn't control how much tax I had to pay the UK, so I rejoiced in cheaper root vegetables and accessible healthcare.

Much of what we covered in the early days was what I considered "sensitivity training." My fellow trainees were a mix of young people interested in a legal career, my fellow unemployed looking for job experience, and retirees who were chronically helpful. We had been weeded out through a series of meetings and applications. Our numbers grew smaller as the training got more difficult.

Once I had "graduated" volunteer training and Ann deemed me safe to work with the British public, I met people with all sorts of problems, many of whom were struggling with British English even more than I was. The UK had a huge immigration boom after it joined the European Union because all EU nationals had the right to travel and work in the UK. My mother's family was 100 percent Lithuanian, but I'd never met so many Lithuanian people as I did in Peterborough. I complimented a young blonde on a beautiful handbag that happened to match a briefcase I owned, but she said I would have to venture to her hometown, Vilnius, to find one.

My heart went out to people struggling with English, and they gave me new appreciation for what my mother's relatives would have gone through when they came to America from Lithuania at the beginning of the 20th Century. A native Portuguese speaker told me that conditions in the house she was sharing were so bad, she "couldn't even go downstairs to use the chicken." I pictured a lower-level bank of nests, with an eager line of Portuguese immigrants getting into fisticuffs over who would have dibs on the next egg. It took about ten seconds for me to realize she meant "kitchen." Another client told us how a man she rented a room to stripped every fixture from her rental property. "He even taking the smoking detective!" she yelled in Mandarin-glish exasperation.

It didn't take long to learn British volunteers work for snacks. My informal study showed a significant proportion of people who volunteered at Citizens Advice Bureau put on at least a stone, or fourteen pounds, in their first year. I was not immune from this scourge. The entire operation was fueled on tea and biscuits, which had to be in continuous supply for maximum efficiency. There were digestives (no aid with digestion detected, just graham cracker taste), custard creams (containing neither custard nor cream), bourbon creams (no cream again, but chocolate instead of booze), rich tea biscuits (neither tea-flavored nor rich tasting), Pontefract cakes (no cake at all again, but little chewy licorice circles) and my favorite, Jaffa Cakes (orangey, but clearly not a slice of cake). The cookie aisle in our local Tesco was roughly the size of the wine section.

After volunteering for a while in Peterborough, I managed to find a full-time position as a herder of volunteers at the Cambridge CAB. In hindsight, the monetary and emotional cost of the hour-long train ride wasn't worth it, but I fell under the spell of my bank account expanding. The job amounted to acting as cruise director for about 120 volunteers, trying to keep them recruited, scheduled, and happy. Cambridge was a better funded bureau, so its biscuit selection was even more expansive than the Peterborough branch's.

My job was helpful in learning to understand the -isms and cultural references that made me feel more at home. The volunteers were officially eclectic, and most were retired from another career. I found my tendency to speak up about problems in a very direct way clashed with the English custom of going through the chain of command and having "a quiet word." I tried to win favor and found myself buying tickets for a school summer fete raffle, secretly hoping I wouldn't win the purely eccentric prizes of a bat safari or polo lessons. A particularly posh longtime volunteer stopped me one day in amazement—she wanted confirmation of a rumor that I was, in fact, an American.

"But, Claire! We thought you were Canadian!"

If there was a "Best of British," maybe there was a "Worst of North American." I was hoping to avoid that title, and if I had to feign being Canadian to avoid my homeland's baggage, so be it. I was tiring of Brits who used my nationality as an excuse to grill me about American foreign policy, as if I had anything to do with overseas raids or controversial wars. At the time, I didn't have enough cultural depth to turn the tables and ask them to account for the cultural damage inflicted by their empire.

When I first took the job in Cambridge, my fellow volunteers at the Peterborough CAB joked that the worst issue the Cambridge office had to solve was old, affluent people coming in to ask the location of the nearest Waitrose, a posh grocery store chain. Overall, the Cambridge volunteers were tony—I took a copy of one woman's passport and noticed she was "Lady Laura." I would have never guessed. She wore Airwalk skateboard sneakers and jeans so baggy they were a trip hazard.

In fact, Cambridge was the land of the haves versus have-nots. While there was a well-to-do aura around the university scene and its professors, housing prices were astronomical. Sleazy landlords still preyed on poor student populations, and ordinary people struggled to afford a decent place to live. Cambridge wasn't a bubble that protected people from the worst social issues, after all. There were far worse problems in town than being heckled by a punt tout cruising for an ASBO.

—ele—

## They Call Althorp a House, But You Decide

An American friend and I wanted to visit Althorp House, a 14,000-acre estate seven miles from Northampton and within an easy drive of Peterborough. It was the ancestral home of Lady Diana Spencer, who went on to become Diana, Princess of Wales. She was buried behind the house, on an island in a small lake called "The Round Oval." Perhaps it was just the modesty of the aristocracy, calling it a house. My house didn't have fifteen bedrooms.

I wasn't quite sure what to expect. Diana was such a public figure with an almost cult-like following. My worst fear was commoditization—things like Princess Diana hot water bottle cozies or Princess Diana fudge in the gift shop. I was no stranger to fudge from stately home gift shops, but there was a line somewhere.

I was initially put off by a crusty OAP at the ticket booth. My stomach was making embarrassing noises. I noticed one price labeled "Concessions." It was a bit less expensive than my ticket and I was in desperate need of a snack.

"Excuse me, what are your concessions?" I wouldn't be interested if they offered a jumbo box of whitebait, little breaded fish eaten whole, popular in a seaside town called Grimsby. We were inland. Perhaps a sausage roll? They were like giant pigs in blankets, covered in puff pastry.

"Not for you!" he yelled back.

A jarring needle scratched across my mental record player of food fantasies. I'd heard a much kinder tone from felony probation officers dealing with their wayward charges.

"Twelve pound, fifty, please." He clenched his teeth. I was surprised he bothered with "please." I'd offended him deeply, but had no way of knowing how. Was I somehow unworthy of a sausage roll?

He'd asked me to pay the highest ticket rate and I gladly threw him money so I could flee, but I was miffed about the MI5 secrecy surrounding the snack bar menu. I probably had to be a member of their "society," or it was some tactic to keep peons like me out of the stately Kit-Kats.

My American friend couldn't pinpoint where I'd gone wrong either, so I told Ben the story after work that evening. He didn't do a fantastic job stifling his laughter. In the UK, "concessions" means a concession in the price due to old age, student status, disability—none of which the old man thought I had. It never referred to snacks.

There were no other worries about decorum, as it turned out. The gift shop was remarkably restrained. In fact, I don't recall seeing Diana depicted on any merchandise. The most touristy item offered was an Althorp tea towel, which I resisted adding to my collection. Diana's younger brother Charles, the 9th Earl Spencer calls his home ALL-trupp, though the locals don't. The upper classes like to swallow their vowels. When I learned Cholmondeley was pronounced CHUM-lee, I despaired.

A long hallway lined with large glass cases contained some of Diana's most famous dresses, accompanied by photographs of her wearing them. Her starched wedding dress was the grandest of all, but I found it creepy. I've never been a fan of the giant meringue look, and the fear factor came from a featureless mannequin with a face of white cloth. The dress was turning from the white I remembered in pictures to yellowy cream. Granted, I sat in my childhood bedroom on her wedding day in 1981, watching her walk down the aisle on my black-and-white Sylvania with about six inches between my nose and the screen. It was hard to imagine someone actually wearing a garment that could double as a special-event marquee.

The earl lived at Althorp with his wife and a few other fixtures of stately homes—peacocks. Female peacocks are called peahens, and although beautiful, they can be prickly. Their dispositions aren't the friendliest and their calls are unmistakably shrill. On a romantic note, Althorp House's current flock of peafowl had been embroiled in a dating standoff, where elder peacock Tim was completely ignored by the new females on the scene. Apparently, the girls were more interested in dating the much younger Jim. *Regency House Party* missed out—the producers could have made their plot even more scintillating with a bit of peacock drama.

The stables were converted to a small museum about Diana's life and times. There was a beautiful John Singer Sargent pencil drawing of Diana's doppelganger and paternal great-grandmother, Cynthia Spencer. Diana had an American great-grandmother on her mother's side, Frances Burke Roche—one of the "American Dollar Princesses" who came to England in the Gilded Age to marry once-wealthy aristocratic men. In Frances' case, she married a baron—The Honorable (in name only) James Burke Roche, but later had to sue him for divorce in Delaware on grounds of desertion. There were lots of family snapshots, personal letters, and most interestingly, Charles Spencer's draft of the speech he delivered at Diana's funeral. The line where he thanked Dodi Fayed for making the last weeks of Diana's life happy was noticeably struck out with black pen.

The interior of the house was awe-inspiring, and so was its rental fee for private parties, events, and weddings. I pitied whoever had to clean the vast Spencer collection. What a nightmare, even with a clever, patented Dyson cushion attachment.

## Peterborough Cathedral

PETERBOROUGH GOT A BAD rap as a newer industrial city without a lot to offer. I didn't find that to be true—I saw history all around me. Despite my soft spot for Peterborough, I enjoyed getting a municipal rib in once in a while. At an outdoor concert, the emcee announced that she wanted us to give a "warm, Peterborough welcome" to the next act. Ben smirked. "What does that mean?" he asked. "Should we slash her tyres and steal her bike?"

I yukked it up with him at the time. But for all the snark, I was fascinated to live somewhere with such a long and interesting history. On one day's agenda, I got milk, bought stamps, and saw Catherine of Aragon's final resting place in the cathedral. She was the first of King Henry VIII's six wives, one of the four who managed to keep her head. I thought our American Revolutionary War era was ancient, but living in the UK redefined "old." Here, one of the pivotal timestamps was pre-Norman conquest in 1066. I sat on the sofa eating my Cheerios, pondering whether some Stone-Age shaman sharpened his flints in the place where our family room now stood.

Thanks to reading all-too-frequent articles about everyday people stumbling onto treasure, I was always on the lookout in our back garden. We lived in East Anglia, an area geographically closest to Scandinavia and famous for Viking smash-and-grab raids. Occasionally they left behind hoards of silver coins pilfered from East Coast monasteries or relics inscribed with Norse runes. I figured I had as good a chance as any at digging

up unexpected surprises, and at long last, that came to pass. Unfortunately, the surprise was a tiny wooden cross reading "RIP Little Hammy." I
shrieked as I threw my garden spade and ran back to the house. I gave up
doing archaeological digs in the garden.

I knew Vikings had been in my host city, courtesy of my tour guide at Peterborough Cathedral. Historians thought Vikings attacked and destroyed
what is now the cathedral for the first time in 870 A.D. In its current
form, Peterborough Cathedral celebrated its 900th birthday in 2018. As
opposed to the usual ground-floor tour, I took a tower tour, which spiraled
endlessly upward to reach the roof. The top of the cathedral was the
highest point in the city. (England enforced the old rule that, by definition,
cities had to contain a cathedral. Everything else was a town or a village.)
The tour guides were small slips of women the size of medieval monks who
issued thoughtful warnings about the tour for those who feared heights
or felt claustrophobic. They didn't advertise that the tour could also be
called "Cathedral Cardio." Or perhaps another version of *Sweatin' to the
Oldies*. I had no problem feeling the burn on the mini-monk-sized stone
spiral stairwells, with treads worn smooth and concave by the footprints
of the last millennium. I waddled up bowlegged—my size 9 US feet didn't
quite fit inside middle-aged monk print.

Benedictine monks used to run the place, but their only remnant was
in the gift shop: little teddy bears dressed in black, hooded tunics. Peterborough Cathedral looked remarkably good for a building completed
800 years before. Henry VIII decided that the city's relatively new church
should be Catherine of Aragon's burial place. He wanted his first wife
"out of sight, out of mind" seventy miles north of London as he plotted
to behead his second wife, Anne Boleyn, four months later. Henry gave
Catherine a lavish funeral when she died at age forty-nine, but he did not
attend. For the history buffs who want to remember which of Henry's six

better halves lost their heads, the rhyme goes "Divorced, beheaded, died; divorced, beheaded, survived." Another local celebrity, Mary, Queen of Scots, cousin of Queen Elizabeth I, was here for twenty-five years after she lost her head in a town about fifteen minutes outside Peterborough called Fotheringhay. Elizabeth was always suspicious that her cousin Mary might make a power grab for the English throne, and their relationship took a serious downward turn when Mary ordered a failed assassination attempt against Elizabeth. Elizabeth dealt with the Mary problem by ordering her execution, though she claimed to be furious when it was actually carried out. Mary's beheading was utterly bungled by her executioner, who failed to sever her head with his first whack. When he finally held it aloft by what he thought was her flaming red hair, he was the one who lost her head—everyone saw her gray-haired head drop unceremoniously to the ground from the wig he clutched. Eventually, Mary's son upgraded her final resting place to a better plot in Westminster Abbey when he became King James I of England and Scotland in 1611.

After my never-ending cardio duck-walk up the tower's spiral staircase, we arrived at what will forever be the highest point in Peterborough due to that snazzy real estate concept of zoning—the City Council will never allow a building higher. I forgot to stake a miniature flag like summiting Everest, but the sherpa-docent ladies were sure to remember me by my "Oh, no..." comments every time I saw we needed to wedge ourselves through yet another 3' x 2' door. (Like in my driving exam, I maintained my habit of narrating my misfortune.) These doorways reminded me of the childhood cheese maze I crawled through at Chuck E. Cheese pizza, with the sound of the Skee-Ball machines dinging in the background now replaced by bell clanging. I felt the bones in my middle ear buzzing.

Despite the surprise workout and hearing loss afterward, I enjoyed my-self. I reluctantly paid the "camera license" of £2 to take photographic evidence of my visit. (There was still something off-putting about being taxed by the British.)

_ele_

## Buck House and the Palacette of Westminster

I WAS GETTING GOOD "value for money" from our television license
and taking in all the history shows the BBC had to offer. I especially
liked where food intersected history, which led me to a segment on Queen
Victoria's favorite decorative, flavored jelly (Britspeak for gelatin mold). I
felt like we might as well see her house to round out my knowledge, so
we headed to the State Rooms of Buckingham Palace. The Queen opened
them to the public when she retreated to Balmoral Castle in the Scottish
Highlands each July and they closed when she returned home at the end
of September. Or, perhaps more correctly, she returned once riffraff like us
couldn't show up on the doorstep anymore. Legendary for her thriftiness,
she unbolted the doors to paying visitors in 1993 to help with the damage
bill after the devastating fire at Windsor Castle in 1992. We ordered tickets
online and took the train to London for the day, which turned out to
be unusually warm for September. We had an interesting conversation
while waiting in the queue. If someone visited your house, would it be
tacky to charge them £16 a head for the privilege, especially when it wasn't
technically owned by you, but by the public? Would your guests feel remiss
that the only thing they had to offer you was their cash as opposed to a nice
bottle or bouquet? But most of all, would you miss not being the one to
open the door?

The answer to all these questions is a resounding no. The Queen had
likely never opened a door for anyone, at least in her throned life. Despite
our best efforts, we didn't spy a single corgi, but we found consolation

in admiring her really nice stuff. King George III, who ruled during the American Revolution, bought a much smaller version known as Buckingham House in 1761 just so his family would have a comfortable *pied-à-terre* near the center of London. Today, "Buck House" has 775 rooms, 78 of which are bathrooms. Despite the surfeit of toilets, there was no public toilet on the tour, only a temporary one in the back gardens for the great unwashed to use. In fact, the gift and tea shops were both mobile, and came down promptly at the beginning of October.

The paid tour came with a "free" audio component, which made the hordes of people relatively quiet and cooperative. At the time of our visit, there was a special exhibition on the Queen's fifty-year reign, displaying her most notable ball gowns. She was downright diminutive, and in her youth, particularly stylish. My favorite dress was a blue and white gown embellished with crystal maple leaves across the hip line, that she'd worn on a 1967 state visit to Canada. She clearly wasn't eating the strawberry jam and clotted cream on scones she now peddled in the tea shop, which Ben said were delicious. Between the snacks, fine art, and knockout knockoff jewelry in the gift shop, there was a little something for everyone.

Most amazingly, we were in the palace for nearly three hours and only saw a small fraction of it. I was disappointed that the swimming pool, the cinema, and the Queen's private post office were behind closed doors.

A FTER SEEING BUCKINGHAM PALACE in the morning, we kept the historical momentum going with afternoon tickets to tour the Houses of Parliament, also referred to as the Palace of Westminster. Or Palacette, as I called it—we got into the chambers of both the Houses of Lords and Commons, only to find them downright dinky. It reminded me of the time I saw Dustin Hoffman in person, chatting in Los Angeles. I was an undergrad in journalism at the University of Iowa, and a kind alumna issued an open invitation to students looking for externships at *Los Angeles Magazine*. I was her plus one at a Director's Guild function, right behind diminutive Dustin in platform shoes.

The rest of the Parliament building was vast. Westminster was indeed a palace until it was converted to use by Parliament, partially burned, rebuilt, and finally took its current form. Our tour guide was a chatty and informative professional Blue Badge guide, the best sort. They were required to pass an exam to earn their credential, much like London's Hackney cab drivers had to pass the test called "The Knowledge" before they were officially qualified. Our guide warned us that straying off the path could lead to getting lost and his dismissal. There'd also be an opportunity to learn the UK criminal justice system as we were swarmed by many formerly friendly Metropolitan Police toting submachine guns.

Parliament offered one of the wickedest taunts of any tourist attraction, much worse than the exorbitantly priced bottles of cold water on sweltering days. Most tourists trekked many miles in their practical footwear, especially in large cities, and craved what the Brits call a sit down and a cuppa (cup of tea). We were at that point when our guide escorted us into the House of Lords and told us to file into the rows of luxurious, red leather-covered, overstuffed benches—but warned us we were not to sit in them. They were strictly the domain of the Lords. And, by the way, the luxe seats we couldn't use were made by the same company who did the car interiors for Bentley. They might as well have been giant chocolate brownies attached to fishhooks, so overwhelming was my urge to risk arrest and dive onto the buttery leather. They would have to pry me out with the speaker's gilded staff. I knew for a fact that Ben did not carry sufficient cash to post bond, so I grumbled to myself and imagined that the Members of Parliament had booby trapped the place with giant tacks on the seats. The House of Commons wasn't much better—same moratorium, different-colored green leather. The crusty British oldsters who carried a cane that doubled as a stool were looking pretty intelligent, after all.

Our guide explained the system of voting in Parliament, which was bizarre but effective. Instead of having a desk with a button to push, all the "nays" congregated in one hall, while the "ayes" congregated in another. They individually filed past a person taking tally, and in the meantime, had a chance to mingle and catch up on old times or new laws. It was the cocktail party approach. The Brits did love a good cocktail, and who knew the cost of wiring such an old building with newfangled electronics like voting buttons? There wasn't room for any desks at all. It was so small, in fact, MPs might get stuck sitting next to their arch enemy if running a bit behind for debates that day. There were no assigned seats. Knowing what little I did of English politics, the icy glances would set the thermostat back a few degrees Celsius.

The tour was great, but I couldn't say the same about the frisking as I went through security. I suppose they were still a bit uptight about Guy Fawkes trying to blow up Parliament in the Gunpowder Plot of 1605. Or when the Irish Republican Army planted a bomb in Westminster's underground car park in 1974. My only regrets were that my potato shoes lacked arch support and I struggled to find liquid refreshment. I needed to find a purse-sized, fold-up pint glass and a weary-tourist stool.

## Lizzie, Get Your Gun

As the days turned a bit colder, or "fresher" as the BBC weather people liked to say, so began my experience with radiators and Cox's Orange Pippin. I saw a roller skate key's older cousin, the radiator key, make an appearance on top of a decorative wooden box that fit around the largest radiator in the house. Our house, like many others, worked on a combi-boiler that heated water for our baths, sinks, and radiators. I was used to the dry, forced heat we had back in our Midwest homes, so I was delighted to notice the difference between radiator heat and feeling like I'd stuffed packets of desiccants up my nose every morning back home.

In contrast, I was petrified by the ungodly clanking coming from the radiators, usually right after we'd needed to fire them up for the season. Ben announced he needed to "bleed" them, and I was relieved when he presented the radiator key instead of leeches or a straight-blade razor. He explained that, occasionally, air got into radiator systems. The key turned a valve that allowed the air bubbles to escape and help hot water flow freely once more, no blades or blood stains required.

I feared nothing about Cox's Orange Pippin, an older variety of apple esteemed for its fine flavor. Of course, I was smitten by any foreign fruit, so Ben agreed to a road trip. We trekked cross-country to Sandringham in northwest Norfolk, the royal family's Christmas hangout and modest hunting lodge. The Queen's orchards were open to the public. Unlike Buckingham Palace, Sandringham was a country house privately owned by the royal family, so they could really let their hair down. While others may have ventured to Sandringham for the manicured gardens or opportunity to tour yet another royal residence, the secret purpose of my trip was to stuff my Tardis of an A-Class with as many pippins as it could hold.

After seeing Buckingham Palace's lavish display of wealth and privilege based on particular DNA, I thought the monarchy had reached the end of its shelf life. I squelched my republican sentiments and we embarked. I was at the wheel when a behemoth Land Rover came barreling toward us on a nauseously narrow Norfolk lane, bordered by steep drainage ditches that would surely beach my car. Not all of the driving advice I received from my father was "quality," but his reminder to stop before I got into an accident stuck in my head. He said I couldn't be accused of hitting someone if my car was at a standstill. I got over as far as I could and we heard gravel scratch as I pounded the brakes. I stopped before we heard the thud of the wing mirror bending toward my window glass. I wondered if the other driver would stop. It took a few seconds, but a rage-filled woman in welly boots launched herself out of the stationary Land Rover yacht.

"Get the bloody hell over!"

I felt I spoke the language and I shook my fist.

"Any further over and I would have landed in the ditch! Slow down!" I resisted the urge to rhyme "ditch" with another word. In her horsey dog set, I was sure that was just another name for her female, fancy-pants spaniel. She muttered something unintelligible as she dove back into the Rover and sprayed us with gravel bits on her departure.

I was shaken, but I recovered instantly as I saw the signs for royal pick-your-own. (I doubted the royals picked their own.) I left a small dust cloud as I turned off the main road and motored down a sandy lane surrounded by woods. I felt like a '49er prospecting for "PYO" signs and felt the adrenaline rush at so much golden fruit in one place. Arriving at 11:30, I was devastated to see the orchards were closed until 1 p.m. I felt like Clark W. Griswold in *National Lampoon's Vacation* when he endured cross-country travails, only to find Wallyworld closed. After throttling the steering wheel in sad rage, I reluctantly agreed to take the house tour to kill time until the apple loading dock opened. Based on his alarmed reaction, I think Ben was catching on that my agenda was entirely fruit-focused.

Sandringham was not an overly large royal home—a mere drop in the fountain of Buckingham Palace. A large array of Asian armor and various pointy metal objects were artfully splayed across many walls. Ever mindful of health and safety, Ben noticed the deadly objects did not look particularly well-secured. Fearing hidden submachine gun-clad police, we decided his observation was best left untested.

We arrived in a room filled with many guns under glass, as well as artistic renderings of the Queen wearing a '70s head scarf and holding up a pheasant she'd recently shot. It was well known she enjoyed the outdoor life. Her expression was downright joyful, much happier than the group pictures of her and the house staff from 1979. Granted, if I were wearing that much polyester, I'd find it hard to smile, too.

The culmination of the house's hunting theme was in a separate museum. It had a wing devoted to exotic game trophies of kings past. I looked into the vacant glass eyes of various mounted, stuffed heads and wondered if they were on remote controls for Halloween parties. Some of the lions were fixed in particularly rageful poses. I flashed back to my experience earlier that day at the empty orchard car park and checked my watch. It was go time.

We found the garden shop sold pre-bagged Queen's orchard apples, and I whimpered enough to get Ben to buy me the economy bag plus one for good measure. Realistically, I would have needed a cider press to process an A-Class full of pippins. In thanksgiving for his companionship, I promptly baked us a blackberry and apple "crumble" with a smattering of hot custard. The truth was I made an American apple crisp topping with oatmeal instead of breadcrumbs, and called it crumble so Ben wouldn't balk. I found crumbles dry, so much so that I had the urge to dig through one memorable specimen with a garden spade instead of my dessert spoon. When concealed with the magical condiment of Ambrosia low-fat Devon custard, my crisp-as-crumble ruse was complete. Either my conspiracy remained undetected or Ben let me blaspheme the blackberries for the sake of international relations.

## Particularly Green Tea in London

T HE DAY HAD COME to make good on the bonanza of Marriott
rewards points we had racked up by living there for seven weeks. We
could be judicious and parcel them out in less-desirable Marriott properties over time, but we decided on the nuclear option—we would use
up pretty much all the pot in one go, posing as the rich and famous at
the Grosvenor (pronounced GROVE- en-or) House Hotel on ultra-tony
Park Lane in London for a long weekend. Grosvenor House was smack in
the middle of Mayfair, overlooking St. James Park. They held the British
equivalent of the Oscars, the Baftas, in its ballroom every year.

I worried reception would uncover my redneck past, and by the time we
got our luggage toted across London via the Tube, we were feeling like
two dim bulbs at a high-wattage address. We checked in without blowing
my cover, but restorative fresh air was in order. The Dorchester Hotel's
gardens next door brought the festive back.

As my grandma would have said, that garden was "cute as hell." Just in
time for Easter, the gardeners had created rabbit topiaries out of green moss
and fuzzy, natural cotton. Green topiary teacups were subliminal messages
to passersby in need of some refreshment—the Dorchester was on the very
short list of places to experience a glorious afternoon tea in London, with
the exalted prices to match. Afternoon tea in the finest establishments was
a frilly meal, and the Dorchester wasn't giving it away at £46.50. That was
almost $75 a pop.

Instead of paying the still-ridiculous fee of £30 per person when we had the urge for tea at our own hotel, our Gold Club membership came with a key to the executive lounge, complete with all the free tea and scones we could handle. The hotel room was a bit disappointing, but mere access to the piles of freshly baked sultana scones with clotted cream made it worthwhile. I felt like I had stumbled in off the street just to use the loo every time I crossed the great marble lobby. We navigated through a lavish Arab wedding party, with a number of female guests sporting the unmistakable red-soles of Christian Louboutins under their long, flowing silks. The doormen gave me only a few wayward glances, so it would seem our rewards points spent as well as the next Middle Eastern sheik's.

_ele_

## Greetings from Sunny Hunny

I WAS INTERESTED IN a beach outing, so Ben suggested a Saturday trip
to Hunstanton, otherwise known as "Sunny Hunny." It was an hour's
drive under clear, blue skies. He insisted on listening to cricket on longwave
radio the entire trip there, but he was driving, so I didn't contest his vote
on listening selections. I resorted to counting fields of leeks and potatoes
out the car window for fun.

Admiring leeks and potatoes from afar wasn't as mind-numbing as it
sounded. Vegetables were in ready supply, grown locally. In fact, Ben got
down if dinner didn't include "meat and two veg." Norfolk was part of
The Fens, the swath of formerly swampy, perfectly flat farmland that grew
a good deal of the produce for the country. I liked feeling surrounded by
produce. When on a country road in the Fens, I'd close my eyes and be
back in Illinois amongst the thickets of corn and soybeans. Besides
potatoes and leeks, I'd spotted barley, wheat, puny corn by Midwest
standards, and vast quantities of rapeseed, used to make vegetable oil. In
April and May, rapeseed fields lit up fluorescent yellow.

Not only was longwave radio irritating because of the topic, but the
radio signal was blocked every time we drove through an underpass. It
came through with the fidelity of a WWII radio dispatch.

I was lucky when I met Ben that he didn't follow any American sports. I
assumed that meant he wasn't much of a sports fan in general, but what it
really meant was that he was merely on fan hiatus while out of his element.
His restoration to sports came when he uncharacteristically grabbed me by

the shoulders and shook lightly to convey elation. (I had seen Ben fervent on rare occasions, mostly while trying to convey the importance of tea.)

"Claire, Claire! The Ashes! The Ashes start in three weeks! Woo-hoo!"

At the time, I remember wondering if "The Ashes" was some sort of annual volcanic incident, but upon expressing ignorance, I was subjected to a ten-minute dissertation on the history of cricket, Australia vs. England rivalry, how the match went on for something like three weeks, and how cool it was that they always stopped play for lunch and tea. No help came. I thought of the line from Nick Hornby's memoir *Fever Pitch* when the sports-obsessed main character's girlfriend points out how football will never love him back.

As we finally arrived in Hunstanton, the call of seagulls was like music to my ears. Hunstanton is the only west-facing sea resort in Norfolk. It was a bit faded from its heyday in Victorian times, when it was a prime destination to cure anemia and rheumatism. We arrived at low tide, which meant the sea had receded more than a mile out. It left behind countless damp, tiny sand dunes, and water channels like briny capillaries. There were tide pools too, occasionally full of little fish, among other organic deposits. Ben and I had a healthy round of "Is it Dead Yet" as we meandered through the rust-colored or sea-grass slick rocks littered with biological specimens. The stripey cliffs above us were red and white chalk on top of what looked like sandstone. I thought they'd been defaced by dripping white paint until I figured out local pigeons were to blame.

Ben suggested lunch during a day at the beach should be a healthy dose of fresh fish and chips. I'd never had bad fish and chips in the UK. In fact, I saw an employee throw a ten-gallon bucket of cut chips into the cooker as we waited in a nearby chippy, so I knew lunch was not loitering under heat lamps. I always ordered mushy peas. I liked them, and as a vegetable, they staved off my deep-fried dietetic guilt.

The weather was breezy and warm, which led us to a park bench and the Saturday *Times*. A young man on an adjacent bench asked me the time and I obliged.

"Nice one! Cheers!"

I hadn't been told "nice one" since the days where my kid brother was paying me a sarcastic compliment after I had deftly fallen down on some mystical hazard. If my deed was extra dopey, he might upgrade his commentary to, "Nice one, shortstop." I had no choice but to interpret this young man's comment as sarcastic congratulations for the ability to read my watch. Perhaps he was especially impressed because it was analog. "Cheers" I knew as the all-purpose form of British "thanks." I cracked up just after he left.

Ben looked at me as if I had sprouted another head, but came to the rescue as usual.

"It's as if he's saying, 'Thanks for taking the time to help me.' "

"You got all that out of, 'Nice one'? Maybe I look stupid. It was probably all that longwave cricket."

In my defense, I didn't think stupid people read the *Times*. Based on what I'd seen, they would be more interested in the *Daily Mail*.

## Stately Home Improvement—Burghley House and Blenheim Palace

I HAD A NEWFOUND soft spot for old houses—rare was the day I didn't pass by a medieval guildhall converted to a Pizza Express or a house full of antique, wavy glass windows. About fourteen miles north of Peterborough is the historic market town of Stamford. It was the scene of our house hunting until we discovered that having a Stamford postcode added at least 10 percent to the price of everything. Posh, sandstone Stamford was nice for the occasional visit, especially after I figured out where to find the public car parks among the medieval streets that looked like a pile of spaghetti hit a map.

There was a public park on the banks of the River Welland where I discovered just how desperate the British were for the smallest bit of sunshine. It was an early June day, unusually bright and sunny, as we walked past a riotous queue at an opportunistic ice cream truck. Ninety-nine Flake ice creams were flying out of the van as quickly as they melted. We crossed a stone bridge to see a green field full of glowing white people, some transparent by nature, stripped down to bare chests and legs wherever decorum would allow. It was a mass of melanoma in the making. One man continued to broil himself despite turning an alarmingly bright red on his face, chest, and arms.

The thing to visit in Stamford was Burghley, the best-preserved Elizabethan manor house in England. It was built by William Cecil, 1st Baron Burghley, the closest counselor and confidant to Queen Elizabeth I. He died in 1598. Again, the term "house" really wasn't accurate, any more than referring to our garden shed as a cow barn. It was a marvelous example of what a man who controlled the nation's treasury could buy. Interestingly, it bucked the trend of many British stately homes, which are usually affiliated with the National Trust charity to pay for their upkeep and preservation. Burghley House is still owned and occupied by members of the Cecil family, who held onto it and managed the restorations themselves, with a marvelous result.

The house is filled with the typical chinoiserie found in the homes of the seriously old rich, along with great portraits of many important people sporting the weak chins of generations of inbreeding. There was a small, solid sterling silver bathtub on display, allegedly the largest silver item of its kind in the world. In fact, it was an enormous wine cooler. Back home, Two Buck Chuck would be awestruck. They brought it out especially during the Burghley Horse Trials, an event that attracts people who are into dogs, horses, and new clothing items made out of tweed. They gathered to admire one others' jodhpurs, scope out expensive riding boots, and acquire more Joules brand sportswear. I was at once intrigued and repulsed by the home's heaven-and-hell staircase with its disturbing overhead mural of the jaws of Satan. I couldn't help but think how cathartic it would be to put cling-ons of annoying people right below the satanic uvula. Our tour guide said the Burghley children used to like to play there. It was excellent preparation for a career in banking.

Overall, the house did an excellent job of showcasing the Burghley lineage. This included David Cecil, 6th Marquess of Exeter. He was most famous for his Olympic hurdling career and his depiction in the film *Chariots of Fire*. On screen, his butler balanced full champagne glasses on the ends of hurdles, recruiting his love of tipple to develop his technique.

Our tour guide told us about one of the ladies of the house, who, spotting a significant regiment on the horizon and knowing they were likely to pillage and plunder, invited them in for tea. Based on the quality of the scones in the Burghley Orangery, now its tea room, I saw why this approach was so successful. I would feel chronically hospitable if I could grow fruit year-round in my English orangery. We roamed the vast deer park, and managed to avoid the flocks of sheep that randomly invaded our personal space. We also visited the "Gardens of Surprise," but the only real surprise was the smoke machine in one corner of topiary.

Naturally, the upwardly mobile idolize Burghley House as the perfect place to have a wedding. An *hors d'oeuvre*, champagne and cake reception cost around £120 ($150) per head when we were there. The designated cake baker also does fondant chicken cakes with individually cut feathers for the country set, just in case a traditional cake isn't quite up to scratch.

Contrast this to Blenheim Palace, birthplace of Sir Winston Churchill and subject of the slogan, "The Finest View in England." Somehow, I doubted the Queen would have appreciated this brazen braggadocio, especially because her predecessors on the throne gifted the 1$^{st}$ Duke of Marlborough the money to build it between 1705 and 1722. Buckingham Palace had a certain cachet that Blenheim couldn't touch. Or maybe the Queen's machine-gun-toting security staff were just that more persuasive to my American sensibilities.

There was a reasonable admission price to Blenheim Palace and gardens. We accidentally took the back entrance into the property, which in my experience can lead to the most interesting and serendipitous discoveries. As we drove down the quiet lane, we had a sweeping view of a lake below us all to ourselves, with a fairy-tale stone bridge spanning its width. Ben slowed down to take in the vista.

Not unlike many old properties in rehab, Blenheim Palace's front entrance was partially obscured by industrial scaffolding. It felt like staring
at an attractive person burdened by hideous braces. We toured the state
rooms, darkened by heavy-duty shades to prevent sunlight from damaging
any of the priceless décor. There was a series of four Flemish tapestries
on the wall, depicting the victorious battle scenes of the first Lord Marlborough, the very acts that led to Queen Anne granting him most-fa-
vored-courtier status, aristocratic title, and pocket money.

Although the palace makes quite a bit of its connection with Sir Winston
Churchill, World War II-time Prime Minister of the UK, he is only a cousin
of the resident family and was born there by accident. His parents were visiting for a dinner party when Sir Winston decided to come into the world
a bit early, or so his American mother claimed. He was born in a modest
bedroom by stately home standards. We saw impressive old portraits of
the family and its circle, including a singular John Singer Sargent painting
of the 9th Duke of Marlborough and his family. He married the filthy
rich American Gilded Age heiress, Consuelo Vanderbilt, an arrangement
neither party was happy with. In exchange for being a Duchess, her wealth
was the Palace's home improvement fund. When he decided to run for
local office, she campaigned for his opponent, amongst many other marital
infractions. Divorce ensued, but the portrait was marvelous.

The state rooms did their duty for king and country in the second World
War, when they were used as headquarters for MI5, the UK's domestic
terrorism and counterintelligence agency. Our guide told us that all rooms
appropriated by the secret service had to be redecorated due to smoke
damage. This was not due to a pile of documents that had to be burned
after reading, but the prolific smokers on staff. It smelled relatively clean
after sixty years to air out.

As a nonsmoker and all-around super sniffer, I was shocked at how the 1930s cigarette smoke still lingered in the drawing room of Bolton House. This was a stately home north of Peterborough that was once the abdication crisis headquarters of King Edward VIII, just after he got into a giant spat with Parliament over wanting to marry American divorcee Wallis Simpson. I could still smell the steady stream of cigarettes, lit off the last one, in the carpets, wall tapestries, and even the piano. Whenever Mummy died, I was sure this would be her idea of the big smoking parlor in the sky.

Blenheim's rooms were in perfect repair, not surprisingly as the family still owned and lived in the residence. We went on an animatronic, interactive tour of the second floor. One scene depicted the first Lord's widow sitting at her dressing table with her back to the audience while her reflection in the mirror spoke. Her chest "breathed" to make her more lifelike, but the mechanical lungs were clearly exposed to all the spy agency smoking. Her back rose and fell with the subtlety of a consumption patient. I had to give Jorvik Viking Centre higher scores for authenticity.

The ceiling of the main entrance, called the North Portico, was home to the most unnerving, spy-worthy stately home art I'd ever witnessed. Maybe this sealed the deal for MI5. A series of six large eyes peered down from the ceiling above. Half were brown, half were blue, and all were surrounded in starbursts and frames. They were commissioned by the 9th Duke's second wife, the American Gladys Spencer-Churchill, once a friend of Consuelo. It wasn't entirely clear what she meant them to symbolize. If they were a window into her mind, it would be useful to know that she died as a nocturnal cat-lady recluse who suffered from mental illness. I couldn't say they made me feel welcome.

I did give hospitality marks to the Blenheim Palace cafe, which expertly served us the single largest slab of Victoria sponge cake I had ever seen. The young man behind the counter simply tipped the piece onto a plate, much like tipping over a New Stone Age megalith. On the blustery day we visited, we used the cake slices as paperweights for our garden map and tickets as we ate on the patio. It overlooked the magnificent Water Garden fountain, which was interspersed with boxwood hedges in perfect byzantine geometry.

What I really couldn't award credit for was the nebulous family history the house presented to the public. Part of the most interesting thing about visiting a stately home was learning more about the life and times of the people who lived there. This history was presented in little chunks: an anecdote here, a factoid there. Aside from the gallantry and battle bravery of the 1st Duke as stitched into priceless Flemish tapestries, I never grasped what such seemingly important people did or contributed other than providing a room at the inn to Winston Churchill's mother in her time of need. There were some allusions to possible bad behavior, like the whispered reference to "the wicked duke." The guides were purposefully terse about the nature of his wickedness. About the most severe activities they would commit him to were "youthful indiscretions" and a few mentions of wild oats. He didn't completely sink the enterprise—he redeemed the family coffers by selling off 200 or so Old Masters paintings, and here lay his wickedness in family circles. I would be interested to know if he tried less drastic measures to shore up finances first. Perhaps a series of stately home bake sales or cloudy lemonade stands? (Stately home baked goods were a winner—I was thrilled with my unexpected gift of a Chatsworth House fruitcake with my new subscription to *The Lady*.) There was also an account of how some of the workmen and artisans responsible for building the home were left in penury after the 1st Duke and his wife fell out of favor with Queen Anne. The newly-minted duke and his wife upped sticks to France to wait for her to die. Meanwhile, she pulled the plug on their building project. Once Queen Anne did kick the bucket, the Marlboroughs sloped back to Blenheim to finish the house with their allowance restored, but still owing workmen they stiffed on the first round of construction. I'm surprised I was allowed to know this much based on the hush-hush vibe. I had the urge to check any closets we passed on the tour for a hefty pile of skeletons.

Sure enough, my gnawing curiosity about what stories were absent was quelled by my new reference on English living, *The Lady*. The issue I received after our Blenheim visit contained a feature on Sir Winston's family, including rumored syphilis and episodes of *in flagrante delicto*. I knew I smelled a rat. Good thing Sir Winston bolstered the family far more than some of his predecessors.

## Pump it Up, But Don't Drink the Water

B EN AND I WERE invited to a wedding and reception in Cheltenham, a few hours west of us in the Cotswolds. Cheltenham was a spa town with the last and best "pump room" of the Regency era—elegant public spaces that actually served water from geothermal springs beneath. The vibe was very Jane Austen. It was also home to a famous race that attracted the horsey set once a year. Zara Philips, the King's niece, lived there in her vocational pursuit as an equine physiotherapist. Long before we arrived, the first order of business was for me to learn how to pronounce our destination in a way that did not sound like an order at a deli. Ben deftly filled the role of my elocution coach.

"Chel-ten-HAM!"

Ben winced.

I thought deeply and prepared to try again. *Swallow the vowels.* "CHH HHHHHHHHelt – num!"

"No, no, you're attacking it." He had to stifle the chuckles. It happened when those folksy Americans tried pronouncing UK localities with no less than five silent letters. It might as well have been in Welsh. "Try again."

"CHELT-num!"

He smiled and left to boil the kettle.

Soon, I began saying "CHELT-num" as an accidental curse word around the house. I couldn't seem to edit out the rage. After months of random "CHELT-nums" in the car, during dinner, and whispered at the movies, I got a "very good!" from Ben and the feeling that I just might have it down.

I had been to five English weddings, including my own. By no means was I an expert, but I considered myself a well-practiced observer. I associated English weddings with hats. I avoided hats because I knew in my soul they made my head look fat. On others, however, they could be slimming—especially when the size of the hat dwarfed its wearer. I enjoyed going on fascinator watch. A fascinator is a small spaceship of a hat that has run into a bird on its way to earth, eventually touching down on a woman's head. They were appropriate for weddings and horse races. They served their intended purpose—I did find them fascinating, especially when several women were wearing them in close orbit. To be honest, these mystical miniature hats freaked me out. I was also looking for crop circles at the salad bar.

The reception was held at the Pittville Pump Rooms, a depressing-sounding, but splendid, venue built in 1825. Jane Austen died in 1817, so the style of this venue's architecture was similar to where they filmed movie versions of her many novels. Cheltenham grew fashionable after the locals noticed a flock of pigeons that hung out at a particular spring-fed puddle seemed to live long and prosper. (It couldn't have been the stray french fry that sustains them today.) People began to "take the waters." Ultimately, Mr. Pitt of Pittville fame built his Pump Room after King George III visited in 1788 and really got the place popular. Thanks to the building code equivalent of Botox, the Pump Room and the entire town are in a remarkable state of preservation. In George's case, he got taken by the waters—his notorious mental illness became much worse the same year he visited Cheltenham for relief.

I eschewed an empire waist gown, but remained on Mr. Darcy-watch at the wedding reception. There were no lambchop sideburns in sight, but a delicious roast beef dinner instead. (Confoundingly, they called this dinner the "wedding breakfast.") British wedding cake is traditionally a fruit cake surrounded by a layer of marzipan and fondant icing, and I managed to breathe deeply and wedge a piece down.

One obviously tipsy male guest latched on to my American novelty and insisted on invading my personal space time and again. I ran out of excuses to flee. I kept stepping backwards around our round table, realizing I'd made a complete revolution before Ben sensed I was in conversational peril. I needed a drink. It could be anything but spa water, the Pump Room's *raison d'etre*. The Pittville Pump Room still had its operational and recently refurbished pump house, or more simply a hot water tap in an ornate marble closet.

Back in my study abroad days, I visited the Pump Room at Bath where I was bowled over by the Roman Spa. My unbridled enthusiasm had continued into the Pump Room dining area, where a dandy dressed in Regency garb taunted me with a glass of water drawn from the hot springs, full of "forty-three vitamins and minerals." At the extortionate tourist rate of £2 per glass, I was swept up by the fancy carved fish fountain dispenser and sudden thirst. I coughed up the money, but choked on the water, which tasted like a warm, rotten egg. I avoided a public spit take and drained my glass out of spite. It was probably a good thing that I had sat alone on the bus ride home. Who wanted to talk to someone with rotten-egg breath?

Some wedding truths were universal. A drunk person might try to engage me in conversation. I might be trapped by a close talker. Worse, these people may be one and the same. Most importantly, my attendance hinged on the promise that there would be cake.

## The Crowland Show

B EN WANTED TO RUN a 12k race in a village called Crowland. The name was ominous and I expected dark events and scenes out of Hitchcock's *The Birds*. To my surprise, I noticed a cheery flyer advertising a dog and pony show. How many people could say they'd been to a real dog and pony show? I couldn't refuse.

We had some time to kill before the race, so we stood outside the equine judging ring, where we watched a matronly woman decked out in tweed ordering around a troop of miniature horses and their handlers. The working horses with furry feet and enormous bodies looked at the spectacle. I could tell they were laughing, much as a group of Mr. Universe contestants would when their stage was suddenly invaded by eight Pygmies. A teenage girl was in charge of an attractive miniature horse that apparently found all his fellow contestants attractive as well, and tried to mount them. Being a completely non-horsey person, I watched in horror as Ben laughed.

"Oh my God," I muttered. "I wasn't expecting *that*."

"Surely that warrants a judging deduction."

Thankfully, the little Casanova calmed down as Mrs. Tweedy approached. We were fairly certain she didn't catch the sideshow or else he wouldn't have won third place.

While Ben went for his trot, I took a stroll among the booths to see what the local folks had on display. There was an old man who had emptied the rusted contents of his garage onto tables and blankets on the ground. I had seen some better offerings in the large bins at the householders recycling center. I wandered past ladies selling Avon, the police eating Kit Kat bars, the homemade dog biscuit booth, and the gluten-free fudge display. I walked past a table of candy where a teenager sat in a lawn chair next to his mother.

"Would you be interested in some rare American sweets, miss?" he called to me with the bravado of a British market stall keeper. Hopeful for a chance to score a coveted Nestle 100 Grand bar, I sized up his wares in silence. Nerds, Hershey Bars, and Tootsie Rolls dominated the display. I looked at him quizzically. It was time to pop his balloon.

"I hate to break it to you, kid, but where I come from, Tootsie Rolls are a dime a dozen." The gall of hawking them as "rare" made me want to nominate him for a feature on *Rogue Traders*. Maybe they were rare specimens... in Crowland.

His face fell. His mother started laughing.

"Oh, you're American." His tone was defeated. I had been reeled in regardless, and the two persisted in trying to sell me photographs of London, wedding photography, and Hershey's chocolate bars while they had my waning attention. They could tell I wasn't a punter.

"I don't know why you bother with Hershey's when you have Cadbury's on your doorstep," I said. Back in the States, Ben pined for a mere square of English-manufactured chocolate.

"I know. It's shite." His mother nodded her head in agreement.

Out of nostalgia, I overpaid for a handful of what might as well have been solid gold Tootsie Rolls and went on my way.

Even though I hadn't had one in years, Tootsie Rolls did make for entertaining conversation. I accidentally dropped a segment under Ben's driver's seat, which he mistook for phantom-animal scat. After his run-ins with delinquent raccoons in the States and the general state of my car, he was vigilant. Once I restored his car to its pristine state, we opted to have a look around the village rather than risk the dog show.

We checked out what was left of Crowland Abbey. It was a fine-looking ruin without a roof. The abbot offered to ply Henry VIII's fixer, Thomas Cromwell, with fish, but it wasn't enough to save the abbey from dissolution. Like many abbeys of its time, it was disassembled and sold for parts by the king in 1539. Although we couldn't get access to the roofed, working church portion that remained, the outdoor carvings of pint-sized saints and martyrs were fresh-faced considering they were 1,300 years old.

We stopped in a charity shop for cat rescue that looked and smelled far worse than our old yurt curtains, a handy yardstick of decay. We had lunch in The Old Copper Kettle tea shop. The name fit—it was so hot inside, I found it difficult to finish my soup. Local oldsters yukked it up next to the fire while wearing a colorful array of '80s-era macs (raincoats).

Water weighed heavily in the fen landscape. We climbed up Trinity Bridge, a curiously medieval three-way structure that used to span the convergence of three rivers. In fact, the entire town was riddled with transportation canals before it had modern streets. I imagined a feudal man guiding his punt up to the Spar mini mart, grabbing a case of the Crowland Abbey monks' special ale before floating over to Hector the Elder's dog and pony show.

## The Magical Mystery Tour

I THOUGHT I'D BE missing a major cultural opportunity if I didn't make a pilgrimage to Liverpool to see some of the Beatles' old haunts. My dad owned a majority of the Beatles' vinyl records. As an adult, I marveled at how hip he was for his time. He had all the first albums of Madonna, Bryan Adams, Journey, and a particularly fun Rolling Stones record that had a real zipper my brother and I used to fiddle with incessantly. At the time, I didn't realize we were amusing ourselves by adjusting some guy's crotch on the infamous "Sticky Fingers." As kids, we considered it a personal invitation, based on the amount of orange push-ups and Flavor Ices we consumed.

I arrived on the island with what I thought was a respectable body of Beatles knowledge, enough to be confident should it come up on the "Life in the UK" test. Despite our road tripping, I couldn't recall one time I'd heard any Beatles songs on British radio. Beatles hits were the foundation of oldies radio back in the States. Had the UK burned out on them?

Always up for cultural enrichment, Ben agreed to take the Magical Mystery Tour through Liverpool. The name whispered "tourist trap," but how often did a tour come with a pre-written theme song?

We bought tickets at £15 each from the tourist information office, located in the red brick fortress of Albert Dock. In the late 1800s, when the port of Liverpool was one of the busiest in the world, the dock was a bonded warehouse. Historical snippets on the walls reported that Liverpool mainly sent goods and people to North America, and in return received cotton, sugar and spices. Naïvely, my first thought was of legitimate passenger ships, but these ships transported slaves. Estimates at the Slavery Museum placed the number of African slaves shipped on Liverpool-based slavers at about three million. The route was triangular—the ships left Liverpool, underwritten by wealthy slave traders and laden with goods to trade for slaves when the ship reached West Africa. Once their cargo of people was forced aboard and shackled, the ships sailed to Barbados or other New World ports to deliver the slaves. They then produced the goods that England and the rest of the industrialized world clamored for.

Liverpool made an attractive tourist area from its old docks by converting its countless square meters of solid brick warehouse space into modern apartments, restaurants, shops, and museums. We were looking forward to the Magical Mystery Tour to get away from the touristy bits and into the neighborhoods where real Liverpudlians lived.

People from Liverpool were "Scousers" from Merseyside, the area named for the River Mersey flowing past and out to the Irish Sea. To my ear, Scouse was one of the trickiest regional accents to understand in the entire UK. Coupled with their dry sense of humor and peppered with a bit of Cockney rhyming slang for good measure, I was relieved to have Ben as a translator. But even he struggled. I came across a guidebook that claimed to translate Scouse. For example, "Eez gorra banger" could translate to he's got an old beater car, he's holding a firework, or he's got a sausage on his plate. Ben filled me in—the guide was written for fun, and half of its contents couldn't be taken seriously.

There were a number of Americans trolling in the shops and sites that day, thanks to a massive Crown Princess cruise ship shored up in harbor. I have a quiet voice, but overall, Americans were a loud bunch. I thought our collective noun could be a "squawk." Brits tended to imitate an American accent like a parrot. Other than by their look of confusion, it was easy to pick them out by the way they pronounced the Liver Building. It was one of the major architectural landmarks of Liverpool's waterfront. They said "liver," as in the organ meat, and indeed the city's name. Locals said it with a long i. Thanks to a BBC news segment on the building's 100th anniversary, I had learned this myself the day before. I tried not to feel too superior, and I didn't see any snickering from the locals. They needed Americans to stay in the gift shops and buy more Fab Four tea towels.

We got on a coach (Britspeak for bus) painted in psychedelic Magical Mystery Tour colors. The interior was a chocolate brown velour which reminded me of the overstuffed backseats of my dad's 1980s-era 98 Oldsmobile, though the "cush" in these seats had left a few decades earlier. Ben got nostalgic, too—a similar '80s-era Volvo coach had served as his school bus.

Just as we were preparing for takeoff, our tour guide, Phil, responded to a couple rapping on the coach door.

"Can we take the tour?" they shouted in stereo. They were breathless, baby-boomer Americans.

The woman looked ready for portable defibrillation. This was highly irregular behavior in the land of rules, and the natives shot each other glances at this attempt to short-circuit the protocol of advanced purchase. Luckily, the tour wasn't full. The laws of commerce trumped tourism conventions and the couple collapsed into two empty seats. The fact they coughed up £30 cash worked in their favor. The UK doesn't burden purchasers with hidden sales tax, so the price they saw was the price they paid.

Our first stop was the birthplace of Ringo Starr, 9 Madryn Street. It was surprisingly easy to get the coach down this old lane of brick row houses built around the turn of the century. The entire city block was boarded up by the Liverpool council and abandoned. It was a stark contrast to the gleaming new buildings and urban renewal going on a mile or so away. There were plans to tear the entire block down to build affordable housing.

If they were like all the other worker's cottages built entirely of brick all over the country, then they weren't going anywhere on their own—the buildings looked solid as bedrock. As fans of old houses ourselves, Ben and I muttered that it would be more "in keeping" with the district if the council could renovate and rent them out. The local council thought it would be cheaper to merely raze the entire block and start over. There was a years-long tug-of-war after the council initially said Ringo's birthplace was of no particular historical importance (despite John Lennon and Paul McCartney's homes being protected by the National Trust) and there was nothing to stop them knocking the block down. Local furor swelled. The council agreed to save his birthplace and disassemble it, brick by brick, for inclusion in a museum. Ringo himself said that was a stupid idea. And so, the block sat idle as Ringo's house collected graffiti. Liverpool opened a billion-pound shopping center in 2008 that was strangely reminiscent of one in the futuristic film *Minority Report*. Could they not spare a few million for the likes of Ringo?

Occasionally, the tour bus would pull over so we could get out and see the sights close-up. We pulled over on a less busy section of Penny Lane, as Phil told us the barber, banker, shelter, and roundabout were at a very busy intersection.

About a dozen of my fellow Americans rode a wave of nostalgia off the coach and right into the middle of the road to get the perfect picture of the Penny Lane sign. A Ford Ka came along and tooted its pathetic little horn, but this wasn't nearly enough to make them realize that standing in the middle of a major thoroughfare was not a good idea.

"Get out of the road!" Ben and I yelled. There were probably a number of Miracle-Ear customers among the squawk.

A Ford Ka was like a mobile jelly bean in motoring and maiming power, so it took quite a few more irate motorists to get the group's attention. The last motorist in particular was completely cheesed (honked) off. As his car parted the herd, he gave the "V-sign," a two-finger salute with the palm facing away from the insulted (i.e. flipping the bird). The wayward herd mistook this gesture as either a hippie peace greeting or flashing the "V" for victory a la Winston Churchill. In grateful acknowledgment of America's help during World War II, they shot the "V" back to the ballistic motorist and let out a tremendous cheer. He shouted an unintelligible Scouse insult as his car spewed a blue cloud of diesel fumes.

We visited all the other birthplaces and childhood homes, with the most oblivious Americans stumbling into Ben's pictures at each stop. I admired Phil's patience. But he wasn't above passive aggression when he told us that he occasionally left some Americans behind. I was not well suited to his profession—if I were in charge, we would have left the entire lot at Paul's house. Just as the coach began to pull away, Phil spied a couple frantically running after us. They had ignored his announcements of departure and got busy photographing the back of the coach. To my mind, that was like going to the zoo and taking a picture of a rhinoceros' behind—it wasn't particularly attractive and you never knew what might come out the tailpipe.

We finished the tour at the Cavern Club, the Beatles hometown venue of choice. We descended the four sets of stairs into its dark cellar. As the Brits say, it did what it said on the tin (a phrase from a famous ad for wood stain). Music from the guitarist onstage echoed off the arched brick ceilings, reinforced by steel rods. In the days before the smoking ban, it would have been a shadowy gas chamber. One T-shirt later, we were out the door and surface dwellers once more.

# Christmas Goes Cornish

I'D RECENTLY JOINED THE cult of British food personality and cookbook author, Delia Smith. She was no revelation to the natives, but for Americans, she flew much lower on radar than the potty-mouthed Gordon Ramsay or voluptuous Nigella Lawson. The BBC ran Lawson's cooking shows as late-night viewing—she flounced around in silk pajamas, raiding the fridge for a midnight snack. I'd never looked like that when I went looking for midnight snacks. On the other hand, Delia was sans gimmick. She was into old-fangled, cozy snacks, and, unlike Martha Stewart, her house cat was fluffy without being pretentious. (At least he was well-groomed in her Christmas special.) I thought of Delia as the anti-Martha Stewart. She doused her fruit cakes with enough booze to flambé for years. I believed her confident assertion that she'd never made a dry turkey. It wasn't hubris—it was the truth. After years of cookbook writing, Delia saved up and bought herself a football team, yet wore clothes that looked like they came from places regular people shopped.

Emboldened by her holiday special, I made Delia's sausage rolls to take to Cornish Christmas. Despite her flawless TV demonstration of making puff pastry by grating frozen butter into a bowl, I took the easy way out and used frozen sheets. How hard could it be? She had knocked out a batch in thirty minutes. After what seemed like a couple hours faffing (messing) around, splitting the casings off two pounds of sausage and crying over the onions I chopped, I had meaty little marvels to show for it. Into the freezer they went. I thought I'd earn extra points amongst the soccer fans at dinner based on the game-day chant classic: "Meat pie, sausage roll—come on England, gi' us a goal."

My first visits to Ben's family were in summer, with so much to do and see outdoors. We piled in the A 170 and began a six-hour drive to the beach. Of all the naturally beautiful English landscapes I'd seen, Cornwall was my favorite. It was rocky and rolling, beachy and unspoiled, even though sprinting around the winding, narrow lanes with an experienced local driver gave me motion sickness.

I'd never seen a moor until our route to the Cornish coast took us past Dartmoor. The landscape was alien compared to what I knew of England so far. The terrain turned particularly rolling and barren. Large, intensely prickly gorse shrubs bloomed small, yellow flowers. Gorse was the equivalent of the botanical undead, immortal and deadly. One of Ben's sporty horror stories involved hearty mountain bikers taking a tumble into gorse, like landing on a bed of nails.

It was a wilderness meant for sheep and the fabled "beasts" that stalk them. Farmers thought these beasts were large cats that successfully evaded capture due to the harshness of the landscape and a buffet of unlimited fresh lamb chops. We would also pass through Bodmin Moor, home of the Jamaica Inn made infamous in Daphne du Maurier's writing. It struck me as the English equivalent of the O.K. Corral—lawless and full of an element who didn't ask questions. They might even pack a gun or two.

Once we reached the sea, perilous cliffs dropped off abruptly to the waves hundreds of feet below. The Cornish peninsula juts like a giant claw into the Atlantic at England's furthest southwest corner. Its north shore faced the Irish Sea, while the south shore faced the English Channel. It was freakishly warm for its latitude, the same as Saskatchewan, Canada. The Gulf Stream gave it microclimates within microclimates. The weather could switch from merely overcast, to small hail, to bright sun in the span of ten minutes. While it wasn't tropical, I'd never seen so many palm trees outside the Caribbean, mostly planted in people's pristine front gardens. The daffodils were usually out in February. Back in Illinois, we'd be lucky to see them sometime in April.

Aside from the ridiculously changeable weather, Cornwall reminded me of the Northern California coast, complete with surfers, New Age enthusiasts, and meat replacement foods. There were plenty of wind farms. The population was more "green thinking" after millennia of hard rock mining spoiled the landscape and wreaked environmental havoc. Hundreds of years ago, Cornwall was one of the richest mining locations in the Old World. Its rock was loaded with tin and copper, so business was naturally booming during the Bronze Age. Things got busy once again when the Victorians discovered the merits of preserving food in tin cans. It was also a source of china clay for fine porcelain. There was even a bit of gold.

Mining left scars on the landscape where centuries-old abandoned slag heaps formed artificial hills. Abandoned mine houses once held state-of-the-art Watt steam engines which had pumped water out of the ever-deepening underground mines, hollowed out to unsustainable depths over hundreds of years. The most striking pump houses were perched on cliffs high above the sea, and had emptied the mine shafts that extended for miles under the sea floor. The mine houses' timber-framed roofs had long since rotted away. The ghostly granite shells remained. They were the gravestones of an industry long gone, taking with it jobs, wealth, and many of the area's young people who sought work in other mines around the world. Their hard-rock skills were in demand—Cornish granite was one of the densest stones on the planet.

The Cornish Riviera was popular with British staycationers. My mother-in-law spun tales of legendary traffic snarls that began the moment school was out for summer in mid-July. My first visit was in late August, lasting until after the bank holiday, which meant the crowds were dying back and the locals were taking a much-needed breather. Traffic was a particular problem because only one major road descended into Cornwall's peninsula from the north.

The locals called points north "upcountry." They were generous in their definition—a town just a few miles up the peninsula from any Cornish location would be labeled "upcountry." I asked Ben about various beaches that had caught my eye on the map, but he knew only a handful.

"When you had the beach five miles away, why would you ever go to one fourteen miles away? We were happy with what we had."

This was a young man talking, but it sounded like a "make do and mend" sales pitch left over from WWII. I felt like handing him a slice of potato peel pie. Clearly, the motto was, "Beach Local." When Ben wasn't looking, my eyes scanned the map for Sennen Cove, Cornwall's famous surfing beach. It was all the way out near Land's End, a staggering twenty miles from his mum's house. It might as well have been on the moon. Beach selection required a bit of local knowledge. Many beaches required a hike down well-worn paths, or were completely submerged except at low tide. I wished someone would produce a map called "The Underwater Beaches of Cornwall."

After beach season turned to Christmas, we headed down there again to visit Ben's family. We would fly to my family in Illinois for New Year's. Ben and I were the harbingers of miserable weather wherever we went, and no more painfully so than in Cornwall. Ben and Cornwall were usually very mild, even milder compared to the rest of the island. We left our house in East Anglia around 11 a.m. in snowy weather and arrived on the West Coast at 6:30 p.m., having covered about 270 miles. Most of this was motorway driving, but we averaged only forty-one miles per hour. A little snow on British roads prevented anyone from going a long way. We inched along roads that weren't salted or plowed with any regularity. Gone were the monster snow plows and preventative road treatments of Illinois.

Our visit promised to be more whimsical than usual because my mother-in-law had become a chicken enthusiast in the last year. Besides the fresh eggs, she started dabbling in chicken watercolors, chicken photography, and she had a particular chicken-tending wardrobe. All her chickens had names. Ben suggested Fricassee, Kiev, and Korma, but they were much more civilized names like Bella and Bossy. After days on end of below-freezing weather, the pond in the back garden froze over and the chickens decided to put on an ice show. We knew they had not been practicing "Bolero" by Torvill and Dean when one began pecking at the ice in an effort to break through. The rest who joined the capon Ice Capades struggled to leave the rink, despite announcements from management.

The roads were surprisingly slick. Salt was in short supply all over, but the council had gritted 800 or so miles of A roads (the major ones). In Cornwall, that didn't quite cut it—80 percent of its roads were not A roads. I don't think a road in Cornwall existed that didn't involve a hill. We were icebound, so we amused ourselves by carefully setting foot outside to watch the fruitless efforts of optimistic neighbors as they tried to motor up a small hill to the main road. About two-thirds up, they would lose traction, fishtail, come to a stop, and slowly slide all the way back down again. This was good fun until my father-in-law attempted to leave for work himself. Out of respect, we let him slide unmonitored as we returned to the kitchen for another cup of tea.

My mother-in-law enjoyed her fair share of Yuletide frivolity, which sometimes escaped her own realm and came to roost on us. I enjoyed wearing her Christmas gifts—puffy, electrified miniature angel earrings and headbands with spring-mounted Santas that swayed with every nod. Our Christmas dinner places were carefully laid with cylinders wrapped in beautiful paper, with gathered pleats at either end. I was assured they were not extra festive toilet paper rolls, nor were they holiday recreations of Sputnik. Christmas crackers are laced with a tiny bit of gunpowder that makes a fine, Class A-explosive bang when pulled apart. Traditionally, they contain a joke, motto or riddle, a prize of debatable value, and a tissue paper crown I always got goaded into modeling, despite my aversion to headwear.

Our crackers came from a local National Trust shop. Their inventory is usually upmarket, but the occasional cheesy item slipped in. Our crackers came with extra cheese. A set of eight contained a small, plastic horn tuned to a different note and a numbered sticker. Each diner was to wear his or her sticker. As my mother-in-law stealthily revealed the baton that had come with this kit of fresh hell, it became clear she would be conducting us in a post-dinner plastic horn concert of popular Christmas carols. She produced the tabulated music, announced the song, and began calling numbers and pointing at each diner when their horn's particular note was necessary. It sounded like a herd of flatulent geese being strangled. We managed to get through all of her musical selections without a single one recognizable as the original work. After an offer of one more tooting, we unanimously declined and voted to serve the Christmas pudding instead. Unfortunately, there was no tragic incident involving her sheet music and the flaming brandy that pooled around the pudding.

A cracker is also British English for all of the following: a dry biscuit; something that is good; an attractive woman; and a firecracker. Once, Ben caught me off guard by declaring that one of the Harry Potter movies was "a cracking film." All the American possibilities raced through my mind—poor projection and sound quality, produced by a crackpot? When I went Yankee and thought cracker, the Premium Saltine came to mind. But deep in the American South, it was a loaded term far worse than trailer trash. For example, asking for a Christmas cracker at the customer service desk of a southern-fried Walmart would result in a visit with security disguised as Santa or worse, an immediate throwdown.

I was crossing the street on my way to another Cornish Christmas dinner, loaded down with a bag of holiday beverages. I stepped on a white traffic hump and felt my shoe move beneath me, followed by sudden bum pain and the sickening clinking of glass. Ben rushed over to help, but I had cushioned the blow by thrusting the bag skyward as I hit the ground.

"Forget me—save the booze!"

I imagined him carrying the wounded bottles out of a frosty jungle battle zone full of Cornish palms and menacing men wearing Christmas crowns. At least my priorities were right. To lose that much alcohol would be particularly tragic at a British Christmas party. Remarkably, not a single bottle broke.

Ben's sister opened the front door to find me spread-eagle in the street, stunned and immobile.

"What are you doing?" she asked.

"Oh, I'm just lying in the street."

From that point forward, my winter walking paranoia started. I was a very large chicken on ice. Ice in Cornwall was about as rare as ice in tea and was met with the same degree of disgust.

On one of our holiday evenings, our family settled into a cozy pub in the little fishing village Mousehole (pronounced MOUZE-ul). It was the home of the legendary Mousehole Cat, whose purring calmed rough seas and saved the village. There was one empty seat at our table. Without warning, a male octogenarian collapsed into it. We suspected he was a local when the bartender took a stein off a high shelf, filled it to the brim, and handed it to him without any money changing hands. Although doddering, he seemed charming enough in conversation, and at first mistook me for a Canadian. I promptly forgave him. Ben and I sat side by side, with Ben's mother across from us. Our guest stared directly at me.

"How nice it must be to get over to visit your son."

There was no thick coating of goose fat from holiday roast potatoes on his glasses. I saw no hearing aid, which may have been the problem.

"I'm his mother," my mother-in-law said before I attempted to explain that I was actually younger than Ben and married to him.

There was no way to recover from this conversational bombshell, so we downed our drinks and cleared off. I was ready to dismiss the senile dementia, but Ben had other ideas.

"We occupied a prime spot by the pub's fire—his, most likely, and we needed running off in a hurry so he could drain his stein in peace."

It was a viable theory. A major rule of UK decorum was not to mess with a local's spot "down the pub." It would be like trying to crowbar Norm off the butt print of his barstool on *Cheers*.

We felt guilty for being away from my family at Christmas. After the eight-hour drive to Cornwall, we drove to London to fly to the States on December 26, Boxing Day. We'd fly back into London at some stupid hour a week later, then drive three hours back home to Peterborough. For our mental health, this feat should never be repeated. There was one loss of consciousness due to sheer exhaustion, but the worst part of the trip hit on the way home from Heathrow. It was about midnight when Ben realized that he couldn't find our house keys.

I blamed myself. Years ago, I suggested a practical travel policy where one of us was voted "travel *presidente*," with a Spanish pronunciation. It was more of a third-world dictatorship than a democracy. The program came to life in the Washington D.C. Metro, waiting on a train to Dulles airport. We had spent an entire weekend swearing to the reliable other that our flight home left at 4 p.m. As we sat in the Metro at 2 p.m. I double-checked our itinerary. It said our flight home left in twelve minutes. I had misre-membered, told Ben wrong, then asked him to confirm. He had repeated back to me exactly what I had told him, creating a self-perpetuating spiral of misinformation that ultimately left us grumpy and flying home standby.

Ben was travel *presidente* for this trip, so I left my own keys at home. In hindsight, I admit there hadn't been an inauguration. In fact, I never bothered to hold an election, or even announce his candidacy. I knew Ben didn't think finding our keys was likely when he gave up rummaging through all our bags on our lightless front porch and dashed into our hedgerow to answer nature's call. So this was what a globetrotting lifestyle looked like. In the end, we were both relieved—I did find the keys in an obscure luggage pocket while Ben was otherwise engaged.

We crossed the threshold of our house at 3:30 a.m. and reported to work the next morning. I temporarily forgot some basic vocabulary like "toothbrush." Ben suggested monkeying around with melatonin for relief from crippling jet lag, but at any given time, I just wanted a snack and a nap. Once again, the driving license exam guide held important pearls of cultural wisdom. In times of travel peril, offer the victim a warm drink to aid their recovery.

# Part Four:

## Sticky Toffee Pudding and its Friends

*Training is everything. The peach was once a bitter almond;
cauliflower is nothing but cabbage with a college education.*

— Mark Twain

## Weights and Measures: The Fahrenheit of Stupidity

ONE OF THE MOST difficult cultural adjustments I had to make was learning to convert into Celsius and metric units. I prayed nightly I wouldn't be asked to do this on the "Life in the UK" test. Given the British obsession with weather, it wouldn't be an unfair question.

I used to think that the weather was the great cultural Rosetta stone—every country has it, and most people feel the need to discuss it, wherever they are. That goes twice for the British, of course. But even in an English-speaking country, there were days I just didn't get it. I wasn't alone in feeling lost—a fellow American expat confessed she'd burst into tears when she purchased a screw-in light bulb for her new lamp from Tesco, only to find it took a quirky UK bulb with a bayonet ending. It was a shining knife through the heart. She felt so culturally incompetent because she couldn't even screw in a light bulb. My particular highs and lows came predicted in Celsius.

Ben hadn't struggled as much converting Celsius degrees to Fahrenheit when he lived in the US, largely because he worked in a cold testing facility where he moved in and out of both scales as part of his job. He could also convert a liter to a US gallon in his head, which impressed me. That was handy for scaring Americans; he'd quote them UK gasoline prices in units they could actually understand.

One evening, a TV meteorologist recapped that the day had brought "short, sharp showers with a high of 18°." I'd worn three layers and left a trail of sweat through the store while it was in the mid-60s outside. Speaking only Fahrenheit left me chronically miserable and inappropriately dressed. I needed to take control of my happiness and learn to convert quickly from Celsius in my head.

In high school physics, Father Thomas Pisors had burned the equation for Celsius to Fahrenheit conversions into my permanent memory: $C = {}^5\!/_9(F-32)$, and its converse, $F = {}^9\!/_5 C + 32$. I used to be able to work these roughly in my head, but it took too much brainpower to convert on the fly when I had to get dressed on a schedule. Britons of an older generation spoke both Celsius and Fahrenheit, but in 1962 the country moved on with most of the world to Celsius. The US, along with the Cayman Islands and Belize, still clung to German units. (Ironically, there wasn't much call for British Thermal Units in Britain anymore, either.)

With limited room remaining on my hard drive, I decided to learn the most pertinent temperatures for my new climate. I got an instant morale boost when I had a clue how to dress in the morning:

10°C = 50°F
15°C = 59°F
20°C = 68°F
and so on, with every rise of 5°C = a rise of 9°F
28°C = 82°F
37°C = 98.6°F

I skew toward the less subjective, but this little poem was also helpful for learning Celsius:

*30 is hot, 20 is nice, 10 put a coat on, 0 is ice.*

It was still possible to get by on inches and feet for the most part, except when the carpet fitter arrived. He measured our entire house in a mental metric storm of square meters that left me wondering if our house had shrunk considerably during the dry summer. I wasn't about to learn these conversions. Any more serious knowledge acquisition would require me to purge other data, like my home address and phone number.

Weights were daunting. I knew academically that a stone amounted to fourteen pounds, but I was lost with any small amounts in grams. One of the most miserable experiences Ben and I had together was baking Christmas fruitcake, almost as nuclear as when all my possessions went to Delhi after I got off the plane at Heathrow.

I am not a good kitchen sharer, and the metric system plunged us into a kitchen snarkfest. Before he knew me, Ben appeared to be well-nourished. He fed himself food that required pots and pans. He cooked me a fine roast chicken dinner early in our dating life, so I had proof that he knew how to operate an oven. Despite this assurance, I shooed him away anytime he offered help in the kitchen. His sometimes-controversial techniques, like using non-Italian cheeses on pasta dishes, inflamed me like when Europeans lopped a burger onto any dish and called it "Americano."

This power balance was civilized until he wanted to steam a "proper" English Christmas pudding for my American family's Christmas dinner. Ben said we should tackle this project in October to have it ready in time for Christmas. Perhaps that was a clue to what lay ahead. Ben excavated his trusty *Leith's Cookery Bible*, with a dozen different riffs on Christmas pudding to choose from. Naturally, he gravitated to one that included stout beer. I tried to veto, but he was calling the shots this time. What did I know about Christmas pudding? My version of pudding was powders that mixed into noxious, inauthentic chocolate swill, in his book. I recognized Ben and Prue held the trump card in this debate, so I resigned myself to backseat chef.

To Ben, the measurements in cookbooks were merely suggestions. I was the daughter of a perfectionist mother who coated her avocado-green bathtub in marine wax to keep it perpetually shiny. Imprecise measurements drove me insane. We had gone to great lengths and expense to collect dried currants, dates, figs, sultanas, apricots, and apples. Prue had seen fit to list all her measurements in grams as opposed to ounces or pounds. Ben didn't own a kitchen scale, or even a bathroom scale. The wrangling started over what constituted 400 grams of dried apricots. I was convinced this was about a cup, but Ben was more convinced that we should toss our entire bag in. It came measured only in ounces, specially packaged from a fancy food store. There was no way I could confirm the bag weighed anything near 400 grams and I raged. In response, Ben was growing hostile that I dare question Prue and his birthright dish by badgering on quantities. Worse yet, some of Prue's recipes suggested using an oven set to "gas mark

5." I couldn't imagine that a gas mark left anything good in its wake. Meanwhile, I gritted my teeth into a tension headache and dumped unknown quantities of dried fruit into boiling Guinness. Surely this would be fit only to serve Ben's hated raccoons. He steamed the resulting cannonball of a cake in a glass bowl, carefully wrapped with a twine and suspended in a pool of simmering water for no less than eight hours. He decided to steam at night, and that made two of us. The next morning, he packed the pudding away in a dark, faraway cellar space I tried to forget.

Christmas came and we unwrapped the pudding. It was nearly black. I didn't want to serve a black cake to my family. I could see all of us falling out of our chairs within minutes, foaming at the mouth, muttering something about payback for the American Revolution. After pleading with him not to douse the pudding in so much brandy it would burn for days, I reluctantly helped him dish it out. It was, unfortunately, annoyingly delicious. My almost-ninety grandma, who had survived on coffee and aspirin for lunch through many presidential administrations, asked for seconds. After ten minutes with no severe abdominal cramping, I had to concede defeat.

Ben was gracious. We agreed to disagree on method, but I got a digital ounce and gram kitchen scale to preserve my sanity.

## Foreign Food Fetishes

A N ENGLISH DINING COMPANION once asked me how I was finding UK cuisine compared to the US. The honest answer was delicious in some cases, but dastardly in others. There was also a food limbo, where seemingly unmatched foods were thrown together and became tolerable to my beaten-down palate, but just barely.

My first case study was the ubiquitous British comfort food, beans on toast. Heinz had cornered the UK market on tinned baked beans. They are in lightly sweetened tomato sauce as opposed to the practically candied barbecue sauce versions that form the bedrock of American cookouts. At first, I thought like many Americans and deemed beans at breakfast just plain weird. But beans are a vital component of a "full English" breakfast. Hot buttered toast has a remarkable calming effect to the British, and adding a ladleful of beans and a smattering of optional mature cheese can be even more tranquilizing. I enjoyed eating beans on toast once I suspended my disbelief that there was a secret cookout lurking just around the corner from breakfast.

Case two was a noxious "condiment" called Marmite. My first experience of Marmite was in the States, when I observed Ben smearing some on hot toast. It looked dark, syrupy and ominous. When I inquired further, Ben made no attempt to describe it, but instead urged me to take a sniff.

"This smells like some sort of... by-product!"

"That's the thing about Marmite—they built their entire ad campaign around people who might hate it."

Sure enough, Marmite is the leftover yeast squeezings of the brewing process. I can only imagine its discovery by some legless (drunk) man doing a face-plant in the bottom of a brewery vat, accidentally licking the floor, and thinking it tasted good enough to mass market. I pray God will keep my path from crossing any more jars of Marmite. It is not to be borne. I'd rather own sheep dip than Marmite in the 500-gram economy size.

Case study three: I learned the hard way that one of the hallmarks of culinary Americana, the peanut butter and jelly sandwich, was repulsive to most Brits, including Ben. Firstly, "jelly" in American translates to preserves or jam in English. (Jelly in English is Jell-O in American, which could lead to a nasty surprise for the rookie American ordering it with hot buttered toast.) After the incident where I disgusted our removals men with a plate full of the offerings, I thought they might come in handy to repel British Jehovah's Witnesses or door-to-door salespeople.

Case study four: cheese, and lots of it. We lived about ten miles north of Stilton, home of the eponymous blue cheese. There were so many UK cheeses; it was hard to keep track— Cornish Yarg, Wensleydale, Red Leicester, and my personal favorite in name only, Stinking Bishop. It was a trend when we were married to name tables at wedding receptions, and some guests at our wedding were seated at a table by that name. I've not worked up the nerve to actually try Stinking Bishop cheese, so it may be superb and befitting a table name for guests of honor.

Artisanal cheese was big business in England. We visited the market stalls at the Burghley Horse Trials, only to get the most amazing whiff of farm-fresh feet. We were directly downwind from an artisanal cheese booth, complete with some wheels that looked more at home as weathered cornerstones of grimy mansions than gourmet food products. I tired of Ben's complaints about what passed for cheese in the US, and high on the list of offenders was "spray cheese." Instead of bone-chilling tales around the campfire, I used to tell him the story of a rather unsavory acquaintance who, in the height of the Atkins anti-carb diet craze, insisted on publicly consuming lines of aerosol spray cheese off his index finger in lieu of a cracker. Ben couldn't even bring himself to say the words "spray cheese," and I sensed I might have crossed the sacred cheese line. Some forms of torture were just too cruel.

In the cruel category, there was my experience of bread sauce. It was a throwback to medieval sauces thickened with bread. I personally encountered it at a turkey dinner, next to the cranberry sauce. It could be served warm, but this was cold, made by simmering a peeled onion dotted with cloves in milk, then thickening the milk with breadcrumbs and a bit of butter. As the English are ever thrifty, it's also a good way of using up stale bread. Even the host admitted that he had made it only out of guilt, and described it as "useless." This bread sauce tasted like cold, onion-flavored glue. It would make a fine substitute for decorators desperate to hang that last bit of wallpaper on Christmas when the shops are closed. I opted for a very small serving and daydreamed about my childhood compatriots who were persecuted for eating paste during art class. I could have broken them of that habit entirely with a little bread sauce.

# American Foodie FanMail

A FTER I'D MOVED TO the UK, I received a number of questions and comments from friends back home about British cuisine.

*Q: I know the Brits aren't known for their food, but couldn't you do worse?*

Indeed, I could do much worse, as I had once found out at a subpar hotel buffet in Italy. Breakfast had been a broken record of hard rolls with butter, deli meat, and unsweetened yogurt.

We had to eat out daily in the first six weeks of our English residency, so I became intimately familiar with "pub grub." Overall, British cuisine was very meaty. (Paradoxically, it was easier to be vegetarian in the UK.) "Back" bacon was one of the things many UK expats in the States missed most about home. It isn't the streaky bacon Americans are used to, but like Canadian bacon in consistency.

As Britain is an island, fish was big. Fish got baked into another well-received British food institution: pie. (Pie wasn't just for fruit. There was pork, chicken, fish, and even rabbit or quail for the tweedy set.) One potentially therapy-saving pie tip for the reluctant fish eater was to avoid something called "Stargazy Pie" at all costs. I first encountered it on the menu before we were run out of the pub in Mousehole. Thankfully Ben's mother was the cultural guide I needed to explain what I should expect if I ordered it—a Cornish fishing village specialty, in which the head of the whole fish baked in the pie gazed upwards out of the piecrust and into the dark recesses of my mind.

As drinks went, I missed the US tendency to give free refills at restaurants. I consumed an extraordinary amount of liquid every day compared to most people. Ben thought he'd purchased a 64-oz thermal mug for me as a gag gift, but "The Big Gulp" had turned into one of my most treasured possessions. I had to purchase each drink separately in the UK, so I switched to ordering pint glasses of tap water with my meals out. When I did pay for a drink, I found the UK's beverage selection enchanting. I couldn't get enough of the various fruity cordial concentrates that transform magically with water. Ben showed up with some elderflower cordial one evening, and at first I was skeptical because I thought it was a weed. I'd been down this hedgerow before when I made the mistake of trying dandelion and burdock in the soda aisle, which tasted like carbonated vegetable stock. Once I plucked up the courage to try elderflower, I found its flavor refreshing. We picked up a recipe for elderflower champagne. Aside from being afraid of mistaking elderflowers for their toxic look-alikes, Queen Anne's Lace, I was equally timid about trying a recipe that could explode. As part of the "Life in the UK" test, I did have to know the various patron saints of the four countries that made up the UK—and their feast days, but I was pretty sure I wouldn't be asked to brew anything.

Ice cubes existed in small quantities—perhaps a couple cubes floating in a glass. If the bartender heard me speak, my cold drink contained a bit more ice than usual. Larger quantities were available on request, and the Brits would never understand the American concept of chewing on "nugget ice." My mother the dental hygienist raged in my head: "You'll break a tooth!" which was right up there with death or dismemberment. But it was hard to shake a long-standing habit of drinking unlimited quantities of liquid loaded with ice. I don't think anyone who grew up in Illinois could survive a modern summer there without it. I tried to keep a low American profile when it came to asking for ice, but once I had a freezer in the privacy of my own home, I was much happier.

I was optimistic when other expats back in the States said losing weight in the UK would be easy. "The portions are smaller, dining out is expensive, and you'll walk everywhere," was a theme I heard time and again. The Brits didn't have the sugar fixation the Americans did and generally disapproved of Frankenfood. "E numbers" referred to the codes the European Union used to classify food additives. Some people used it as a synonym for all artificial things they didn't want in food, but E numbers covered natural additives, too. I bought British granary bread (whole wheat bread with cracked grains) at Tesco, and it had a third of the shelf life of any American counterpart. That was probably a good thing.

What the expats failed to mention was the dietary trap of British desserts. The puddings, as they are called, were so much more varied and tastier than back home. They could be fruity in infinite ways, and steamed, then doused in hot custard, pouring cream, ice cream, whipped cream, or clotted cream. Cookies and brownies were American inventions that invaded the occasional British pudding menu, but I preferred the classics. My all-time favorite was sticky toffee pudding, originating from the Lake District in the north of England. It was a rich, moist, dark brown cake, sometimes flavored with dates, that completely broke British pudding convention on reduced sugar. The color came from black treacle, which sounded like an ingredient in road asphalt, but was similar to America's blackstrap molasses. Some recipes called for the addition of brewed tea. (Could the Brits resist the chance to add hot tea to anything?) The best part was the sauce—a toffee (caramel) sauce so dense and sweet, a fork plunged in a saucepan of the stuff would stand at attention while my pancreas contracted in fear. The amount of heavy cream in traditional toffee sauce would make a cardiologist wince. It was edible rocket fuel that produced the shakes and an ass as big as the Lake District when consumed in quantity, so I rarely partook. There was simply no rival in its class. It was a fixture on every pub menu Ben and I spied for the first year of our island existence. In its absence, I'd listen for the thud of the earth shifting from its axis.

The caloric garnishes got to be a bit much. I felt like a heathen when declining cream poured over pie. But then came a case of pie stink eye.

"Well, what do you put on your desserts in America?" the cream enthusiast asked.

"If it doesn't have a sauce, we don't feel compelled to make one," I replied. "We'll probably just give you an even bigger portion to make sure you get at least as many calories." I never liked to play apologist on behalf of my entire home country, but I thought my explanation was authentic.

*Q: I know you can get a great cup of tea, but can you say the same for a great cup of coffee?*

Coffee was a rarer bird, not nearly as popular as the revered "cuppa." I'd had it readily offered with dessert and it wasn't half bad. They had the empire of Starbucks on the occasional street corner, so all was not lost if some wayward American needed a frappuccino to avoid imminent system shutdown. I tried *cafetière*, or French press, coffee served at a tea room. The brew was muddy. To be fair, so was my French.

*Q: I know there are McDonald's in London... is there a Krispy Kreme?*

There were at least a hundred locations, according to the company's website and Tesco carried them at 500 pastry counters. I couldn't help but wonder if wayward American expats had petitioned to bring them to the UK (but the Brits do love a good jam doughnut too).

I NOTICED THAT SOME Americans got hung up on recreating Americana outside America, and worse, felt affronted when they couldn't find it. There was no denying that parts of American culture spread worldwide, like music or the occasional bit of language (some more famous examples being okay, telephone, and a beeline). I was as guilty of this with my stash of Country Time lemonade mix as the expat who told me to hoard Old El Paso taco seasoning. It was easy to fall into a trap of magical thinking, that everything familiar should be accessible wherever we were in the world. In truth, the only thing that reliably followed Americans worldwide was our Internal Revenue Service tax liability. I was happier when I adopted an "absence makes the heart grow fonder" policy over "absence makes the heart want to shove American culture down everyone else's throat."

_ele_

# The High Holy Festival of Beer

EVERY YEAR, OUR NEW home city put on the Peterborough Beer Festival, otherwise known to Ben as the "High Holy Festival of Beer." This title was often muttered in reverential tones, similar to the Jewish faith's tradition about mentioning the name of God aloud. When we lived in the States, he would get misty regaling me with times of prior Festival of Beer mirth. There were stories of friends who booked the entire week of the festival off work so they could worship to the fullest. There was also the year of a totally coincidental, company-wide computer failure that happened to perfectly correspond with the Festival dates.

In my mind's preconceptions file, I noted the English liked a drink or two. Or three or four. Ben and his friends worked their charms on American waitresses in bars when they drained their glasses and said, "Excuse me, miss, but this one's broken. Could I have another?"

American beer festivals had helped keep me in work in Illinois. My main job for years had been prosecuting a never-ending stack of DUI cases, and many began when people got carried away at a festival beer truck. I'd also worked as a volunteer at a beer booth with Ben's US running club one year. I couldn't pour, serve, nor take money fast enough, despite a very efficient assembly line operation probably dreamed up by some engineers on the serving staff. While serving, I was positive that I recognized one of my frequent-flyer DUI defendants—too blotto to realize who had just handed him his beer. I also knew he was on probation and wasn't supposed to be drinking at all. Was using an off-duty DUI prosecutor to serve alcohol entrapment? In any event, I didn't have a chilling effect on sales. There were plenty of police around to discourage the extra unruly. It wasn't the most pleasant way to spend an evening.

I had already made a few observations about the sale and consumption of alcohol in England. I did my weekly grocery shopping at a Tesco Extra, a store that followed the American superstore model of trying to sell a bit of everything to everyone. Alcohol took up about fifty yards of shelf space, times four rows per shelf. There were wines of dizzying provenance from all over the world, a staggering array of beers, spirits for what seemed like miles, and even Weight Watchers chardonnay. It was easy to purchase alcohol on any given day at any time. Legal drinking age was eighteen. Technically, someone over eighteen could buy beer, wine, or cider for sixteen- or seventeen-year-olds to drink with their meals at pubs. Most places I saw found it easier to keep under-eighteen patrons out of the bar areas after certain hours, or altogether. Brits would think the "blue laws" banning the sale of booze before noon in the US were the Puritans' moldy leftovers. They wouldn't know what to do with "dry" cities and towns.

I was also shocked by the ultra-low alcohol prices. Of course, there were offerings that would always be expensive because of what they were, but many bottles of wine were priced under £5 (less than $7.50). Sometimes, grocery stores and bars ran buy-one-get-one-free specials, but alcohol-awareness groups pushed back against this practice because it encouraged binge drinking. Back in Illinois, it was illegal to give away alcohol, as it was in many other states. There were Federal and state restrictions galore on the sale of alcohol, although not all of them made great sense. In England, I noted an all-time record for cheap drinks at a wedding reception held at the Royal Naval College in Dartmouth, the equivalent of Annapolis, a hallowed British naval institution. Technically it was a cash bar, but an entire pint of beer was an unbelievable £1, while 50p bought a soft drink.

Granted, the Royal Navy has always procured a vast amount of cheery beverages cheaply and passed them along for sailing services rendered.

Out of cultural and professional interest, I decided to partake of Peterborough's festival as a comparative study. I expected to be a wet blanket because I detested beer, but so-called fruit beer was a different story. I was also a fan of cider, almost always sold as the hard variety, and perry, cider made with pears. With more than 250 beers and ciders to choose from, the locals assured me I wouldn't have a problem finding something to drink.

Belgian lambic was completely un-beery, and the cherry variety in particular was delicious. (I pictured a horde of Belgian monks scurrying around a cherry orchard, steadfastly pitting cherries in between bouts of vespers.) I knew lambic back in the States, but grew to appreciate it even further after a trip to a surreal Belgian restaurant called Belgo in the Covent Garden area of London. We used an elevator to descend to the basement where the wait staff, dressed as Trappist monks, brought great bowls of *pommes frites* to our table. I happened to be suffering from one of the worst head colds of my life, but my selection of a large goblet of cherry lambic was inspired, like a party version of Vicks cherry cough syrup. I found it mixed particularly well with Lemsip powdered lemon cold remedy.

The British beer festival experience was considerably different than what I'd seen in America. For starters, I could buy either a full or half Imperial pint glass upon arrival. After that, I could sample adult sizes of whatever I liked and pay as I went. There were thousands of people, but no real drunk and disorderly moments. Not one person got into their own car and drove away afterward—every cab in town was booked. People were jolly, but not to the level of shabby.

Binge drinking happens everywhere. But I thought the difference between British and American drinking culture was that Americans tend to use the fire-hose approach to drinking, whereas the Brits have the faucet on a steady drip. Both approaches have their downsides. Drunk driving is far more taboo in the UK. Unlike Illinois, motorists under suspicion of what's called drink driving in England had no right to refuse chemical testing. Civil liberties aside, I thought the Brits drank more per capita, and there was more social pressure to drink. I never was a big drinker—my drug of choice was cake. I regularly turned down offers of alcohol, and I'd been asked several times if I was "teetotal." Ben hung his head and said he couldn't drink at all anymore after he'd lived in the States for years, like it was a talent he'd been neglecting.

Thanks to the steady drip effect, tolerance levels were much higher. But tolerance was a mental attitude as well as a state of bodily adjustment. A poster at the train station in Cambridge warned drunken passengers to take extra care on the platforms. I think the American version would start with temperance and a plea not to drink at the train station. The ad would never have enough guts to accept that some passengers may be completely drunk upon arrival. I didn't know whether it was more noble to address the root of the problem or to be pragmatic and accept the fact that there are drunk people in train stations. In reality, I hadn't seen many tipsy people interested in reading and contemplating public health announcements.

As part of my tip-toe into British pub culture, I learned about a game called "country skittles." The first time I heard that term, I pictured people rolling enormous Skittles fruit candies as big as bowling balls at some unknown, pastoral target. I think my American brainwaves made the connection that country equaled somewhere like Texas, so that a country skittle was like a giant piece of Texas toast. Wrong again. It was bowling, all right, but with tiny little wooden pins and a ball that looked like it was shot out of a cannon during the Napoleonic wars. One variant of country skittles used a grotty (Britspeak for shabby) wooden replica of a small cheese wheel to bowl at the pins. I never cracked the code on the cheese—perhaps it was a homage to the annual event in Gloucestershire where punters flung themselves down a perilously steep hill to catch the giant wheels of Double Gloucester cheese that get a one-second head start.

In fact, I wish they did make my version of country Skittles. They would be an excellent accompaniment to a Texas-size lambic, served by a hospitable Trappist monk.

## Hedgerow Cuisine

F ROM AUGUST TO OCTOBER, we were surrounded by blackberries. They appeared in nearly every hedgerow from Halifax to Hertfordshire. As I was driven to snacking on many walks, Ben and I spent quiet hours gathering serious quantities of blackberries for our freezer. They were on public footpaths and in parks and completely free for the taking. Eventually, my pain tolerance kicked in. The bushes were thorny themselves, never mind the wild roses and stinging nettles they liked for company. After all our efforts, I thought an apple and blackberry crumble was in order. Almost as popular as sticky toffee pudding, it could well be the national pudding of England. Crumble was a product of rationing in World War II, when pie crusts took up too much coveted flour and sugar. Ben made custard (a warm vanilla pudding) to finish it "properly," a word that appeals to the instinctual cultural norm of following the rules and doing things the right way. The Church of England celebrated Michaelmas on the 29th of September, and it was said the devil has spit, stamped, or done worse to the berries if they're eaten after this "expiration" date. As a fruit addict, I took a chance.

I was glad Ben was in charge of the custard because I hadn't quite got the hang of making it. The most "proper" custard was homemade, but those who prefer to avoid stirring away twenty minutes of their life use Bird's custard powder. I was told by a Brit back in the US that instant custard making was an art form best left to fathers and brothers. Once I'd transcended the misogyny hopefully limited to that family, I figured I could whip up a batch using literacy and measuring spoons. The directions called for a strange sequence of mixing hot and cold milk in separate parts. It was more complex than producing homemade nylon in college chemistry. In any event, there were handy microwave directions. We had guests coming to dinner, so I welcomed the chance to put less on the stovetop. After I heated and stirred, it was still watery, so I spooned in a bit more custard powder to speed things along. With a bit more time in the oven, I opened the door to find a solid, orange brick. I wedged a spoon into its center, only to pull up and remove the entire glob from the glass dish. It had instantly congealed around the spoon, creating a giant over-baked custard pop.

"Can we eat it with a knife and fork?" I asked.

Ben was appalled I had wasted that much of his precious imported custard powder. I found Ambrosia canned custard, and everyone was happy.

Besides blackberries, English hedgerows were remarkably fruity, full of things I'd only ever read about. In our first few weeks in England, Ben and I heard a mysterious crunching sound as we walked past the exercise yard of a riding stable. As we drew nearer, we could see a pony snarfing damsons, pits and all, from a nearby tree. Damsons are a type of plum, popular for making jam. I had never attempted jam making. For one thing, I lacked a thatched cottage with millennia-old lichen attached, so clearly I wasn't qualified. There was also a rarer, golden version of damsons around our parts, called mirabelles.

Sloes were similar to damsons in color, but much smaller. I learned the term "sloe-eyed" refers to someone with eyes as dark and deep as sloes, which sounded either gothic and romantic or a bit like Japanese anime. Our local hedges were dripping with them, but after several failed taste tests, neither Ben nor I could figure out how they could ever turn into anything edible. They tasted like extremely tart, used tea bags. Their best and highest use was sitting in a bottle of what would become sloe gin or vodka. I was familiar with a sloe gin fizz because it fit neatly in my beloved fruity beverage category.

I was frustrated when a particularly domesticated friend of Ben refused to reveal the secret location of a Queen Anne cherry tree. Queen Anne cherries were wonderfully sweet, light yellow fruits with a pale red blush. He'd found enough for a pie. I blushed pale red with jealousy. While Ben was at work, I went on a fruitless odyssey to find this legendary tree, careful not to be spied by nosy neighbors or other free-range fruit hoarders.

One summer day, I was walking into Peterborough's city center when I saw a strange formation of mobility scooters in a nearby field. A group of supposedly immobile grannies were off their scooters and on little step ladders they had somehow stowed as cargo, carrying baskets and messing around in lush trees. I was afraid to investigate the scene because their canes looked scary, but I learned the reason behind the granny convention from a shop clerk at our local Italian food store.

"Those are morello cherry trees. The minute those cherries are ready, they strip the trees in minutes."

"Maybe I could get there in time next year?"

The clerk shook her head and let out a breath to warn me off, just as she might warn a young person wanting to compete with organized crime. Our neighborhood hosted displaced Italian immigrants after World War II, and the remnant old Italian ladies lusted after the cherries for preserves and syrups. Only after picking their fill did they return to impaired mobility.

I seethed with more free fruit envy. I would have to be happy with the six containers of GladWare full of blackberries in my freezer.

_ele_

## Chocolate Wars: Hershey's versus Cadbury's

B EN THOUGHT HIS YEARS in the States were a chocolate famine, full of inferior, lecithin-laden excuses for the real thing. Not to say this had stopped him from consuming the occasional Twix, but it just wasn't the same.

This cultural chocolate divide became clear when he'd get an occasional Hershey's miniature chocolate bar in a goodie bag from some running race. Untrue to form, he'd turn up his nose.

"What's wrong with Hershey's?" I felt loyalty to the brand Americans grew up with.

"It tastes like earwax."

"Earwax?"

I was horrified. I accidentally licked the end of a used Q-tip once, and I didn't think Hershey's and earwax shared a common flavor profile. I chalked up his contrariness to his love of being contrary, but he didn't backpedal in future chocolate conversations. They were brief and always to the point.

"Earwax!" he proclaimed, shoving any Hershey's chocolate product toward me. I was not completely upset by this arrangement. I liked to pick out the milk chocolate bars from the Hershey's miniature mix because I was a milk chocolate purist. Excessively high cacao counts reminded me of a childhood incident where, despite my mother's warning, I covertly sampled a bowl of melted baking chocolate while she stepped out of the kitchen. After the molten goo swamped my taste buds in bitterness, I had to wipe my tongue with a napkin. Was Ben's palate that affronted?

"What kind of chocolate would be acceptable, then?"

"Cadbury." He was adamant.

Bearing this in mind, when I spied a sale bin riddled with Cadbury Dairy Milk at the local grocery store, I swooped. I presented Ben with a bar ceremonially, hoping for a glimmer of appreciation. He didn't gush like I did. It would be too much to ask for him to throw his arms around me and pronounce me his chocolate savior. He examined the label and pointed to the fine print.

"It's made by Hershey's, you know. It still has earwax overtones."

"You've flipped it over and inspected its bottom for a mark of quality?"

Upon a close examination of a so-called Cadbury wrapper sold in the States, I saw that Hershey's was licensed to produce US "Cadbury" on British Cadbury's behalf. I was crushed, but he did manage to consume half the bar.

Was it possible that my chocolate palate was that unrefined?

In the days when a Costco World Market lurked near our US home, Ben would do the near impossible and light up with glee in its candy aisle. He couldn't help exclaiming the names of the merchandise aloud, like he was greeting old friends.

"Curly Wurly! Double Decker! Lion! Bounty! Fruit and Nut!" He showed restraint in his purchasing, but insisted I get his favorite Double Decker bar to see how the other half lived. It was a magnificent and extremely delicious bar with a layer of vanilla nougat covered in very smooth milk chocolate, mixed with crisped rice. I studied some of the ingredients and noticed the conspicuous absence of soy lecithin, otherwise known by Ben as earwax.

It was a sad day when our World Market closed, but I was delighted a new store had opened nearby. It was called "Devon Grocery," surely a home away from home for pots of clotted cream, scones, and decent fudge a la the English county by the same name. Instead, I was greeted by the unmistakable scent of curry and coriander as I stepped over its threshold.

At the front counter, I noticed the characteristic purple wrapper of Cadbury products. Surely this chocolate would be imported, just like the rest of the store's inventory. As a former British colony, maybe Indians were just as big of fusspots about their chocolate as Ben was. I victoriously purchased a Dairy Milk and waited to be congratulated.

"Where'd you get this?" He gave me a suspicious look and sniffed the wrapper. As the rest of the store's inventory, it wafted a very faint odor of bygone coriander. Before I could answer, he flipped the bar over.

"This was made in New Delhi." He pointed to the wrapper, but still opened it for a sample. He chewed and pondered.

"It's a bit off."

"How?"

"It's more like..."

"Let me guess. Earwax?"

---

ONCE WE MOVED TO England, Ben's chocolate-related happiness was restored. Convenience stores carried a mind-boggling array of chocolate bars that I'd never tried or heard of before. I felt like a kid again. There was a difference in the amount and type of emulsifier in Hershey's chocolate versus British-made Cadbury. Genuine Cadbury melted at a lower temperature and was much silkier tasting than Hershey's. To turn a blind taste bud made me feel like a traitor, but the internal angst of noshing a covert Cadbury's was like eating the forbidden Yorkie bar.

After being so cruelly shut out of Nestlé Rowntree in York, I'd been intrigued for what seemed like years by a magical-sounding place called Cadbury World. The Cadbury factory and its World were near Birmingham in a town called Bournville, which also happened to be the name of a line of Cadbury cocoa products. Cadbury World aspired to be a Disney-like homage to CDM, Cadbury vernacular for its flagship product, Cadbury Dairy Milk. These chocolate bars were in every post office, convenience store, grocer, petrol station, roadside snack stand, and even at the snack bars of better home improvement stores. There was little hope that I'd ever be off the cocoa bean for good—junkies would find it difficult to stage a sincere attempt at recovery surrounded by so many dealers.

It was an exciting Saturday morning when we drove to Birmingham and presented ourselves at Cadbury World. I had heard urban legends that tastings involved molten Dairy Milk. I detected strong whiffs of sugar and cocoa. It was like smelling fresh roasted coffee beans in Mexican border towns, without the threat of gunplay. First, we saw a hologram presentation of amateur dramatists reenacting the discovery of the CDM formula. Despite the cheese, I was rapt.

At its conclusion, large doors swung open as the light from beyond illuminated our theater like a sunbeam from heaven. We were herded into a room that was part laboratory, part sweet shop. This was the promised land. Young people in white lab coats and hair coverings offered us a small paper cup filled with liquid CDM and our choice of mixers, which included round cookie bits, wine gums and jelly babies (fruity baby shapes, like gummy bears with the texture of gumdrops), among others. The workers dispensed my filling of choice into the cup, covered it in a considerable amount of CDM plumbed through copper pipework overhead, and inserted a spoon. I went for the wine gums, a soft, fruity candy that I was disappointed to learn contained no wine. (The same was true for Jaffa Cakes, a small, dark chocolate-coated soft cookie filled with orange Jell-O that contained very little cake.) The liquid CDM was nirvana. I wanted a hot tub full of the stuff for snacking and relaxing.

We toured parts of the factory orchestrated for the public, and immediately, the smell of sugar with vanilla and chocolate overtones transported me to childhood. When I was growing up, my dad worked for Pillsbury in a flour mill and cake mix production plant. Occasionally, he'd take me to work on a Saturday when he needed to pick up a paycheck. The best part was visiting the testing lab, where the workers had to bake up cake mix, brownie mix, and doughnut mix out of every lot the plant produced. There was a ready supply of baked goods that were free for the taking for the right person at the right time. My dad was always capable of great charm, especially where sugar was involved. Almost always, our visits left me with a warm, industrial brownie in my hot little hands. On special occasions, he'd bring home an entire cake.

The last part of our visit involved a substantial queue for some sort of ride. I was due some good automated ride karma, especially after the offensive stench and animatronic crouching and straining at the Jorvik Viking Centre. We climbed into a car on a track and motored through a series of scenes showing animated cocoa beans engaged in wholesome activities like ice skating and bursting into song. It was a welcome opportunity to sit down after being on our feet for several hours, but aside from the joint relief, we were cheesed out and underwhelmed. The worst part was when we were directed to stare at a fluffy talking parrot that would squawk as an automated camera took our picture. The resulting shot was surreal digital embarrassment that we declined to purchase. My face showed perverse fascination as I stared at one particular cocoa bean that bore a striking resemblance to Mr. Henky, the talking turd from the animated series *South Park*. Ben did the sensible thing and shielded his face from the camera as if we were stalked by a band of confectionary paparazzi. I left with lots of chocolate souvenirs and the hope those pictures disappeared into the digital cosmos.

_ele_

## Enchilada Envy

BESIDES WHETHER I OWNED a gun, one of the frequent questions
I got from British locals was, "What do you miss about the US
the most?" Decent Mexican restaurants were right up there. Back when I
was studying abroad in London, I had several passable Tex/Mex meals at
the Embassy of Texas Cantina, right across from our school building off
Trafalgar Square. In true London form, the restaurant building really had
been the Embassy of Texas when it attempted to break away from the rest
of the United States in 1836. Unfortunately, Taco Tuesday in London was
a long trip from Peterborough.

To avoid disappointment, I made Mexican food at home, thanks to
my neighborhood Tesco. I figured out American expats were a suspect
source of advice on my very first grocery run—there was Old El Paso taco
seasoning, right in the middle of the Mexican food section.

Americans who loved Mexican were in the same category as Britons who
loved Indian. Both were foreign cuisines that caught on among the locals.
Just as there were excellent Indian restaurants in the UK, it wasn't hard to
find good Mexican food in America. Some of the spices overlapped. Indian
entrees used coriander, known as cilantro in Mexican cooking.

Ben went through Indian cravings in the States. He found Indian cuisine
there just didn't measure up. The local newspaper reported one Indian
restaurant that British expats actually liked couldn't pass repeated health
inspections. Among other infractions, they found both dead and live
cockroaches in the kitchen. At least some of the bugs were fresh.

To satisfy my cravings in the UK, we tried a restaurant in York that claimed to specialize in Mexican. My dinner came loaded with "salsa" with the heat and spice of vindaloo but the look of bolognese sauce. It was just wrong. The restaurant's refried beans were passable, just like pond water tastes good to the deathly thirsty. I would have preferred them without the flavor of liquid smoke, a vile American condiment that no Mexican ever used. I finally understood the complaint desk mentality of our English friends in America. Thankfully, I found peach margaritas on the menu, and that atoned for some of the sins on my plate.

Ben and I attended a dinner party where our Indian host made chicken fajitas and Mexican rice. He supplemented the punchy Mexican spices with Indian chilies and plenty of coriander. It was a noble attempt, but a bit too much of a mashup when mixed with basmati rice. I always smiled when I heard the Brits attempt to pronounce "chimichanga" with a twangy American "a" sound. I didn't correct them. I was learning there was virtue in adapting wherever I was.

_ell_

# Death by Rhubarb

S OME PEOPLE HAVE IRRATIONAL fears, and some of those fears are
stranger than others. I was mostly paranoid about small dogs after
having some scary encounters as a child. Ages ago, a co-worker of mine
had Crock-Pot-o-phobia, the fear of slow cookers. This person would not
only steer far away from Crock Pots at work potlucks, but shiver at the
prospect of eating food that could have possibly been prepared in one. He
feared an undetected power cut during cooking would render it a cauldron
of salmonella disguised as hot dip. He didn't seem to have the same phobia
of electric skillets. I did not probe his psyche further by taunting him with
an electric wok or a fondue pot, but I assumed the latter would set him off
by its mere resemblance to a Crock Pot.

I was snacking in our UK kitchen when Ben walked in and I offered
him a choice of yogurts. He wouldn't touch my low-calorie ones, but
instead preferred the Müller Fruit Corner, strawberry cheesecake variety
if available. To give him as much yogurt agency as possible, I recited all the
flavors I'd acquired at Tesco, including rhubarb. He began to gag. He was
so triggered at the mere thought of rhubarb, he sent himself into some sort
of psychogenic epiglottal spasm. I decided we shouldn't speak of it again.

Rhubarb was a beloved flavor in the UK, and luckily, I enjoyed it. It
flavored gin, tea, trifle, ice cream, and hard candy. Its ubiquity didn't
explain Ben's extreme reaction, which was similar to what I would have
done with a chihuahua puppy. Try as I might to delve deeper, Ben was
clearly stalked by rhubarb for no apparent reason. It was too bad. I was

planning on test driving a recipe for rhubarb fool, a type of parfait. I didn't want to be "the rhubarb fool" in perpetuity, assuming he could even bring himself to say the word. I hid any food products rhubarb had "tainted" behind diet items in the refrigerator. In case I ever wanted Ben repellent, I needed only to make a cross out of rhubarb stalks.

Just when I thought I had to break up with rhubarb, my birthday rolled around. As a teenager, Ben had been a gardener at a large home in his village and liked to dabble in dirt, so my presents were two peach trees in giant terra cotta pots and two rhubarb plants. He even planted them for me, muttering something about how our estate (neighborhood) used to be gravel pits and he could see why. I was touched. I expected him to wear a hazmat suit during planting, but garden gloves were adequate. Within a month, I had viable rhubarb I could foist on people at work. (Out of an abundance of caution, I left my Crock Pot at home.)

—*ele*—

## Thanksgiving, Observed

B EN DIDN'T MIND GOING to work on Thanksgiving because it never was his holiday to begin with. On the other hand, I moped around feeling sorry for myself at the office. I commiserated with a young, Canadian law student at Cambridge who worked at CAB on her Thanksgiving Day in October.

To recover, I cooked a curative Thanksgiving dinner for five British dining companions the next weekend. I had never dabbled in turkey roasting before and with my first attempt, I learned to appreciate my mother for all the years of slinging giant poultry. I took deep breaths and repeated my mantra: "It's just a large chicken," but I ultimately chickened out and bought a turkey breast crown versus a whole bird. The menu included crudites with cream cheese chive dip, fruit and nut mix, mulled cider, gingered cranberry pear sauce, roast turkey breast and gravy, stuffing, honey-glazed carrots, green beans with bacon and shallots, mashed sweet potatoes with a touch of maple syrup, scalloped potatoes, Pillsbury croissants (that looked just like crescent rolls), pumpkin banana mousse tart and vanilla ice cream. It was a lot of food. It would be authentic.

By far, the most controversial menu item was anything that contained pumpkin. It rarely appeared in British cuisine—Ben had never eaten it before he lived in the States—and was mostly used to make Halloween jack-o'-lanterns. However, Starbucks imposed its American will on British consumers, and the ubiquitous pumpkin spice latte started appearing in their UK shops during autumn ("fall" in Britain means to quickly lose altitude). I wondered if pumpkin spice would ever be the full-blown phenomenon in the UK that it was in the States. Ben shrugged dismissively.

"Starbucks doesn't change its marketing—it thinks, 'We'll keep plugging away at selling until British people actually buy pumpkin coffee.' "

Just a couple years before, I had lived in Morton, Illinois, Pumpkin Capital of the World and home of the largest pumpkin-processing factory. Now, I was struggling with the prospect that I lived in a little world where canned pumpkin was nearly impossible to find. An English co-worker remarked the reason for the island's fairly pumpkin-free existence was that they just had no idea what to do with it. Notwithstanding it could appear in food items like pie and cake, it still wasn't remotely enticing.

So far as pumpkin cuisine went, a few fresh Jack-be-Little's found their way into UK supermarkets and snuck into savory foods, but the prospect of roasting a whole pumpkin was a dealbreaker for more than just me. The American expats emailed emergency bulletins of where canned pumpkin had been spotted and how many units remained in stock. I happened to be in a small Waitrose grocery store where I saw a cache of "squash" canned somewhere in the Czech Republic. It looked like a pumpkin in the picture. I bought them all, told no one, and hid them at the back of our pantry. I never thought I would stoop to canned pumpkin hoarding.

As I wrote out my shopping list, I thought, *"Damn. That's a lot of food for six people."* I pooh-poohed my instincts and sent Evites for our "Totally Tremendous Thanksgiving." Best not to disappoint.

I had no expectations of how the offerings would go down with the Brits. A roast turkey was hardly foreign—it was the stuff of a traditional Christmas dinner. After a brief show-and-tell segment, the diners willingly queued at the sideboard. Several rounds of enthusiastic snarfing later, I was delighted to see completely clean dinner and dessert plates. I braced myself for some candid commentary. Brits mince beef into what the US calls hamburger, but they rarely mince words. It might be veiled in passive aggression, but the subtle insult was king.

Pointing to the fruit and nut mix, Ben asked me, "What are those giant brown things in here? They kind of look like turds. You can have those."

"They're dates, Ben. Thanks for being so graphic."

One guest I called Mrs. Tart said, "I quite like the cranberry sauce. It's not weird. We have that, you know." She announced to the diners that her husband had just dropped cranberry sauce all over the table. From a crime scene perspective, the stain appeared next to Mrs. Tart's water glass while her husband was still at the buffet. He didn't look surprised at finding himself under the bus yet again.

I got more spousal support from Ben, who declared the turkey "decent." I heard muffled echoes of, "Yes, very good," from the table as one man returned for seconds and doused his entire plate in gravy. He saw me staring, but I couldn't look away.

"We just pour it over everything," he said unapologetically. I knew this to be true. At the Royal Naval College "wedding breakfast," I was seated next to an officer named Dan who was attractive and charming until he poured the entire contents of the gravy boat over his second helping of roast beef. His terrace of sliced beef was so high it created a gravy fountain that spilled all over the table. He used his butterknife to scrape it up like wallpaper paste and sling it back onto his plate.

I got a few questions about the stuffing, baked in a pan like a cake. The box of Paxo stuffing mix led me to believe I should be making little spheres of stuffing, but I asserted myself.

"I refused to roll it into little balls," I said defiantly. After all, this was Thanksgiving observed. The green beans with bacon and shallots were a success, but one diner corrected my pronunciation to "shal-LOTTS."

My scalloped potatoes were a disaster because my neurotic prep the day before had me mindlessly slicing the potatoes without the benefit of keeping them underwater. It was a rookie culinary error. Ben tried to help me feel better.

"Yes, they are ugly. But they taste good."

I was most nervous about the reception of the pumpkin banana mousse tart from my Barefoot Contessa cookbook. Ben advised me away from hardcore pumpkin pie for this group of greenhorn pumpkin eaters, so I opted for a lighter, less squashy iteration. Once again, Ina Garten didn't let me down. A fracas broke out over who got to clean up the crumbs.

"Hey! Whoa! I want that broken crust, please," Ben said to the diners, exercising host privilege. I had no luck in finding graham crackers for the base, so I'd had to resort to pulverizing their British cousins, digestive biscuits. Just like clotted cream, they managed to put a vile-sounding word into the name of a delicious food item. Clearly, these names emerged before the era of focus groups.

Overall, I was surprised and relieved by my dinner's success. I subjected Ben to yet another authentic American Thanksgiving experience: the up-cycling of the turkey leftovers. Once again, he said they were ugly, but they tasted good.

# Part Five:

## Cultural Conundrums

*They say travel broadens the mind... but you must have the mind.*

— G. K. Chesterton, English critic and author

## Churchy England

I WAS BORN CATHOLIC, though I skewed Episcopalian in my older age. As for Ben, he was exposed to the Church of England (C of E, or Anglican Church) as a child, but his parents weren't regular churchgoers. Sometime in the first six months of our acquaintance, I transcended the juvenile idea that organized religion was a necessity for being a good person on the basis that he was far more prone to string-free generosity than I had ever been.

One of his earliest churchy memories was while visiting his great uncle in the seaside town of Aldeburgh (ALL-brah). He happily agreed to his mum's suggestion that he visit a "camp" on a Sunday morning. There was a large body of evidence that would suggest young Ben would have really enjoyed a real camp, based on photographs of pint-sized him rappelling down cliff faces and fearlessly kayaking downstream. Instead, this camp was actually Bible camp, and the nearest he would get to water sports was discussing Jonah and the whale.

Unlike the megachurches of the American Midwest with in-your-face flashing neon signs and televised worship hours, I noticed that Christian England was harder to find. It was easy to locate the nearest mosque in large cities by looking up, but the C of E was more subtle. Unlike the US, there were no political parties that took their cues from religious groups.

Ben had a theory about the Church's poor transmission to adults of our generation. In their youth, the British were made to endure services in ancient stone churches with no heating and only little, cross-stitched pillows to cushion their knees against the frigid stone floor. Of course, these cushions had been crushed by generations of knobby knees.

Old churches were respected as architectural treasures and sociological relics, but overall, their fan clubs lacked numbers. A woman at work told me that she had recently signed on as a bell-ringer in the tower of her local parish church, but she enthusiastically added she didn't attend or belong to the parish. I found that tone-deaf. It was as if the original purpose of the group, to remind people to attend church, had been completely thwarted, and all that remained was a social club for people who enjoyed noise.

Besides, I felt for the neighbors. We lived a hundred meters from a parish church. Every Wednesday evening, Ben and I were subjected to bell-ringing practice that began in timed pentatonic sequence down the scale, but soon, accidental syncopation set in. It was a cross between fusion jazz and a Japanese tone poem. Was there such a thing as Kobe-be-bop?

I went to a C of E sanctioned event, a "crib service" in Cornwall just before Christmas. The stone walls radiated cold that settled around my icy feet, but the press of people raised the temperature to just tolerable. My mother-in-law had a gig playing in a bell choir at the back of the church. A middle-aged, female vicar recounted the nativity story, calling up various children dressed as pivotal characters. One of the shepherds looked about three, and the cozy terry towel on his head and robe around him brought on a nap. More children processed forward dressed as sheep, but the back of the flock included the little-known nativity tiger and rare-breed Christmas brown bear. Surely, the Christmas lobster in the movie *Love Actually* had paved their way.

I would occasionally sample mass at my nearest Roman Catholic church in Peterborough. The priest was young and exacting. One Sunday, he looked nauseated during a visit from diocesan seminary dignitaries, there to celebrate a soon-to-be-minted priest who had been apprenticing under ours for weeks. Just one week before he was ordained, the priest-to-be was put in charge of mixing the water and wine together. The usual protocol was for the priest to pour a considerable amount of wine into each chalice, and simply deposit a few drops of water in each thereafter. The trainee looked pained and struggled with the recipe. An older man sat directly in front of me and felt compelled to comment. Thanks to an ill-adjusted hearing aid, his volume was on par with a PA system.

"Why, he couldn't mix squash in a pub!"

I tried to sit well away from others because the occasional parishioner wanted a kiss on the cheek during the sign of peace. Even outside church, I dreaded this custom. I could never make it in France, where greeting kisses were as common as croissants. I was not a hugger by nature, and I embraced the wingspan personal space rule shared by many Americans. Aside from a simple handshake, I reserve personal contact for those I know extremely well. It had been difficult to dodge the many kissers I'd encountered, especially men I felt were overstepping their bounds. I never found an elegant way to decline. In fact, one man's goodbye kiss zigged when I zagged and I accidentally kissed him on the lips. I screamed on the inside until I'd left the building and could let the sound out, but the phantom grossness burned my lips for hours.

In church, I once sat adjacent to a disheveled older man out of necessity—I had arrived exactly on time and the place was packed. He was acting loose, swinging his feet beneath his seat like a child on a Ferris wheel. He sang with the enthusiasm and quality of someone in the wee hours of a stag night (bachelor party). Based on his lyrics, I wasn't completely sure he was a native English speaker. His nose was red with rosacea, and his stomach protruded from his sweatpants. I braced myself for the sign of peace, and politely extended my hand in his vicinity. Without warning, he grabbed me around the shoulders and pinned my arms to my sides. He kissed me slimily on one cheek. When he freed me, I stood stiff and stunned. Surely if I lived in Stone Age times, I would have been dead long ago with such an underdeveloped flight reflex. My eyes were my only body parts still functioning. In my petrified state, I witnessed this man proceed to place a petite, elderly woman five feet from me in a half-nelson with a violent jerk toward his lips. I could not help but think of the American evangelical Christian slogan, "What Would Jesus Do?" In this case, I felt confident that even the Son of God himself would have cleaned this man's clock and turned his wine to water. Once I regained control of my extremities, I found it hard to resist plunging my head into the baptismal font.

~*~

W E FOUND OURSELVES ON a four-day jaunt to the Republic of
Ireland for a friend's wedding at an old cathedral. I was sure that
in a traditionally Catholic country, the priest would run a tight ship.

The groom was Church of England—in fact, the son of a vicar. Not
only was there full Catholic mass, but the groom's father split labor with
the Catholic priest. It was the shortest full mass wedding I'd ever been
to. (The Catholic diocese in Peoria, Illinois, had been a surprisingly tight
ship. My wedding back there hadn't allowed the full monty of mass with
communion—we got only a service because Ben wasn't Catholic.)

I was most surprised at communion. Back in conservative Peoria, I'd
heard priests make announcements that non-Catholics could not par-
ticipate in communion. Instead, the Irish ceremony turned into a wafer
free-for-all. We were sitting on the groom's side. An Irish boy in front of
us turned to his mother.

"Mam, what's going on?"

"Why don't you go up there and find out?"

Had the hardliner bishops I'd seen in the States been in attendance, they
would have used their crosiers to personally fish all of the Protestants out of
the communion line. I expected religious relations between Catholics and
Protestants to be fraught, especially so close to the border with Northern
Ireland, but it was delightfully equal opportunity. I cast a look to a couple
rows behind, where a family of Hindus were stirring in their saris as if ready
to spring into action. What wasn't so clear was the father of the Irish bride's
speech at the reception—I couldn't understand one word. Once again, I
found myself wishing for subtitles in an English-speaking country.

_elle_

# The East of England Antiques Fair

I PINED TO OWN a genuine English antique. I spent a lot of time watching TV shows where people scavenged antiques fairs and auctioned their treasures for many times the purchase price. Ben and I knew the British version of *Antiques Roadshow* from PBS, but I added *Bargain Hunt*, *Flog It*, and *Cash in the Attic* to my viewing repertoire. The best episode of all these involved a man who took a set of family heirloom silverware to nearby Ely Cathedral, only to learn it was pre-Russian Revolution Fabergé. It sold for about three times its original estimate in a nearby auction house, thanks to an electrifying bidding war.

Inspired by my viewing, I rummaged through the moving boxes in our garage for anything with auction value. During my pre-move liquidation phase, my secretary back in Illinois begged me not to sell my child-sized Tupperware baking set in early 1980s earth tones at garage sale. Horrified, she plugged the item into eBay's search engine. Similar sets were selling for around $80.

My aunt's 1967 Easy-Bake Oven also fueled my lust for sudden auction riches. Granted, its UK marketability was limited—it was wired for a US plug on US voltage and used a US light bulb. Never mind—it was just the sort of quirky thing I thought the *Antiques Roadshow* people would adore. After all, an old man had whipped out a mummified dog's penis in the previous week's episode. Ben had quietly suffered the Easy-Bake moving transatlantic with us, but remained unconvinced of its value. I noticed that what the English considered antique was at least one hundred years old.

Back home, my dad's 1967 Camaro reached antique status at twenty-five years old. Perhaps Ben had a point. I returned the giant, dusty box to its shelf and hoped that someone would finally appreciate its merits in sixty years or so.

I asked Ben if he'd be interested in perusing the East of England Antiques Fair at the nearby showground, with more than 1,700 vendors. My eyes were taking in the surfeit of other people's old household goods when Ben muttered something about an orange man heading our direction. I looked down, scanning for an Oompa Loompa. Instead, Ben had spied Tim Wonnacott, a colorful character and host of the UK show *Bargain Hunt*, who glowed in a perpetual shade of too much self-tanner. (Despite hosting a show called *Real Deal*, the antiques presenter David Dickinson faked his own patina, too.)

We were after something small due to our downsized English life, but it would figure that the most attractive thing we first spied was a Regency mahogany flip-top table with gleaming French polish. For £400 it was impressive, but we couldn't think of anywhere to put it. Parting with that booth was bittersweet. I mourned the French polish, but congratulated myself on our self-restraint. I was unlearning the American habit of acquiring so much stuff—I had offloaded more than half my wardrobe and shoes to charity shops before and after we moved to the UK, and I still didn't have enough space for the clothes that remained.

In housewares, I spied a number of the most wonderful, massive coffee mugs, priced around £50. They far exceeded the size of my *Friends*-era models. Often, they had beautiful, intricate patterns and I loved the oversized handles. Some had lids to keep the contents warm. They would easily hold a liter, if not more. I picked one up with care and held the edge to my lips. Ben screwed up his face and disappeared into a musty clothing rack.

The booth proprietors looked disturbed. It was tempting, but I didn't take one home.

The outdoor antiques stalls were in the cattle barns, faintly scented of their most recent occupants. We were browsing toward the end of the day, which made the bargain hunting easier. As we sashayed through the aisles, I noticed a brown paper grocery sack thumb-tacked to one stall's wall. Its tag read, "Real American grocery bag—£2." I was outraged on behalf of all the consumers enduring stinky conditions to look at so-called antiques. That bag was from a Cashsaver and didn't look any older than last year. Millions like it were readily available in every grocery store across the US. I silently judged the booth keeper. I had some rare American sweets she could sell while she was at it.

Ben was fascinated by one booth's display of militaria. He held up a reproduction Roman breastplate to his chest. He was a natty dresser by nature, so he always struggled with striking the right tone of casual at work.

"Maybe this is what I should wear on dress-down day."

The stallkeeper's antique clothing rail was an affront for the nose, but a feast for the eyes and a marvel for those with an upcoming costume party. On a recent night out in Stamford, as we were walking toward the town center, Ben had seen a group of young men who clearly recognized him from work. One was dressed as Rambo and another as Danger Mouse. They exchanged pleasantries, and after a few slurred comments, went on their way. I was sure Danger Mouse would not remember this encounter come Monday.

"What's with the getups?" I had asked.

"It's fancy dress night." My brain whirred. *No tux, or even a tie? Perhaps this was the fanciest they could do, being poor placement students.*

"Costumes, Claire. Fancy dress means costumes."

At the antiques fair, Ben returned the centurion outfit to its rack. He looked disappointed. His dream of being invited to a gladiator party would have to wait.

Next we found a booth with an ornate brass box. The geometric pattern was byzantine. It didn't look almost one hundred years old. I took the tight lid off to discover the interior was lined with tin. I had an idea of what this item was, but I called Ben over for a consultation. He concurred—it was a tea caddy, meant to keep the once-expensive commodity fresh and safe from the rampant moisture of the British atmosphere. It was marked £18, but I managed to get it for £12. I declared an antiques coup. Ben seemed happy with my purchase. Now, my so-called fruit tea wouldn't have to mingle in the same cupboard space with his proper black tea.

Next, my eye darted to an attractive mahogany tray. It was oval-shaped with brass handles and green felt pads beneath. The center was satinwood marquetry inlay in the shape of a conch shell. It was meant for transporting tea circa 1910, which made it about the same age as Ben's semi-detached house. The price tag said £80, but the couple on the stall told me they really didn't want to pack it up and take it back home. I managed to pay £50. Later, eBay confirmed my good deal.

About a week after the fair, I was watching a television show about life in a Georgian stately home. A woman in a grand parlor reached behind a curtain and pulled out a beautiful, giant coffee mug that had been sitting on the floor. These "mugs" were chamber pots, which meant I had pretended to drink out of a portable toilet in the presence of hundreds of people. I was failing the practical portion of my own "Life in the UK" test. I curled up in a ball on the sofa until I remembered I'd likely not see anyone who witnessed my pantomime again. Then again, it was a small country. We couldn't go back next year.

## The Lady

**M**Y FATHER-IN-LAW GIFTED ME a subscription to a weekly magazine called *The Lady*. I'd never heard of it before.

"It's a funny old magazine," he said. "Very English. I hope you'll like it."

The cover model on my first issue was Dame Maggie Smith. I thumbed through and took in some of the advertising. I saw chair lifts, retirement properties, baths with accessible doors, and matronly cotton nightwear. My heart went out to the people needing the help of the Distressed Gentlefolk's Aid Association.

I got talking about *The Lady* with a co-worker in Cambridge.

"It's a funny old magazine," she said, then reminisced about finding an au pair placement while at university by consulting its advertising section. Sure enough, many pages of ads were from obscenely wealthy families looking for cooks, nannies, housekeepers, gardeners, house minders, and a nebulous term called "mother's help." I imagined this last one was a particularly thankless job when I reflected on all the gross things my mother got stuck doing in my childhood. Would the duties include extracting tiny pairs of soiled underwear from the washing machine after they had somehow become stuck and disabled the agitator? The pay wasn't particularly good, with sometimes the only remuneration being use of a "cozy" cottage on the estate. Some of the ads were very specific about the type of hooligan they were trying to eliminate: "No one under age forty-five need apply."

Despite my urge to place *The Lady* on a piece of doily-clad furniture next to the Queen's silver jubilee Wedgwood plate, I continued to enjoy reading it for sheer entertainment. I became well-versed in the best features of stair lifts and mobility scooters. I enjoyed sidebars devoted to knitting patterns for Royal Wedding action figures, complete with a small pack of corgis to surround the Queen. The article on England's Best Marmalade contest was light and breezy, as was the fashion feature on what outfits were sleek and stylish to wear to a second wedding.

While on the train to work, I was pantaloon-deep into an article on Colin Firth. A lady of *The Lady's* target demographic age shared a table directly across from me.

"I have that nightdress!" she said, pointing to the back cover. I jolted in my seat, then flipped the magazine over to spy the raft of practical cotton nighties *The Lady* peddled on a monthly basis.

"So comfortable, and great value for money," she added. I smiled and nodded in agreement to pacify her, until I saw it went for £79. I'd seen the same pattern on a tea towel in a National Trust gift shop. The matching robe would set her back a mere £139. Only people who took their loungewear very seriously would consider paying this much for a wearable tea cozy. I continued to thumb through my copy, occasionally catching her pained glances. She was either in the throes of jealousy or passing a gallstone. As the train pulled into Cambridge and I gathered my things, I was compelled to do my Christian duty.

"Would you like my copy?"

Her eyes lit up with megawatt brilliance.

"Oh, I couldn't." Her hand started to twitch.

"Really, my new issue arrives tomorrow, and the article on Colin Firth is well worth reading."

That comment sealed the deal, and I left a very happy pension-aged Englishwoman on her way to Stansted Airport.

## Vocation and Communication

A N AMERICAN FRIEND ONCE wondered if Brits ever asked me unnecessary questions just to hear my conspicuous accent. It certainly happened to Ben in the States. Some Americans were more interested in admiring the way he was talking than what he was actually saying. In Britain, I felt more like a novelty act.

I was buying a box of tissues at a chemist near Piccadilly Circus when the teenage clerk slipped me a note and asked me to pronounce what it said.

"Awesome?" Had I lost something in translation?

She succumbed to a fit of giggles. "AAAAHH-sum! AAAAHH-sum!" she chanted.

It didn't feel so good to be mocked, but I was charitable and took my leave without a word. I was sure she needed a jolly in between pointing people to the hemorrhoid suppositories and flu remedies. Ben said "awesome" was a word the British rarely use, especially not with the drawn-out American "Aaaahh" at the beginning. I didn't use it much myself, as I thought it was just a bit too slangy. Brits were as bemused as Americans were to hear the little twists of phrase for the same meaning. I got a kick out of "turning on a sixpence" instead of a dime, "trolley" for cart, "pot" for container (as in yogurt pots), and the US phrase that always made for British comedy, stick shift. "Shift" in Britspeak meant to move, as in, "We've got to sort how to shift this extra inventory." "Sort" meant to figure out, not literally stack into corresponding piles. My mother-in-law heard me say our car was a stick shift and smiled. She whispered, "That sounds a bit naughty!"

—⁓⁓⁓—

A FTER NEARLY TWO YEARS of UK residency, and just after returning from a US visit, I dreamed I was in central London, leading a totally confused cluster of Americans. The locals were trying to communicate with them using the same tones and slow inflections they'd use with a group from Outer Mongolia, but absolutely nothing was sinking in. I had raised my tour guide's umbrella and a hush fell over the group. One of the locals had told me what he was trying to say, and I repeated his words verbatim in my American accent. The group let out a collective sigh of comprehension. I woke up feeling useful and needed. That wasn't an everyday occurrence in my UK life, so I enjoyed it while it lasted.

Unfortunately, I'd seen Americans that confused when it came to existing in day-to-day English culture. I was grateful for Ben, my personal tour guide and tutor, who accelerated my learning. If language was a radio frequency, it took time to retune the ear to the right wavelength. Sometimes being different was exhausting. It inflamed the part of me that hated being the center of attention in situations I couldn't control. If I was feeling worn down on any particular day, I'd keep my mouth shut to avoid outing myself as "other." I had a new appreciation for immigrants who struggled with English and looked different, too.

Sometimes, feeling "other" kept me up at night. One solution was trying to blend in sonically, but I was reminded of my foreignness every time I spoke in public. I felt guilty for trying to imitate an English accent, yet it wasn't long ago that I had been ridiculing Ben's American neighbor who'd felt compelled to do a horrendous East End fishwife imitation every time she saw him. My English friends said I shouldn't disguise myself.

In desperate moments where I craved anonymity, I thought about feigning an English accent. I'd read that Renée Zellwegger perfected her *Bridget Jones's Diary* accent by hanging out in London and trying to blend with the locals. At church, I would practice reciting The Lord's Prayer in the crowd to see if I could fake the accent. It was far less threatening to speak in the safety of a group, but God was watching.

I thought about trying a local accent at train stations, especially if I was having a problem. I didn't want a British listener to dismiss anything I said as the manufactured gripes of a pushy American. On the other hand, I would lose the threat of gun play that Brits associated with disgruntled Americans. I would also lose the starry-eyed treatment that some British gave us Americans just because of our accents. I didn't need to rely on my lack of glottal stops or twangy a-sounds for sympathy. Poor me. Or as the Brits would say, "Bless."

Just when I thought I was ready to try my linguistic experiment in public, I heard a notoriously brash British acquaintance mock the way Americans pronounced "water." North Americans convert the "t" sound to a "d" sound, and the twangy short "a" got stuck in the British ear. Apparently, we sounded like parrots. During a dinner out, our companion concocted a performance art piece for the entire restaurant where she strutted and squawked, ordering water over and over in what she thought was an American accent. I wanted to waterboard her with a nearby carafe. This was what bad accent imitation sounded like to a native listener. I was put off imitation for life.

There was only one small exception. The word "Orton" had to enter my vocabulary, because it was in the name of our UK address. Out of sheer need to be understood, I had to drop the hard "r." It came easy, thanks to a lifetime of listening to my father who grew up in Massachusetts and Rhode Island. According to him, I had a muthah, fathah, bruthah, and a cah full of gah-bage. If I fudged just one word, I could sleep at night.

Texting caught on far quicker in the UK than America—I remember Brits texting like mad back in 2001, the date of my first extended visit. Texters were amazingly fast in the UK, back in the days where it wasn't possible to tap a bubble to build a sentence in under five seconds. Based on what I saw on the streets, I was sure the ERs were full of swollen thumbs attached to chatty people who hadn't said a word aloud all day. I did my imitation of the locals texting with two thumbs for Ben, who quickly corrected me.

"We only use one thumb. Anything more is amateur."

All this professional texting was seriously degrading the mother tongue, and the US would be right there in another ten years. Fractured "text language" felt like a literary hangnail, and predictive text was a scourge on written English. My phone always changed Ben's name to "Benevolent," just a step off the path to sainthood. But its fickle switches weren't always flattering. We knew a man who took joy in consuming vast amounts of food without gaining weight. His wife called him by a short-form nick-name that predictive text translated to "lard."

My mother-in-law had a firm grip on her mobile phone and was not afraid to use it, despite her alter ego as "Nun." I contrasted this to my own mother, who was afraid of the spooky, glowing box called a computer that my father insisted on having. Asking her to send a text message would be like asking a passenger pigeon to start using Federal Express.

On my first try typing the words "predictive text," my Nokia magical-ly—and appropriately—changed them to "predictive vex." When I used Ben's phone to type the town "Porthleven" in Cornwall, it changed the word to "Portishead."

"How does your phone know the band 'Portishead'?"

"Huh? You can teach your phone names, you know."

"You taught your phone 'Portishead?' "

"Yeah, it came in handy."

"I didn't know you were a fan."

"Not really." He sighed as he drove. "Look at where we are on the map."

We were driving down the M5 when I spied it—Portishead, just outside Bristol on the west coast of England. It was the home of a large motorway service stop Ben frequented on drives down to Cornwall. Maybe predictive text was smarter than I thought.

—ⅇℓ—

# Ben's Old House

W E HAD A LETTER with the bad news that the old lady who owned our rented house had died. Her children wanted to sell and they gave us notice to vacate. We had some wild ideas about purchasing it ourselves after we red-bagged the fusty yurt curtains. It was satisfying to daydream about demolishing the kitchen, with its permanently sticky, chip fat-infused cupboards and flesh-colored linoleum. But bungalows in England were one of the most expensive types of home because they occupied a large amount of land proportional to their internal space. The house easily needed £20,000 worth of updates, coupled with a £250,000-asking price.

Our most obvious option was to move to the property Ben already owned. It was a 1911 duplex that had been his bachelor pad B.C. (Before Claire). It was narrow but long, on a busy residential old high street. We guessed it would need a bit of tidying after being occupied by four sets of tenants in six years, but Ben had been paying a rental agency to look after the place in his absence.

When we saw the state of the house for ourselves, our hearts sank. Thanks to subpar record keeping by Ben's agency, we couldn't pin any of the property damage on a particular tenant. The study light fixture had too many broken glass parts to count. Our interior doors were filled with yet more broken panes. There were endless rotten skirting boards, a rotten floor, detached carpeting, yellow and sagging ceilings, all amid the funk of 40,000 years, thanks to a family of prolific smokers. Mummy would feel right at home. We needed a machete to navigate the overgrown path from the back door to the garden shed, but that was nothing a major prune couldn't fix.

Time was ticking away. We had a month before our own lease ended to whip Ben's house into habitable condition. I had nightmares about an episode of *This Old House* where the master carpenter Norm Abram kept finding rotten skirting boards as a timer counted down the minutes. I woke up sweaty and fearful of low-rise work trousers, but I was extremely motivated to move into a house I actually liked.

I took on lots of tasks I'd never tried, like replacing a light fixture and a doorbell. I gave myself carpal tunnel syndrome by obsessively scrubbing the once-beautiful hall floor made of encaustic tile. One hundred years before, pieces of completely black, red and yellow tiles were cut and carefully arranged into an attractive tessellation. Now, they were covered with a century of dirt, floor wax residue, and the occasional gob of chewing gum. The tile store sold me industrial kneepads, a restorative acid wash that singed my nose hair, and an indestructible wire brush to lift the grime away, inch by inch. After multiple treatments to raise the dirt embedded in the porous tile surface, I applied a coat of sealer to the bright colors and watched it gleam.

Meanwhile, the carpet estimator came to look at our bedrooms. When I opened the door, he cast a long glance down the front hall and halted.

"Don't tell me you're talking about covering up this floor!" He admired my work, and it was the gold star I was waiting for. He told me many homeowners ripped up encaustic floors as they fell out of fashion or became damaged. He said people were paying £300 per square meter to have these sorts of floors re-installed because all the tiles were cut by hand.

I asked every tradesperson who entered our house to repeat the same mantra: "I've seen worse." I found it comforting. The clerks at Screwfix and Homebase knew me by sight and gave me sympathetic nods with every new paintbrush or cleaning tool I bought. I was learning valuable life lessons, like dried wood filler was awfully hard to get out of my hair.

The interior walls were a vision in Artex, a decorative finish plasterers used decades ago. It produced spiky edges and an ugly, wavy texture, only useful for grating courgettes (zucchini). The bottom corner of every window had large, spidery cracks where it touched the plaster walls. The people responsible for replacing the old, single-pane sash windows with newer PVC models used chipboard to shore up the frames. It swelled and contracted with high moisture levels. Our carpenter told us it was a poor way of doing things, and if we wanted to fix the problem permanently and stop the wall from cracking, each window frame would have to be stripped back and replaced with something more substantial. This was the same man who had saved us from falling through the upstairs floor like Tom Hanks in *The Money Pit*. I was grateful, but it was hard not to cry as I wrote him an astronomical check.

Before our near-total replaster, we had the huge job of stripping off a houseful of wallpaper. There were rubbery red sheets embossed with *fleur-de-lis* that gave a bordello feel to the family room. Some rental agency maintenance goon had filled an entire ceiling with wallpaper strips to hide water damage from an overflowed bathtub. I was armed with a wallpaper steamer, which Ben helpfully described as just a large teakettle. Conjuring thoughts of tea made it less scary. I had permanently achy arms and scalding water burns from holding the steamer directly overhead to remove the strips of hideousness clinging to the study ceiling. I knew my overhead wallpaper project would end with my arms on the floor, fallen off in a final act of rebellion.

Ben found two young plasterers who possessed the single most attractive trait when auditioning home improvement personnel—they were available that Thursday. They used a very rickety metal frame to reach the highest spots on our nine-foot ceilings. As opposed to slowing themselves down with the two minutes it would have taken to cover our hardwood floor with drop cloths, they forged ahead. They mixed plaster indoors in great buckets, blowing powder everywhere and sloshing the wet product onto every horizontal surface. They coated the oak floors with enough splatters of reddish pink plaster to rival any Jackson Pollock painting. I tried to come to terms with the mess, grateful the work was getting done at all on such short notice. Had I known how many late nights we would spend scrubbing the floor on hands and knees with pads and pots of water, I would have thrown an exhausted fit and insisted they use drop cloths.

My job was to keep the project on schedule by removing wallpaper at a rate to prepare each room for its replaster, and cleaning the skirting boards and molding of each room they had skimmed in preparation for new paint. I was also mist-coating the new plaster, which amounted to rolling it with diluted paint to prevent the highly porous surface from sucking all the color out of our paint selections.

I liked the men, before I had realized the catastrophic clean-up they would cause, so I occasionally joined in a conversation or two. I happened to mention wiring money back to the States, wondering about the exchange rate aloud.

"As of yesterday, it was 1.63 dollars to the pound," replied the more diminutive plasterer, Little John. His tall companion burst out laughing. It sounded right to me.

"Wow. You have an impressive knowledge of foreign currency markets," I said. The laughing across the room turned to a chortle. By now, I'd become expert in detecting missing information. Little John's co-worker confessed on his behalf.

"It's not the market, it's Poker Stars, love."

Little John was a frequent online and in-person gambler. He chose to convert his British pounds to American dollars when playing online poker because he got more currency by volume. We had been paying these guys a steady stream of cash at their insistence. We'd spent well over a month of my salary for smooth walls, a trashed house, and John's pernicious poker habit. I bit my tongue and returned to scrubbing skirting boards.

For those over eighteen, gambling was completely legal in the UK as of 1960, but it'd been a popular pastime for hundreds of years. Betting shops populated almost every high street, especially in low-income areas. They were like payday loans stores in the States, only the money usually flowed in the opposite direction. There were a wide variety of machines to plunk money into, as well as any number of horse races every day. The betting shops took wacky wagers, like which song would hit number one on the charts in the week of Christmas, or the odds surrounding Royal weddings.

It's a destructive vice with a long cultural history of famous people who have died in ruin thanks to "deep play" in exclusive clubs or aristocratic drawing rooms. I read the biography of Georgiana, Duchess of Devonshire, born in 1757 and Diana, Princess of Wales' fourth cousin. Georgiana suffered from extreme gambling addiction. One theory as to why Georgiana tolerated her husband's mistress living with them was his willingness to bail out her gambling debt. Upon her death, the duke got the full picture. In 1700s money, she still owed £9 million to gambling creditors. He was able to clear the debt while barely clinging to his ancestral home, Chatsworth House.

T HE WALLS OF OUR front room had been varying shades of mint green and light tan over the rubbery *fleur-de-lis* pattern wallpaper. The fireplace would have been cast iron, but former owners pulled it out long ago when the original fixtures fell out of favor. They installed a hideous manufactured stone fireplace, mantle, and hearth and painted it tan. It looked like a set in an amateur production of *The Flintstones.* I called the fireplace "Fred," and I hated him. It didn't take skill to destroy things, so I chiseled Fred apart and hauled him away in giant bin bags, like I was concealing evidence of a horrific crime against decorating.

At one time, before radiators, the house had contained three more working fireplaces. Carpet and furniture covered the slate and tile hearths that gave their locations away, but we knew better than to go opening up walls to restore them, for fear of what we'd find. I was in the market for a cast iron fireplace insert to take Fred's place.

———

I USED THE PHONE book to find a large salvage yard in the middle of the Fens. I drove through a series of roads that ran parallel to large drainage ditches dividing endless fields, carefully following Google directions to the letter. I arrived in a very small village with three houses, one of which had a large warehouse sitting behind it. I drove straight past, thinking I would find nothing but farm implements there, but after quickly running out of other contenders and leaving the village, I figured I'd passed my destination. I drove into a gravel lane while playing children suspiciously eyed me from their trampoline in the front garden.

As was often the case in England, the extent of the location was carefully concealed from the road. The car park was a surreal graveyard of old bird-baths and poor replicas of Grecian statutes mounted on giant cast cement clam shells. I only remembered witnessing the likes of this chaos when Ben pointed out a travelers' camper van site.

Could this be a travelers' camp? The phenomenon of travelers didn't really translate for Americans. They were a people who lived mostly in flashy recreational vehicles. They were politely referred to as Romani Gypsies, Irish Travelers or, simply, travelers. Some were Irish, some were English, some were from central Europe, and some claimed ancestry back to the ancient Roman settlers of Britain. They were a conservative and religious group, yet the young women dressed provocatively. Their children didn't attend school for any length of time and they didn't live at a fixed address, so they managed to avoid paying council tax. Their culture dictated their nomadic lifestyle. In the UK, trespass to land is not generally a crime, so travelers tended to camp in the most open stretches of public land: parks, walking and cycle paths, anywhere there was a stretch of grass wide enough to hold their trailer. Because trespass was a civil matter, the police were unable to remove the cache of travelers blocking any number of paths until after the legal process ended.

I'd first encountered travelers when I noticed a solid line of prosperous vehicles and campers with satellite dishes parked directly on a local cycling and walking path. With each passing day, I noticed more rubbish accumulating all around the vans. It took time for a local council to serve notice and evict them from public lands, so professional travelers generally knew exactly how long they could stay with impunity in any given location. Meanwhile, the cycling path was completely impassable, and their free-range dogs menaced passersby. Once I spied two ponies tethered to a light pole on the lawn of a used car dealership across the road from a campsite. I drove by a month later to find the travelers had gone, but they'd left a wake of rubbish, dirty diapers, and empty propane canisters. Traveling was protected in the UK as not only a lifestyle, but a culture, with the option of "Gypsy Traveler" always appearing on demographic forms. They claimed they suffered from discrimination and prejudice, which I believed. I also believed how easily taxpayers get honked off when the councils get stuck with cleanup duty. As a drastic measure, Peterborough mounded earth over their favorite decampment in an effort to make the area inhospitable to them in the future.

Related to trespass as a civil offense is the uniquely British fear of squatters. Unlike in the US, it was perfectly legal for a person to gain entry to a vacant property through an open door or window. Once established, squatters can be particularly difficult to get rid of, thanks to a set of laws colloquially known as "squatters' rights." The policy argument for allowing squatters to remain is that a building is best used when occupied, and there should be some protection for those willing to live in vacant buildings to prevent them from becoming derelict. On the other side, squatters rarely have altruistic intent to maintain a property. From what I'd seen and read, most trashed a place beyond recognition during their stay.

Peterborough had some problems with recently arrived eastern European immigrants taking up residence in various city center garden sheds. If they stayed twelve years in exclusive occupation, they could sue the owner of record for adverse possession. Most notably, a seventy-year-old mostly homeless man won a case for adverse possession of property on London's exclusive Hampstead Heath in 2007. The value of the house the court awarded him was estimated at more than £2 million.

Back in the Fens, I managed to find the office of the salvage yard by climbing over the obstacle course of castoff garden bits. The older woman at the desk looked bored, as did the pudgy dog asleep on a rug in front of her. I asked about cast iron fireplaces, and she directed me to the third barn on the left.

Salvaged doors in various states of repair were stacked like library books against partitions of a giant outbuilding. The center row branched off deep and dark corridors. Some of the holes in the rotting floorboards were rehabilitated by bits of cardboard laid over the top. I crept inside to get a better look at the "fireplace" department, only to find countless cast iron specimens with missing or damaged tiles and what looked like a thousand years of rust clinging to every cranny. A man approached, topless and about ready to lose his jeans in an impressive display of cracks that rivaled the state of his antique tile collection. I figured he worked there.

"What's the price of this one?" I asked, pointing to one of the less damaged specimens.

"Three hundred pounds."

I was dumbfounded. This was clearly a special price for Americans who weren't about to lose their jeans. Even this finer model looked like it had been rejected by the war effort, in too sorry a shape to melt down for Spitfire planes.

"It needs an awful lot of work."

His tanned skin shimmered in the sunlight shining through a giant hole in the barn's roof.

"Just a bit of elbow grease, love."

Only a molten salt bath could help, and they didn't sell those at Screwfix. Despite my burning desire to replace our current fireplace, this was not the project for us. This man had elbow and other forms of grease in spades. I politely gave the excuse that I'd need to consult my spouse, ran the gauntlet back to the A170, and drove it down the lane with a cloud of gravel dust swirling behind me.

Our house was built in the reign of King Edward VII, and Edwardian cast iron fireplaces could be surrounded by beautiful decorative tiles inspired by the arts and crafts movement. With a bit of research, I found that reproductions were a far superior option to a crusty, cast-iron relic. The tile sets cost about £100, and the fireplace insert cost £400. Complete with a granite hearth and wooden mantel, the entire project would run about £1,000 installed. I stumbled upon the most glorious insert and tile set pulled out of a modern home, and bought it on eBay for £112. We had to drive to Leicester to claim it. Ben approved my plan when I outlined the potential cost savings.

Sherpa Ben and the grateful seller managed to wedge the cast iron anchor of an insert into the back of my Tardis of a car. The deal came with a wooden mantle. With a bit of coaxing, everything fit, including us. But the thrill of my bargain was fleeting.

"Certified" fireplace installers were employed by fireplace sellers. Businesses that sold fireplaces wouldn't install random units like ours. They kept their installer roster in the safe with the family jewels. I invited three builders to give us a quote for the project. One looked, left, and permanently disappeared. Another studied it like an unsolved Rubik's cube and asked me troubling questions that even I knew the answer to. A third couldn't get to the job for several years.

I began to panic. The UK was a land of rules, and I had purchased a cast-iron albatross. All the certified installers were captives of their employers. I pictured a dungeon full of Gas Safe fireplace technicians, escorted by their warden to their next "approved" job. In the land of chimney sweeps and chimney stacks as far as the eye could see, why was no one willing to install them? I daydreamed about gooseneck flues and smoke testing. I was desperate—I couldn't even find a nice, available fireplace installer online.

A builder neighbor made a passing comment that he didn't know the first thing about putting them in, but his much-older builder uncle might. His uncle was gray and balding with a long ponytail and a jaunty ear piercing. He stared down the hole that used to be occupied by Fred, whipped out his tape measure, studied it thoughtfully, and pronounced everything standard size and easily fitted for the bargain price of £300. I agreed with a handshake, though I was tempted to offer him a kiss. It was a typical rainy day, and although uncle and nephew had come in the back door through the kitchen, I offered to save them a few steps out in the rain and let them leave through the front door.

"No, no, no, no!" they both exhorted in stereo.

I stood there at a loss for words.

"Got ta gout the same durr ye com in, luv," the uncle explained as his nephew nodded. "It's bad luck!"

They scuttled back out the kitchen door in the pouring rain.

When the uncle returned to do the job, it was easy to see he had years of tobacco and building experience behind him. I asked why it was so difficult to find a regular builder to simply plug a cast iron insert into an already-working chimney breast.

"Awe vey've eva done is ripped 'em out, luv," he replied. The DIY stores were populated by gas fireplaces, neatly contained in clear frames. They simply mounted on a plumbed wall. The worst-case was an LCD screen that plugged into a socket and projected a picture of a moving flame, complete with a speaker that crackled like wadded-up cellophane.

Elated by my builder dinosaur who had actually installed *Flintstones*-era fireplaces, I hopped back on eBay and bought a sleek, black granite hearth to replace Fred's mound of fake flagstones. All told, the job cost us £511, far less than half the price of a package job from the evil fireplace dealer/captors. About two weeks later, I learned we lived in a smoke control area. Our beautiful wood-burning fireplace could never legally burn wood, or anything else for that matter.

Regardless of how our money got spent, old problems crept back—more wood rotted and more gutters dripped. There was the occasional new problem, like when a questionable carpet dealer leaned on a freshly replastered wall with the tip of his car key during mindless conversation. Our professionally installed, super deluxe (and super expensive) bathroom suite streamed water down the walls directly below when we had the audacity to use the shower. Months later, I found an occasional gob of gum stuck on some incognito surface, or dirty, toy body parts strewn across the garden by the boys of our former tenants, like a battlefield cemetery for superheroes killed in action. At this old house, the war was never truly over.

_—ele—_

# When One Door Closes, a Flesh Wound Opens

I T WAS LATE AT night and all I wanted was to go to sleep as quickly as possible. I didn't bother to turn on another set of lights after flicking the kitchen light off. By this time, I could navigate in the dark down a hallway to get to the bedroom, or so I thought. Until my body made the sound of a bin bag filled with stew hitting the pavement, punctuated by a groan and expletive.

I knew exactly what had happened. Ben was at it again. British houses had far more doors than Americans expected and their inhabitants weren't afraid to use them. He defended himself with a classic "blame the mother" strategy and repeated what she'd told him growing up: "Only people born in barns don't close the doors behind them."

I agreed that the sound I made hitting the door could have come out of a farm animal. I tried to expound on my injuries at his complaint desk, but it too was closed.

We started duking it out with doors back in the States after we got married and I moved to his 1920s era house. There, the doors were hollow, so they made a cheery ball-cracking-a-baseball-bat sound when my forehead hit them in the middle of the night. It was our first crisis—I never shut interior doors and he couldn't resist closing them. He explained that British homes had radiators and it was helpful to close doors to trap the heat. I tried to appeal to his engineering sensibilities, reminding him that his American house had a furnace and forced-air heat that didn't work as well behind closed doors. He was unconvinced. Meanwhile, I inspected the toes on my right foot for broken bones.

I'd forgotten that trauma until it happened again in England. Both of my English homes had doors that separated every major room as well as hallways. I knew closing them kept things warmer when the radiators were on, but not enough to risk being body-checked at 1:30 a.m. when I got up to use the bathroom and forgot Ben had been on rounds. I compared notes with another American who plowed into closed doors at night because her British husband had the same habit. When asked why he insisted on closing all doors, he told her he wasn't born in a barn. We shook our heads. We needed to negotiate a peace accord.

Ben did relax his militant closed-door policy, and we settled on which ones I should expect to be closed at night. Fortuitously, he even agreed to remove a hallway door on the main level. I attempted to go to the kitchen in the night for a cold drink and rode to the bottom of the stairs on my rear—thanks to slippery new berber carpet. I made the same bin-bag-full-of-stew sound when my ride ended on the hallway floor. I had no idea berber was the worst possible selection for rugburn. If not for Ben's compromise, I would have put my foot through a pane of the old glass-paneled door.

For Christmas, I planned to give him an advent calendar with all the doors permanently closed.

—*ele*—

# I've Got a Nut on a String

I SHOULD HAVE KNOWN something was brewing. Ben made a habit of scouring the ground under horse chestnut trees in the autumn, looking for conkers (that is, buckeyes). Like a large child, he would silently sidle up to me and hand me a conker, smile, and then carry on his business.

"But we have nuts at home," I protested.

"No, you're here with me at the moment."

Did he want me to put it in my handbag? Was it mine, or was I merely the nut butler? Were we to keep these to placate the vicious gray squirrels that might cross our path later?

On the second Sunday of October, Ben suggested we attend the World Conker Championships in a minuscule village called Ashton. It was held in a large field, not far from The Chequered Skipper pub where it began in 1965. A group of fishermen had deemed the weather too foul and played conkers down the pub instead. It must have been incredibly bad to put off fishermen, who were used to standing outside whatever the weather.

The first thing we saw as we parked was a crane that suspended a massive conker on a long string. I could tell the event was bonkers, which made it delightfully British. (If the "Life in the UK" test ever asked a multiple-choice question about the origin of national events, the answer was probably the nuttiest explanation possible.) In conkers, the participants draw from a bag of nuts that have been drilled and strung through. The object of the game is to crack the other person's nut—you take turns wailing on your opponent's stationary nut.

Conkers fans were not a subdued bunch. The world's finest conker talent coalesced into high energy teams that dressed in the most unusual way possible. One team came as a retrospective of the many looks of Michael Jackson. I watched as Michael from the "Bad" album went to town on some poor kid in neon yellow leggings. Despite the chilly autumn weather, one team of men wore only thin capes and stripey Speedo underwear. Their nuts didn't fare so well...

I heard the sound of kids yelling nearby and followed my ears to a miniature mechanical bull in the games area. It did a fine job of hurling its pint-sized punters stratospheric. In this "safety-first" country, I was surprised this idea passed muster. Hordes of kids lined up for the privilege of being flung off and reduced to tears. Had they not witnessed the precedent set by their fellow youth? Luckily, their usual crash pad was near the hot chocolate booth. One sugary drink and a trip to the bouncy castle later and they were back in the saddle.

We had a small collection of conkers on our dining room table that evening thanks to Ben's collecting efforts. It was enough to launch our own tournament, but if you asked Ben, there was no need to adjudicate who was the nuttiest.

## Chew on This

I WAS READING THE *Peterborough Telegraph* when I learned that our city had been chosen as one of fifteen areas to take part in the Keep Britain Tidy Chewing Gum Action campaign. The word "tidy" got used a lot in England, but not quite so much as "lovely." Tidy was a desirable state of being, especially for Ben. Local councils were spending £7 million on chewing gum messes each year, with 87 percent of streets "stained" by it. (I felt for the worker who had to gather that data.)

I agreed that no one liked sitting or stepping in gum. But one man's defacement was another man's high art—a giant mass of confetti-colored gum was considered a piece of "folk art" in Charleston, South Carolina. It wasn't hard to appreciate that lots of tenderness and TMJ went into this work; the value of the Dubble Bubble alone had to be at least $10.

The timing was suspect—someone must have alerted the local authorities to my arrival. I was indeed the 1981 Illinois State Fair Bubble Yum Bubble Gum bubble-blowing champion. The judge measured my bubble on stage with a giant pair of calipers, and I was on the front page of the *Rochester Hello*, holding my ribbon while the Illinois State Fair queen put her arm around me. I was not yet six years old. No one used the term "prodigy," but I later expanded my *oeuvre* to blowing a bubble within a bubble within a bubble.

Thanks to rigorous training by my tidy mother, I have always thrown my gum away in bins or stored it on purpose-made ceramic "gum parkers." I used it to deface my own property just once. Around age six, I went to bed with gum in my mouth. My mother woke me in the morning to find a massive gob embedded in my long, flowing hair (that had also won the 1981 Illinois State Fair prize for longest ponytail in age group). Maybe gum chewing and hair growing were not necessarily good hobbies to pursue simultaneously. After a major flap involving moaning, hand-wringing, and the ineffectual use of peanut butter and ice cubes by my mother, she schlepped me over to my grandma's to see if the kid oracle might have the solution. Nope. They got out the scissors. I had a major hunk of hair missing for a few months, but I didn't mind—as long as it didn't interfere with my gum chewing.

Peterborough was concerned with a number of "gum hot spots." Council employees measured the amount of gum and cleaned it over the next three months. They even had their own website. Once again, I pitied the poor soul who got that job assignment. Was her official title "Council Gob Stopper?" Did she measure by ruler or merely by volume?

I thought I had a solution: personal gum parkers. They would save countless hours devoted to policing all the unauthorized gum parking. My first gum parker was a little ceramic baseball mitt. The gob of gum looked like a colorful baseball in the center—perhaps a shooter marble, if I'd been prolific. (I tended to chew as much as my mouth could hold.) Years later, I upgraded to a little ceramic cat lying on its back, which one of the English removals men unearthed in our kitchenware. Wasn't that where everyone kept their gum parker?

Ben abhorred my gum parker and everything it stood for. Well, never mind him. I thought he was all for recycling.

# Fashion Foibles

Tesco, the giant UK supermarket chain, made headlines by officially banning shoppers who showed up in their pajamas. When the presenter read the story during the morning news, Ben looked up from his cereal bowl with a smirk.

"As if!" I sputtered defensively.

I was on shaky moral high ground. There was no use denying that I loved pajama time. If I was at home without plans for the evening, I'd been known to declare pajama time as early as 7 p.m. Pajamas calmed and cleared the mind far better than Valium. I completed the look with my Easy Spirit slide-on slippers. Those occasionally needed vacuumed due to wear and sock lint. Thanks to their almost shoe-like sole, I'd worn them to take out the trash or return a library book. My footwear spirit was a bit too easy, according to Ben, so my entire wardrobe judgment was rendered suspect.

Maybe the Brits found the website, www.peopleofwalmart.com. Ben knew about it, and it fueled his enthusiasm for the Tesco pajama ban.

"We can't be having *that*!"

I nodded in agreement. Despite my pajama enthusiasm, I agreed with Tesco. How could I forget my young DUI defendant who wore flannel pajama bottoms emblazoned with bottles of Corona beer and lime wedges to his court date? Couldn't he switch to SpongeBob, just for one day?

In other news, a trade organization suggested banning women's high heels as part of mandated corporate uniforms due to their threat to the female foot. I wasn't offended, but I predicted this sentiment would have gone over like a pair of Velcro-fastened, nun-friendly Soft Spots.

Fashionable footwear was a must among some sets in England, while "sensible shoes" carried the day amongst older pedestrians. When a friend had said all my shoes looked like root vegetables, and started calling my footwear "potato shoes," her put-downs were in vain. I was firmly planted in the "potato shoe" camp due to an old foot injury.

I sought refuge in Clarks stores. Amongst the most fashionable feet of the UK, mine stuck out as far as my accent. At least my bunions weren't burning, and my permanently bipartite sesamoid bone thanked me daily.

By my count, Ben owned almost as many pairs of shoes as I did. I attributed his interest in footwear to his time as a youthful shoe shop clerk. He'd worked as a shoe dog for a man named Mr. Cheeseman. Not only had Ben's love of cheese followed him into adulthood, he also collected footwear. He was chronically helpful while shoe shopping, an expert in sizing and testing for fit. Mr. Cheeseman would be proud.

However, Ben didn't relish dealing with British women in search of fashionable footwear. There were too many va-va-voom pumps in shop windows to count. Even ankle boots came with spiky heels. On cobbled streets, these defied any sense of practicality, one of Ben's defining qualities. We were on our way to dinner one evening on a medieval street when we saw a young man checking that all the scantily clad and shod females in his company had footwear that could handle cobbles. Some women didn't make the cut and hitched a piggyback ride to their destination. There I was in my brown Børn Mary Janes, comfortably mobile. I could hear my old friend saying, "Hello, tater tots," in my head. But on cobbles, I thought crunchy, brown footwear was the right fit.

## Pub Quiz

O UR FRIENDS DANGEROUS DAN (the Brits love nicknames) and his wife Lanie invited us to a pub quiz at The Falcon Inn in Fotheringhay, the same village where Mary, Queen of Scots lost her head. Quizzing was an unofficial British sport, and we could win some major coin without those pesky American laws against gambling. We sat down with our scorecards and a drink, but I planned to keep my head. The quiz master announced the pot would be £96. The cash signs rolled over our eyes and we began.

In this version, the quiz master called a number. If it appeared on a player's scorecard, he or she wrote the answer down to the question that followed. It was possible a player wouldn't have the number, which was especially peeving if I knew the answer to the question being asked. It was like trivia bingo, minus the American troll doll good-luck charms. There were a few highly unattractive men in the vicinity, some with long hair. I wasn't tempted to rub their heads for good luck.

It was helpful to be the "token American" on a UK quiz team—quite a few of the questions had to do with American movies, pop culture, or general knowledge. I whipped up the answer "Meryl Streep" for one question, and that seemed to earn me some quiz cred. But it was fleeting—for questions that required any British cultural knowledge, I was out of my depth. There must have been pub quiz brainiacs in attendance. If this was the standard, there was no way I could pass the "Life in the UK" test. I admitted defeat as I chugged my pub drink of choice, a hard cider with a shot of blackcurrant Ribena. The quizmaster cleared his throat.

"What is the name of the dissident Spanish terrorist organization commonly referred to as the Basque Separatists?"

Yet again, I couldn't come up with an answer. The quizmaster announced that the Basque Separatists were also known as the ETA.

"Oh, no!"

A high-pitched female voice called bats as she squealed to her male companion. I silently judged her based on her vocal range and footwear.

"You told me it was the Suffragettes! Humph!" She thwacked the man beside her with her answer card.

Ben and I shared an eye roll. He lowered his voice.

"Equal rights for women isn't exactly terrorism."

I knew there was a reason I married him. From that point forward, the Suffragettes made for an all-purpose bogus answer whenever we were stumped. That happened a lot—I didn't get a single British question right. Dangerous Dan was a Cambridge grad and didn't get anywhere close to winning. The questions were so tricky that no one won the pot that night. Perhaps that was part of the pub's plan.

# Real Estate Spookulation

W E LIVED NEAR A "chocolate box" village called Alwalton, which meant every house looked like the charming, quintessentially British homes that appeared on Cadbury Milk Tray boxes a half-century earlier. I was enamored. A number of locals told me it had always been exclusive, so it was a waste of time to imagine living there. On a local history website, I stumbled across a census-like listing from 1279. In my book, 1279 was officially older than dirt. I noted that, back then, someone's rent was three hens and one cock yearly.

Alwalton had a great pub we enjoyed called The Cuckoo. If I needed to send a package, buy a few groceries, or satisfy my need for a sudden crumpet and tea, Alwalton's post office had me covered. I'd even taken guests there as a treat. Upstairs in the tea room, we'd nosh on reasonably priced pillows of fruited tea cake with real butter, which were like enormous, fruity English muffins. I could also vouch for the quality of the carrot cake and the Bakewell slices, which were an almond cake layered with raspberry jam and a bit of icing. Just when I was worried about not fitting through the doorways horizontally, I noticed the sign on the low ceiling beams warned, "Duck or Grouse!" The thatched roof was beautiful, flammable, and expensive to insure. Based on the amount of thatch in the vicinity, anyone who shot off fireworks would be run out of town.

Not far down the street from my beloved Alwalton post office, I saw a property listed for sale at £175,000. It was an absolute bargain. Better yet, the estate agency was hosting an open house the following Saturday. I read Ben the listing with my own editorial comments:

*A charming* [dodgy] *Grade II listed* [historical Big Brother is watching to see you don't do anything naughty like put in vinyl windows], *semi-detached stone cottage in need of full modernization* [because it's a dump] *with large garden (overall plot approximately 0.3 acres). The cottage is thought to date back to the mid 17th century with 19th century alterations.* [Could this be right? Was it really last improved in the 1800s?] *Built of limestone rubble with ashlar dressings and a Collyweston slate roof.* [It's not going anywhere fast.] *Situated in the heart of the picturesque village of Alwalton adjacent to the small village green. The accommodation now needs full modernization.* [That keeps coming up. The understatement of the year?] *A particular feature of the property is the large garden that in all extends to just over 0.3 of an acre* [postage stamp.] *To the front of the property there is a small garden* [suitable only for microgreens] *enclosed by a low hedge* [that doubles as Restoration-era obstacle course.] *Gated access to the side of the cottage leads to a large garden in all measuring just over 0.3 of an acre* [which we can't stop emphasizing because it's one of the only features.] *The gardens are extensively laid* [overgrown] *to lawn interspersed into which there are a number of mature trees with a small timber garden shed* [only useful as kindling.]

I studied the photo, and something jumped out at me.

"Do you see what I see?" I asked Ben.

"There's honestly no telling."

"Orbs! On the roof. Freaky!" I'd started watching an episode of *Ghost Hunters* where the hosts said translucent orbs were evidence of ghosts on film, but I was too chicken to last more than five minutes.

Ben and his rational mind stared me down.

"It's just a spot on the lens. Still want to see it?" He was intrigued to see what 19th century additions looked like.

We showed up to a bustling open house—apparently, word got out that a property in Alwalton might go on the cheap. The wiring looked like the handiwork of a novice bombmaker and the plumbing looked Roman. There was a spider in the bathtub the size of a small Toyota. I crept around each corner, on the lookout for orbs. Something resembling a tree held up the roof, which was bowing like an overloaded donkey's back. I pointed and ran for cover, but Ben didn't budge.

"If it hasn't moved in the last 400 years, why would it start now?"

The structural surveyor had peeled back manky (rotten) newspaper from 1953 used to smooth out the wavy walls upstairs. There had been modern improvements, after all. Ben started chatting about his vision for the place—what walls he would move, how it could look. For once in the decade, I became deathly silent while trying not to concuss myself on the low ceilings. He paused as he stared in my direction.

"Please don't construe any of my comments as actual interest in buying this place."

"Oh, thank God."

We heard it sold for over the guide price. I hoped whoever bought it had more vision than just the orbs floating around upstairs.

—*ele*—

# Craving Junk Mail

T HE DAY CAME WHEN I would have killed for a UK credit card application. Or a magazine offer. Perhaps even a come-on for new windows? In a two-week period, we had mail delivered twice. I'd read about European workers' hair-trigger tendency to strike, even when they worked in vital occupations. There had been walkouts among the dog-poo scrubbers in Paris, the public transportation workers in Paris, heck, amongst any occupation in Paris. My charmed island life was strike-free until the Royal Mail workers walked out. The formal term for a strike was "industrial action." More correctly, inaction.

My American brain couldn't grasp how the government allowed this to happen. I knew the old motto of the US Postal Service by heart:

*Neither snow nor rain nor heat nor gloom of night stays these couriers from the swift completion of their appointed rounds.*

I wondered if adding "industrial dustups" would ruin the poetic flow. But it was true. I thought of the stacks of important bills, checks, new driving licenses and reissued passports just lying around in warehouses. There were stories on the national news about people whose birthdays were ruined for lack of a single card. As for me, I'd been waiting on my permanent Tesco Club Card for more than a month. My temporary paper one was pulverized, so the scanners at the checkout never gave me the two-for-one price when I shopped for the week. I couldn't go on like this much longer.

The local BBC news reported that more than a half million pieces of undelivered mail were sitting in Peterborough, with twenty million waiting in London, a million in Bristol, and a quarter million in Leeds. Royal Mail, privatized years ago, was cutting jobs, hours, and overtime, and the Communication Workers Union wasn't going to take it anymore. Or take any more deliveries, for that matter.

I thought the sniping was ill-timed considering the number of people who lost their job in the recession. Royal Mail's perks seemed generous by American standards. A friend of Ben worked there for many years until she and her husband moved to the States. She merely had to return to work a couple weeks a year in order to retain all her seniority and benefits. I was fairly sure no employer would ever agree to that back in the US. Most Americans didn't know that new workers anywhere in the UK began their jobs with at least a month's paid holiday, as well. So much for the two weeks Americans got starting out, if they were lucky. I didn't see how Royal Mail's grievances warranted taking an entire country's mail hostage.

There was also volcanic disruption to worry about. In May 2010, all international mail and travelers disappeared from UK airspace. Volcanic eruptions in Iceland spewed tons of ash into the sky, which drifted in dingy clouds over the UK and Europe. The microfine particles could potentially damage plane engines trying to cut through the soupy atmosphere, so all air travel was grounded until the learned volcanologists and meteorologists gave the all clear. Ben's field was engine development, so he was particularly interested in engine damage from cavitation—pitting from all the particulate matter floating in the air.

Not everyone took such a practical view. I had an email from a friend back in the States, asking if our landscape was now "a post-apocalyptic waste land, like the true Earth in *The Matrix* or the world of *Mad Max*." I never anticipated my move to England would feature volcanic fallout, but I had yet to see Mel Gibson roaming the streets with a mangy mutt. There was a thin veil of volcanic ash settling on the cars overnight. Was it what remained of Iceland's economy now that air travel was completely suspended? I let ash build up on the A170 out of novelty, but that was really just an excuse to avoid cleaning the car.

Iceland could be confusing. One evening we were invited to dinner at Dangerous Dan and Lanie's house.

"I love the potatoes," I said as I cut into a perfectly browned roastie.

"They're just from Iceland."

"Wow." I tried to remember if Iceland's permafrost made underground crops nonexistent. "I guess they have greenhouses for all their produce. Maybe they power them from the hot, volcanic springs."

Yet again, the entire group of people around me burst into spontaneous laughter, leaving me stuck in a frosty crevasse of cultural misunderstanding. Iceland was a UK chain of stores specializing in frozen food. I made a mental note that if anyone in the UK announced they'd just come from Iceland, check either their passport or freezer for definitive confirmation.

As an unabashed fruit enthusiast, it hurt when I learned the UK's tropical fruit shipments were being diverted to Spain from Africa or South America on account of the volcanic ash. Worse yet, they were dumping produce altogether due to lack of air logistics. My favorite fresh fruits disappeared from the store shelves. It had been two weeks since my last golden kiwi, which made for a good opening line if I wanted to start my own fruitarian support group. It was a few weeks before I saw jet trails in the sky again, but television news still carried stories of the backlog of UK tourists stuck on beaches in Tenerife. The government sent a naval ship to pick up a load of stranded Brits from Spain. I hoped they wouldn't just dump them on the docks because they were long past optimal freshness.

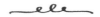

# The Quest for Coziness

THE ENGLISH HUNKERED DOWN for winter, though it hadn't come close to freezing yet. I wasn't really getting their anxiety, given that it was late October and the daytime high was 61°F. But rest assured, I could tell they thought doom loomed from under the drafty door. As evidence, I saw the most impressive window display of decorative and functional hot water bottles I'd ever seen at a local shopping center. I'd last used a hot water bottle sometime in the '80s.

There were at least forty different bottles for the chronically chilly to choose from. Some were wooly and others were swathed in faux fur. For those who thought that the Paris Hilton-inspired range was a bit too woofty (Britspeak for something like "candy-ass"), there was an edgy, black bottle cozy with a skull and crossbones embroidered across the front, just in time for Halloween. One model in the shop window wore its own little stripey sweater. A tiny matching scarf hung jauntily around its neck. Ben gifted me a plush white cat based on a cartoon called *Miffy*, whose back split apart to hold a hot water bottle. I appreciated his gift, but I misremembered her name as "Niffy" (Britspeak for stinky). Ben looked offended. I only made that mistake once.

When it came to hot water bottles, I wasn't quite sure how most people used them. Did they snuggle up to their skull and crossbones at night? Did they take the edge off a chilly car ride, or were they just an excuse to carry a personal hot water supply for tea at all times? Local friends assured me that the level of complaints about the cold would steadily rise as the temperature dropped. The coldest mornings were just around freezing. American Midwest winters with their windchills of -40°F would have halted all life as Brits knew it.

Scarves were a popular fashion choice, on people as well as hot water bottles. They were wool, silk, and every fabric in between, worn equally by men and women. In fact, I could spot a European man on a night out—I looked for pointy, shiny shoes, a blazer with dark jeans, and a carefully draped scarf. I had developed a scarf aversion from too many years of riding the prisoner transport we called a school bus and worrying if my scarf would be used by the future felons to asphyxiate me. But as I spent more time in cold UK weather, I began to appreciate a warm neck.

My friends were right, and I started hearing a steady stream of complaints about the cold. What happened to a stiff upper lip and extra layers? In fact, I thought the stiff upper lip business was brought on by the unique torture that was damp British cold. Winter was balmy compared to my homeland. When Ben bought me two peach trees for my birthday, the lady at the garden center assured him they would be absolutely fine in large clay pots over the winter. Our back garden might as well be Italy. Back home, the only thing we grew over winter in pots were icicles. I didn't want to try to convince my English friends how good they had it, but I felt zero degrees of sympathy. It was time to cinch up the scarf on their hot water bottles.

## Dark with Mizzle, That's fo' Shizzle

M Y FATHER-IN-LAW LIKED TO use the word "mizzle"—a hybrid of mist and drizzle. This reminded me of my mother, who had watched an entire season of a show featuring the rapper Snoop Dog and began using Snoop-isms to spice up her vocabulary. (Something like this had happened before. The summer when I was twelve, she read a fat Southern novel called, "...*And Ladies of the Club*" and started referring to me as one of its main characters, Ms. Voorhees. I thought being addressed as a random name in a deep southern drawl would wear off after a few weeks, but I didn't revert to being Claire until school resumed in the fall. I don't remember being as reluctant to go back that year.)

It is true that the British love to discuss the weather. It is a safe topic, appropriate for any occasion. It could be particularly expressive: provoking joy, loathing, regret—the whole range of human emotion. I'd noticed a national propensity toward moaning, most usually about the state of the weather. It got described as foul, dirty, miserable, vile, and regularly compared to bodily waste fluids. I had to agree the weather wasn't great much of the time, but I'd never heard it described so colorfully.

I was excited to buy a pair of fashionable welly boots back in the States, but once I hit England, the shine wore off. Why get excited about a fashion item meant for the foulest weather? I'd only remembered to wear them once, when we went to hear the New English Concert Orchestra play on the lawn of a stately home under overcast skies. It evolved to mizzle, sprinkles, drops, and finally, a downpour. Amazingly, all the stalwart Brit picnickers around us formed umbrella tents with complete strangers and carried on drinking their Pimms and champagne in what any American would consider a monsoon. We spied one particular reveler eat an entire Victoria sponge cake during the mizzle segment. Once the downpour began, he danced the Blue Danube waltz solo. Even Ben started to crack up at the craziness of his fellow countryman. The orchestra gave up and we did too, careful not to wipe out on wet grass or goose turds on the way back to the car. We were soaked through. I questioned whether we should have bothered, but both shows were entertaining while they lasted. Ben had a favorite saying: "If the English planned their lives around the weather, they'd never leave the house." When Ben ran the occasional road race, he didn't mind the rain, and even hoped for it. Rain sped him up among the fussy competitors who preferred to remain dry. But by the time my absence from the States was measured in years, I missed the cloudless swaths of clear blue that appeared above the American Midwest, especially in winter. I didn't care if the outside temperature made me feel like a ready-made frozen dinner. I had a feeling that, if they could, the Brits would trade in their oatmeal-colored skies for a blast of frigid, unbroken sunshine too.

The English climate produced some other interesting outdoor phenomena that thrived in mizzle. For instance, I'd never seen a real-life snail until I lived in the UK. At first, I thought the small, shiny paths I saw on the concrete were inexplicable, much like crop circles. Ben enlightened me that they were really snail squeezings. I started seeing snails everywhere, even tiny ones stuck to the lid of our wheelie bins (mobile trash cans).

The magpies insisted on leaving round balls of moss they had plucked from our tile roof right in front of our door every morning. My only explanation was that they were housewarming gifts. If I were a magpie, I'd like a choice wad of freshly-harvested moss for my new nest, too. I had another cultural epiphany I could use on the "Life in the UK" test—I finally understood that line of Elton John's "Your Song," where he kicked off the moss while he sat on the roof. No wonder the verses were getting him quite cross—I couldn't possibly concentrate surrounded by damp balls of muck.

Damp and dark was a particularly depressing combination. On December 3, it was 8 a.m. and black outside. There wasn't an eclipse or apocalypse scheduled. We were crawling toward the winter solstice on December 21, the shortest day of the year. Sunrise was at 8:04 a.m. and sunset was at 3:53 p.m. We had our northerly location on the globe to thank for this lightless winter existence, but the jet stream saved us, staving off the drastic temperature swings.

Margaret Dashwood was one of my favorite characters in Emma Thompson's film version of *Sense and Sensibility*, little sister to Marianne and Elinor. Margaret treasured her atlas, as did Ben. In fact, one of his purest joys in life was consulting the atlas, even though his was circa 1984 and the Balkans were wonky. His atlas said we were near the 53rd parallel, roughly the same latitude as Saskatoon, Saskatchewan, the Aleutian Islands, and Upper Mongolia. Early December daytime highs were around 44°F in my part of the UK, but it was a puny high of 24°F in Saskatoon with heavy snow showers.

The bright yang to the dark yin was my long London summer of 2001, not only full of city adventures, but never-ending daylight. On the summer solstice in June, sunrise was at 4:43 a.m. and sunset was at 9:22 p.m. The twilight faded so slowly, it was still light at 10:30 p.m. The Scots to the north would have yet another half-hour of daylight. The closest I'd seen to that much light was a summer visit to Minnesota when I was a kid. I remember my great aunt's neighbors started mowing the grass at 5:30 a.m.

It was turning into the winter of my discontent. The days were going nowhere and what little serotonin I had left for Spain. Add mizzle to the equation and I finally understood why Irish poets were so angsty. Ben knew help was in order when I wasn't even interested in fruit after dinner anymore. The dark days brought on an urge to burrow into bed or look like a bloated seed on the couch, curled up and sprouting a tap root into the cushions.

My days and moods were so stagnated that I dragged myself to my GP (general practice doctor) and asked for some insight. Like many British in winter, I had seasonal affective disorder, which was depression brought on by lack of daylight. SAD was more than just my state of mind—it was my official diagnosis. I declined his offer of antidepressants, but took his suggestion of more trips to the gym and a therapeutic light box. It was a large, bright lamp that I sat in front of for a minimum of thirty minutes per day.

At first, I was skeptical of my light box, especially when I sat too close and felt drawn to the light wherever I looked. It worked by increasing the bright light that reached my retina, which in turn, lifted my serotonin levels. After a couple of days, I noticed that my mood had improved because a pear sounded like a good idea again.

From that point on, I mothballed my sunglasses—every stray sunbeam was a serotonin hit. I was as happy in England's winter as I could be.

# Confessions of a Former Duvet-theist

ANOTHER SYMPTOM OF SAD is an urge to hibernate. A UK home goods store called Habitat drove a surge of European duvet enthusiasm in the '70s, and they've been popular ever since. Before I met Ben, I did not believe in duvets. I made my American bed in the old fashioned, conventional way: fitted sheet, flat sheet, blanket, comforter. The end. Goodnight.

One day, I saw Ben with a pile of cloth on the floor and the corner of a white, cushy comforter in his right hand. He held up one end of the comforter, muttered something about corners, and in an act of performance art, sprang into what looked like a new indoor camping accessory. He reappeared thirty seconds later, ready to button the comforter into the cover and get on with his life. He detested flat sheets and blankets because they caught on his so-called "big" feet, but I never mistook him for a son of Sasquatch.

Habitat claimed people could use a duvet to make a bed in less than ten minutes. I thought that might be possible after ten years' practice. Sure, Ben could whip off the cover and put it straight into the wash without the worry of dry cleaning or washing a bulky comforter, but getting the pesky cover on was another matter. At first, I thought that to properly case a duvet, training began in utero. The same went for understanding the rules of cricket.

In wintertime, Ben would upgrade to the winter-weight duvet. If I could transcend the pain of sheathing the thing, making the bed was a snap. The anti-bedmaker in me rejoiced. Besides, duvets were just so darn fluffy. I was a convert. Hallelujah.

My first attempts at duvet training made it clear that Ben and I had wildly disparate domestic abilities. I felt swallowed by the duvet, like silent drowning. Once I could see daylight, I thought of it as pitching a decorative indoor tent, but I hated the idea of glamping. I'd never surpass Ben's speed, but in time and with practice, I managed a new personal record of a sub-five-minute duvet change. (This was a prime skill for a dastardly examiner to include on a practical "Life in the UK" test, right up there with knowing how to score cricket.)

# A Teeny Halloweeny

I RECEIVED AN EMAIL from a curious American friend asking, "So Claire, what do they do for our American pumpkin holiday over there across the pond?"

My first thought was to tread lightly before stepping into a colonial quagmire. I spied provocative words in her query, specifically "our American." Halloween wasn't the Americans' to claim. True to our heritage, we merely borrowed it, made it bigger, and loaded it full of artificial flavors and preservatives.

I trusted Wikipedia on the subject, which said that Halloween was "linked to the Celtic festival of Samhain or Samuin (pronounced sow-an or sow-in)." The article went on to say the name was from Old Irish and roughly translated to 'summer's end.' Ancient Britons joined in, as did the Welsh and Druid priests.

Back in my old hometown of Morton, Illinois, the pumpkin capital of the world, 85 percent of the world's pumpkin was canned in the local Libby's processing plant. Outside my house, the autumn air was always heavy with the earthy smell of cooking squash. Every September brings the Morton Pumpkin Festival, an entire weekend of events designed to pay homage to the lowly fruit. Besides more conventional pastimes such as selecting the next Pumpkin Queen and eating pumpkin chili, ice cream and pancakes, there was Punkin' Chuckin', a contest that appealed to the engineer in Ben. Purpose-built machinery launched the orange gourds as far into the stratosphere as possible. Slingshots, air guns, trebuchets—no method was off limits. In England, I missed seeing so many pumpkins set out on front porches for Halloween. I never heard of English Halloween pageants in schools. Based on what I could tell, Halloween in its fullest commercial form was an American holiday.

Thanks to my new font of cultural enrichment, my weekly diet club meeting, I learned that troops of kids in "fancy dress" would be going door-to-door in some neighborhoods. My entire reason for joining this club had been to pound the brakes on steady weight gain acceleration. I liked to scout and hoard tasty Tesco ready-to-eat meals, mostly Indian. Unfortunately, I kept eating them. Instant korma was going to get me if I didn't act. I had been to a weight loss group back in the States, so I was interested to see if the vibe was different. My American experience was high in entertainment value—stories of slip-ups on sliders at Burger King, heartfelt confessions of emotional baking, and laments about how lardy one participant felt after consuming an entire pound of grapes. (Okay, that last one was me. I took "unlimited fruit" a bit too far.)

My thoughts and pen had turned to the new British delicacies I could buy on a regular basis, in haiku form:

*Diet shot to hell*
*Granary bread is toasting*
*Toffee's just like crack*

Or,

*Custard on the hob*
*Feeling like a giant blob*
*Gym clothes way too tight*

My meeting gathered at Orton Hall, a small stately home turned hotel with stoney, dark interiors and rumors of phantasmic activity. Halloween was an inspired time to join up at this particular outpost. I banged my head on an original Gothic stone arch as I trekked to the meeting room.

They had less to eat in the 17$^{th}$ century, so perhaps the ambience would be helpful. I imagined Restoration dieters racking up activity points with lively games of croquet on the sprawling twenty-acre grounds.

The first order of business was our weigh-in. Despite moving to metric in most other measurements, the Brits still expressed people's weight in stones. I wasn't good enough to convert the stones to pounds in my head, so I left the scale with no idea how much I weighed.

I found a seat and heard a soft, but steady, crunching noise. Everyone who had weighed in was chowing down on bags of diet crisps (chips) they had purchased from a little kiosk in the back of the room. This was entrapment for the perennially hungry, a brilliant stroke of business acumen. I snarfed an entire box of "diet" chocolate-covered toffee bars procured from the "crack shack" at that week's meeting. I needed to blend with the locals.

At my second meeting, I was studying an interesting outfit of medieval knight's armor when I became enraptured by a buttery smell floating from the hotel kitchen.

"So, Claire, what will you be handing out to the trick-or-treaters?"

I jumped. In a rare bout of sharing, I had confessed to consuming imported Cheetos and still losing five pounds the previous week. I was an easy target for the meeting leader.

My mind went blank. What was the correct answer? Was this a trick question? I hated being wrong in class. This was a diet club, but surely the answer couldn't be "bran muffins." I spouted the first thing that popped into my head.

"Six-packs and fried eggs?"

I waited for a wave of laughter, but heard only confused silence. The knight's eye sockets burned a hole through me and into my metal chair. I guess the "Coneheads" Halloween special from American *Saturday Night Live* didn't translate.

"It's a bad joke. I'll probably bake mini bran muffins."

People finally laughed, but I wasn't about to confess it would be Cadbury's Dairy Milk for everyone at our house, including me.

Ben convinced me that we wouldn't have many trick-or-treaters in our estate. We could pay a visit to our old neighbor, Mummy, and drop a pack of smokes through her mail slot. As childless killjoys, Ben suggested we go to dinner and a movie instead of cowering with the lights off, candy and cigarette-free.

On our way to the restaurant, we spied a handful of lit jack-o'-lanterns and a few mobs of kids in costume going door-to-door. We also saw an older group of girls, one dressed as a tarty barmaid. It was barely 50°F and she was mostly naked. I forgot my manners and pointed as we drove past. I still hadn't gotten over that public possession of alcohol was perfectly legal in the UK, for the most part.

"Look at that! She's got a drink in her hand!"

"She would have needed a few drinks to wear that outfit."

There was no aftermath of smashed pumpkins or an egged house on our return home. Ben reported that signs in the local shops said they would not be selling eggs or flour to children in the lead-up to Halloween. To my American sensibilities, it was the "nanny state" at work—using institutions to force the public to do what was best. At least the worst of the aftermath was massive inconvenience for pint-sized bakers.

I managed to get through Halloween before the sugar monkey returned to my back. For the record, I did bother to decorate with my pumpkin candy bowl (empty, thanks to diet-club guilt) and a light-up plastic jack-o'-lantern—realistic, yet useless, thanks to its US plug and voltage. I even dug out my miniature Halloween tree strewn with candy-corn garland. I craved real candy corn, the soft, sickeningly sweet triangles, but they just didn't translate. UK candy apples (known completely inappropriately as toffee apples) were covered in disappointment: hard, boiled sugar—like giant, organic lollipops. I missed the far rarer caramel ones. If the sales kid at the Crowland show had been hawking caramel apples versus Tootsie Rolls, I'd have personally funded his university.

_ele_

# Not Another Random Guy

I 'D BEEN HEARING THE pop of the occasional backyard fireworks display. When I asked what it was about, Ben replied:

"Remember, remember the fifth of November;

Gunpowder, treason and plot!"

All British schoolchildren learned this rhyme referencing the notorious
anarchist Guy Fawkes. Guy Fawkes Day (or Bonfire Night) was November
5. It celebrated the unraveled Gunpowder Plot of 1605, when a mercenary
from York named Guy Fawkes (also known as Guido from his days fighting
in Spain) was found in the cellars below Parliament with a smidge of
gunpowder. Maybe thirty-six barrels was more than a smidge. Guy was
Roman Catholic, and he and a dozen of his closest friends were tired of
being put down by the Protestant Elizabeth I. When her successor, James
I, didn't treat them any better, the thirteen decided that the best way to
channel their rage was to torch Parliament. A tipster ruined their plans and
they gave Guy the usual treatment—he was hung, drawn, and quartered.
He managed to avoid maximum torture by taking a dive off the scaffold
and breaking his neck early in the process so he wouldn't survive the short
hanging and being disemboweled alive. How sensible. Every year at the
opening of Parliament, there was a ceremonial check of the cellars just to
rule out any bad Guys.

The word "guy" is an eponym—a word based on a real person. The
term "guy" used to carry more baggage. In Britain, "guy" used to mean
a man displaying odd dress or behavior, but the weirdo connotation was

eventually lost. In commemoration of the big boom that wasn't, children began to make grotesque effigies of Guy to burn on a bonfire. On Guy Fawkes night, we drove by one of the largest bonfires I'd seen in years, visible for at least a mile at night. After exhausting myself by calculating the number of hot dogs that fire could roast, I tried in vain to think of comparable celebrations. It was odd to declare a country-wide feast day dedicated to something that didn't happen.

In terms of revelry, American Halloween edges out Guy. I would prefer a piece of Cadbury Dairy Milk to a firecracker any day.

—ₑℓℓ—

## The British Excel at Remembrance

O N THE ELEVENTH OF November, a televised Queen was at Westminster Abbey to commemorate Armistice Day, which honored
the end of World War I at the eleventh hour of the eleventh day of the
eleventh month. People didn't get the day off work, but the entire UK
observed two minutes of silence at 11 a.m. I found it amazing that so many
people remembered to be silent, which was increasingly hard to do.

Little red, paper poppies appeared on lapels in the middle of October,
and most public places had a veteran selling them for the Royal British
Legion, a charity that supports service personnel. TV presenters wouldn't
be caught without one. They symbolized the generation of young British
men who never returned from World War I, made famous by the poem,
"In Flanders Fields." It was written by the Canadian physician Lieu-
tenant-Colonel John McCrae after presiding at the funeral of a fellow
soldier in Ypres, Belgium:

*In Flanders fields the poppies blow*
*Between the crosses, row on row*
*That mark our place; and in the sky*
*The larks, still bravely singing, fly*
*Scarce heard amid the guns below.*
*We are the Dead. Short days ago*
*We lived, felt dawn, saw sunset glow,*
*Loved and were loved, and now we lie*
*In Flanders fields.*

There were well-organized Remembrance Day festivities in London. They passed by the Cenotaph, the country's most important war monument for fallen soldiers. It was built as a World War I memorial and inscribed "The Glorious Dead." After seeing the solemnity of my first UK Armistice Day, I understood why they jailed a young man who threw a wheelie bin, kicked a window, and dared to use a Union flag to swing from the Cenotaph during a student protest. Perhaps his sentence was meant to be an example—after all, he was Charlie Gilmour, a history student at Cambridge and son of Pink Floyd guitarist David Gilmour. Thanks to his staggeringly poor judgment coupled with his privileged status, he was a contender for the often-awarded British title: "upper-class twit." He had plenty of time to stare at just another brick in the wall while imprisoned for sixteen months.

Remembrance got more attention in Britain than in the US. I found the reflection refreshing. The BBC was full of documentaries and programs on war themes. I'd started watching *Coal House at War*, which subjected three modern Welsh families to living conditions typical of 1944. It was no *Regency House Party*. The children were carrying around little cardboard boxes that I naively thought held their lunch, but were actually for gas masks. A lady got fined fifteen shillings for not adhering to the blackout laws at night. It was also stimulating to learn something from these "reality shows" instead of their brain rot-inducing cousins like *Big Brother*. Or *Victorian Pharmacy*, which showed the British viewing public how to brew their own Worcestershire sauce in the basement. We didn't have a basement, and I didn't think I could get Ben to tolerate fermenting anchovies in the cupboard under the stairs. But it was still useful information for someone, right up there with elderflower champagne.

_ele_

# Scary Valentines

I HAD A SNEAKING suspicion that my parents liked Ben better than me. He'd receive a rapturous welcome from them in our early days of dating, where I might have gotten a cursory "hello" and a head nod. In the run up to our first Valentine's Day, I was at Ben's house when I spied a red envelope from my mother peeking out from a pile of bills. It was a bit embarrassing, but I wasn't surprised that my mother sent him a Valentine's card. She was chronically festive. I handed it to him.

"Here."

"What's this?"

"It's from my mom."

He raised an eyebrow as he peeled off a flashy foil heart sticker and opened the card. I read over his shoulder. It struck a friendly tone. He set it aside and looked at me in pain.

"Yeah, this really freaks me out."

"Why?"

"Your mum just sent me a love letter."

I explained how American elementary schools had Valentine's Day parties, and students were encouraged to give Valentines to everyone in their class. Once Ben appreciated how wide the US Valentine net was cast, he agreed to see my mother again. I saw an American lapel pin boasting that Jesus was the wearer's Valentine, so the net was getting wider all the time. If Jesus could be a Valentine, what problem could Ben possibly have?

No wonder Ben was freaked out. Based on Tesco's greeting card selection, Valentine's Day UK style was reserved for the truly lusty. The cards were chock full of references to underwear, or the lack of it. I tried to find a Valentine to send my parents, but all the cards with pants (meaning underwear) were pants (also meaning worthless). I gave up and got a Ribena to ease my nerves.

# Continental Breakfast

O THER THAN MY VISIT to Paris, I had never been to any other part of
Europe. When Ben floated the possibility of visiting Luxembourg,
I didn't need convincing—European travel was one of the major perks for
Americans living in the UK. His beloved atlas showed Luxembourg was
firmly lodged in the middle of Europe, so I would have another opportunity to decipher why he was so quick to disown the rest of the continent. The
primary purpose of the trip would be for him to add the ING Marathon to
his race collection. I had one recollection of Luxembourg from sixth-grade
geography class: it was a small place. I agreed to work as Ben's marathon
support staff and we booked our tickets on Luxair.

We flew with a carry-on from London City Airport in the middle of
Docklands. There weren't many travelers—a massive contrast to my usual
experience of slogging through the mayhem of Heathrow. Just when I
thought our airport experience would be ultra breezy, I saw four Metropolitan Police officers slinging submachine guns, as they chatted with a
massive German shepherd and his statuesque owner. She told the dog he
was being "a very good boy," which made me even more grateful I hadn't
stuffed my leftover bacon croissant in my bag for in-flight snacking. We
tiptoed past them to our gate.

I shouldn't have worried about airline food—Luxair won my award for
the finest in-air sandwich ever served. It was tender ham and very tasty chive
spread on a fresh, miniature baguette. By popular demand, the crew made

two generous passes with the sandwich cart. The seats were leather and the pre-landing candy was a toffee caramel. I liked Luxembourg already.

Luxembourg City was the tidiest municipal venue I'd ever visited. There wasn't a speck of rubbish on any pavement. The public parks and gardens were immaculate, with life-size wooden pirate ships to fascinate the herd of small children on the playground. We arrived at our first hotel, only to learn it was full, so we were upgraded to the four-star Parc Belair nearby. The lobby walls were covered in crushed red velvet wallpaper and rococo gilt mirrors, like the decorators were freshly off their latest gig at a fine Parisian bordello. A nude mermaid fountain in dire need of de-algaefication made me seek out the toilet. The desk staff answered the phone in German, responded to a customer in French, and proceeded to book our rooms in English, all within the same thirty seconds. The official language of Luxembourgish sounded like some hybrid of German and French, though I couldn't be sure what I was hearing in the language *soupe du jour*.

We knew we shouldn't criticize people who speak at least two more languages than we do, but we couldn't resist judging the English translation of an in-room brochure. The picture showed a bucolic scene with a couple on a picnic, laid with an acceptable quantity of organic fruit and un-American cheese. "We have all the resources to help you plan a successful expedition," it said. Were there unsuccessful expeditions? What were the judging criteria? Ben and I spent the next half hour conjuring examples of unsuccessful expeditions. Ben suggested arriving in European wine country, only to discover his fly had been down for the entire trip. We started warning each other before going out to avoid that kind of unsuccessful expedition.

Luxembourg City was home to 146 banks, a marvel considering its full-time population was under 100,000. The city made its revenue from banking, reinsurance, and holding companies. Most of its workers commuted in from any of the surrounding countries. I'd read a statistic that its cost of living was in the top 4 percent of all cities worldwide, so it was much cheaper to live elsewhere. Wi-fi was free for everyone in Luxembourg City and someone had to pay. We saw a man squatting outside the City's Notre Dame Cathedral offering a coffee cup in his extended hands, but he was so well-groomed that I dared not make a contribution in case he was a banker on a break, still drinking his expensive cappuccino.

We figured out the bus system with ease, incentivized by a €1-bus ticket that was good for two hours. Our fare worked out to about $1.50. The service was fast, frequent, and financially feasible. The buses were linked in impossibly long, articulated segments by huge circular plates in the bus floor. I learned the first lesson of bendy bus riding by tumbling into a pile of other people's luggage—don't stand with one foot on the joining circle and another on a segment's floor, as one foot moved every time the bus took a corner. It was strange to see the driver on another street while my segment of the bus hadn't left the first one.

We had just disembarked in the business district and started exploring the mix of new and old architecture when the unmistakable clattering of skateboarders approached from behind us. I wondered what Luxembourgish hoodies would sound like until they got close enough for me to hear "dude" and "awesome" in authentic American English. I was disgusted. I had made such efforts to travel to a petite jewel of medieval Europe, only to have the place overrun by young American boarders.

As it turned out, Americans were everywhere—in the plazas, beside us at dinner, and offering us their prime table at a museum cafe. The music festival for marathon weekend was a tribute to New Orleans, complete with an authentic funk band from somewhere in Louisiana. The lead singer's name was DeWayne, and he urged us to buy his CD because he had child support to pay. Ben munched away on his chili from the southern food booth. I shook my head over the only alternative lunch food I could find, a McDonald's hamburger. No matter how long I stared at it, I couldn't will it into a *croque monsieur*.

Back in the hotel that evening, I studied the regional map. I still wasn't sure exactly where Luxembourg was. Just as I did during London study abroad, I liked to commit maps to memory. I spied Luxembourg on a sliver of land between Germany, France, and Belgium. When my eyes cast downward to Switzerland, I smiled when I saw a place called Schaffhausen, as in Dr. Emil Schaffhausen from the Michael Caine/Steve Martin comedy, *Dirty Rotten Scoundrels*.

At first, calling the front desk gave me anxiety. I'd feel better asking about breakfast by semaphore. I'd heard a little English, German, French, and what I assumed was Luxembourgish at the front desk, but most of the time, the clerk rattled off rapid-fire French. I didn't assume people at the front desk wanted to speak English—that would be an ugly American tourist thing to do. I sweated a bit and dialed zero.

"Hallo?"

The linguistic wheel of fortune spun in my mind. I went with French.

"*Parlez-vous anglais?*" Despite knowing what to say and rehearsing my Franken-French with a variety of inflections, I pictured the person on the other end of the phone holding up his hand to shield himself from my verbal shrapnel.

"But *of course*, madame." Clearly, the exasperated man at reception could not contemplate a reality without the language of *les rosbifs*, a slightly disparaging term the French reserved for the British. I found out what I needed to know and hung up, but I felt like a multicultural clown.

─ℓℓℓ─

S PECTATING A MARATHON WAS a bit like a mobile scavenger hunt. It wasn't as uplifting for a runner to hear supportive cheers only at the start of the race. In the prior two marathons I spectated, I staked Ben out at a number of places, using his pace to calculate his ETA at various locations. Once I arrived at a stake-out, it turned into a large-scale game of Where's Waldo (Wally in Britain). The marathon didn't even begin until 7 p.m. It would be a late night, flitting in and out of medieval city streets lined with flaming torches. I expected armored men to arrive on horseback at any moment.

I scanned the start area for firearms, having had some surprises spectating marathons. At the moment the Cape Cod Marathon began, a fogey from the Falmouth Historical Society had detonated a miniature brass cannon five feet behind my head. Every inch of my body spasmed like I had been hit by lightning. I gripped my chest and felt my knees buckle as I toppled sideways. A herd of pedestrian preschoolers must have been used to the sound of anti-aircraft fire because they pointed at me and laughed. But I had the last laugh. After the race, the old cannon perpetrator overheard Ben talking and interrupted him.

"Say, you from New England?" His tone didn't exude hospitality.

"No, I'm from *Old* England."

The fogey nodded with satisfaction and shuffled off.

There were no surprises along the Luxembourg City Marathon route, and I was able to navigate the course to find Ben four times as he ran past. At the halfway mark, he was smiling and looking as fresh as a Luxair baguette. He was running ahead of schedule, which meant a quick re-figure of his pace and projected ETA at various kilometer markers. To spy him again, I hopped on the free shuttle bus and bypassed a few jaunty samba bands that lined the route. From there, I hoofed it up the street and down several bus stops, past the kids banging on sand buckets and shovels in time to a samba beat. I got plenty of exercise spectating—I once walked twelve miles to see him at various points along the Chicago Marathon route. Finally, I saw him just past the end of some medieval streets, near a group of Germans chanting something unintelligible but ominous. I managed to miss his finish due to a bit of confusion over where the shuttle bus stop was, but the marathon organizers kindly put everyone's finish on downloadable video. He could replay it for his friends at the next Bushfield Joggers ("Bushies") cocktail party back in the UK.

THE DAY AFTER THE race, Ben requested a "gentle" walk in the city's parks, many of which were located at the bottom of a sheer cliff face. He needed to keep moving so his muscles wouldn't seize up. It was easy enough on the way down, but I blew a gasket on the way back up. I pined over the little green tourist trains, thinking of ways to hijack them for their uphill motoring power. We made it to the top of the hill with me puffing and Ben limping, only to be accosted by Mormon missionaries eager to discuss, in our choice of language, whether or not we had been saved. This was a genius move from their standpoint. Nature had worn down their victims so they lacked the lung capacity and muscle coordination to attempt a getaway. This outing wasn't my version of a "successful expedition."

The next day, we went to the indoor public pool. It was the most beautiful municipal pool I'd ever visited. The water was drinkably clear and chlorine free. I suspect one stray Band-Aid would get the patrons shrieking quicker than a pet piranha. The pool contained two tunnels that formed a watery corridor to a shallow area with six submerged lounge chairs. We reclined while millions of bubbles blasted through the tiny holes in the lounger underneath us. The second floor was Astroturf baked by overhead infrared lights. Two pasty young men laid out on towels, oblivious to our gawking. It was a novel idea, but the lamps were just like the kind McDonald's used to keep the local *pommes frites* warm.

As we waited to catch our flight home, I noticed Luxembourg Airport's floors were even shinier than the shoes in the financial district. The woman who checked us in didn't bother to ask us the mandatory safety questions about who had possibly trifled with our bags. She just checked them off in the affirmative, smiled at us sweetly, and wished us a pleasant flight. I don't think our safety was compromised. Luxembourg City's last crime wave was probably a bit of wayward dog poo in the park.

_ee_

## Is it Really That Lovely?

I READ THAT "LOVELY" was voted the most beautiful word in the English language. To me, it was a homecoming queen of a word in England—it started off attractive and popular, but had grown tiresome after so much overexposure. I first noticed it out of place at Tesco while food shopping. I held up my newly minted chip-and-pin debit card (no signature required), and the cashier noticed.

"Ah, that's lovely," she said, punching a few more buttons.

I knew my card was new and shiny, but how could she admire it so intently from several feet away? I noticed many shop personnel made the same comment when I made a move to pay, be it with cash or plastic. Were they used to being stiffed by shoppers with ugly forms of payment?

Over time, I heard "lovely" used to modify parsnips, teapots, weedkiller, paper checks, cricket bats, flooring, paint, and fabric softener. My literal American ear told me that "lovely" should be reserved for modifying truly beautiful things like sweet scents, well-behaved children, and nice diamond rings. But Americans used "awesome" with impunity, to describe everything from spring break to a really good fruit smoothie. Did those things really inspire awe? I couldn't exactly claim the linguistic high ground.

The final straw came when I called to make an inquiry about my upcoming gynecology appointment. I spoke to a chirpy nurse and wondered aloud if my time of the month would interfere with any testing the doctor might want to do.

"No problem at all. That's lovely," she replied.

I had heard periods described in many ways, but they were never twinned with the word "lovely."

"Really? But it's my period. There's nothing lovely about it, is there?"

I felt remorse the moment I'd said the words. She stammered and laughed, but never answered my question. No British person would ever question another's use of the word "lovely," *and* I had dared her to disagree with the obvious as a rhetorical weapon. My chart would be flagged "problematic" for eternity.

In fact, the Good Ship Problematic had sailed already, straight out of their toilet. During my first physical at the local doctor's office, I was instructed by my friendly nurse that she needed a urine sample. There were no lights on in the bathroom. It was so cavernous that the light from the nearby hall wasn't enough to illuminate the light switch. With the door closed, it had the ambiance of a Cornish mine at night. I felt the walls in vain for anything that would betray an electrical connection. About five feet away from the door, I felt a pull cord hanging from the ceiling. Just as I tugged it, I wondered why any sane electrician would place a light switch in such an inconvenient place. A deafening buzzer went off as I stood dumbfounded in the doorway, pee cup in my hand. I stared at the floor and waited for a horde of nursing staff to rush in and ask what I had broken in my fall off the toilet. After about a minute (I could have died if I had really fractured my cranium), the same nurse who had assigned me to pee came to claim me. She had a disgusted look on her face, and simply tugged the cord again to make the alarm stop. She walked over to the doorway and punched a wall switch about six inches above eye level. Properly illuminated, I now saw the cord was red. It matched the shade of my face.

I had run into trouble in English bathrooms before. Most visits had me furiously patting the walls in the dark for a wall light switch, only to flip what I thought was the lights and discover I had disabled the hand dryer main fuse. Ben had to give me a bathroom debrief at his mother's house. The lights, shower and fan were all controlled via a common pull switch that dangled from the ceiling. UK building regulations require this feature to prevent wet hands coming into contact with an electrical switch and a resulting shock. He and his mother grew tired of hearing me drop countless items off the bathroom counter because I wouldn't admit I was in the dark.

Now noted as a brain donor in NHS records, I beat myself up about the light switch incident because I should have known better. When I had attended the wedding reception at the Royal Naval College, after a couple glasses of pinot, I managed to make my way past the armed guard station to the unisex bathrooms in the front foyer. My cubicle was barely illuminated. Based on my bathroom electrics lesson at Ben's mum's house, I tugged the cord dangling next to the toilet because "it controlled everything." The lighting situation didn't improve, but I heard a faraway alarm and carried on the best I could, reasoning some drunken reception-goer set off a fire alarm somewhere. I remember hearing a scuffle and a burly man's voice.

"Is anyone hurt?" He could use the same tone to order a submarine missile launch.

I stood up, hastily adjusted my dress, and opened the door to find a man with a gun staring at me. He knew more than I did. He nodded and returned to the guard station. Had I pulled the emergency alarm? He wasn't messing around, and his response time was impressive.

_elle_

# The Doctor Will See You Now

I KNEW A FEW simple truths about healthcare. The red string in the doctor's surgery loo was a cry for help, not a path to illumination. The NHS was the UK's national healthcare program. Because I had a spouse visa, I was treated the same as citizens and I'd never see a bill for healthcare. In contrast, privatized healthcare back home was a jungle of red tape for Brits living in the US to machete through. The bills used to drive Ben mad.

The debate over national healthcare was heating up in the US, so I was naturally curious to find out what those who'd experienced it thought. The expat swami who advised so much taco seasoning had private health insurance through her employer, so I sought another opinion. I worked with a woman who'd spent years of her life in Australia, another country with national healthcare.

"I'd never do without private insurance in a country with socialized healthcare," she said. She described long waits to see specialists and two medical systems that ran in parallel, the best of which, she said, were private hospitals, private clinics, and private doctors who only accepted private insurance. (This wasn't true—most private doctors in the UK also work in the NHS, and the standard of care is the same in both systems. Private insurance buys you faster treatment, not better, and a nicer room for your hospital stay.)

Her opinion launched me down a rabbit hole of the various healthcare policies we could buy on top of the free NHS service. I didn't think healthcare was actually free because I saw the money that came out of our paychecks every month. It tipped our total tax rate to near 40 percent. Private insurance turned out to be prohibitively expensive. I decided not to worry. After all, the NHS had been taking care of an entire country since 1948. Ben had survived to adulthood. How bad could it be?

I asked a couple of friends who'd had children on the NHS what their experience was like. Mothers-to-be were asked to bring a laundry list of baby care items to the hospital, including cotton balls for wiping newborns without the chemicals in baby wipes. UK culture generally frowned on the extra chemicals, preservatives, and dyes that riddled American store shelves. Instead of hauling their newborns out for mandatory exams at the pediatrician's office, the NHS sent visiting baby nurses to their homes to do their medical checkups. New mothers didn't have to worry about taking such a small child out of the house, especially if they'd just been through major surgery to bring them into the world. It was an example of how the NHS system went out of its way to be helpful when it came to preventative care. In contrast, I felt like the American system was expert at chemical restoration after the damage had been done.

Despite my reservations, I had a great first impression of the NHS. There were surgeries (doctors' offices) in most residential neighborhoods. At Ben's old house, we shared a back garden wall with our local one. If I had an acute problem, I could call that morning and be seen the same day. I'd injured my ankle, and the next morning I was assigned to see a jolly sports medicine doctor who also treated the Peterborough United Football Club. When I was in the winter of my discontent, a same-day appointment had me feeling better as soon as I switched on the light box my doctor had prescribed. It was comforting to know medical bills were a thing of the past. Ben had never heard the term "deductible" before he came to live in the US.

I was referred to two specialists while I lived in the UK. I waited about six weeks to see the first one, which I thought was on par with how long I'd wait to see the same specialty back in the US. The second came when I got a referral for mental health services while in the throes of seasonal affective disorder. Thankfully, I took the GP's immediate advice and started feeling much better before I was invited to a counseling appointment three months later. If I had been much worse off, three months would have been an incredibly long wait.

I'd read newspaper stories, sometimes inflammatory ones, about cancer patients who couldn't get life-saving drugs because their local NHS trust wouldn't foot the £100,000 bill for the latest treatments. American insurance companies could take care of those kinds of bills—if the patient's particular coverage was good enough. But for the legions of underinsured or uninsured, medical bills were the leading cause of bankruptcy in the US. There were no easy answers.

The pharmacy counter at the chemist carried everyday drugs that were only available by prescription in the US. The pharmacy was the counter within the chemist where I'd pick up prescriptions, dispensed by the pharmacist. I kept telling Ben I needed to go to the "drug store," and he gave me a stern warning.

"No one ever talks about a drug store. If they do, the police want to know about it."

My experience of UK pharmacies was mixed. Foreign pollen was a menace, and a helpful pharmacist found me something I could take for much less than I'd pay for its prescription counterpart back in the US. Upon arrival to the UK, I took a daily thyroid pill, and a nurse practitioner at my surgery said hypothyroidism was a chronic condition that entitled me to a medical exemption card. This meant I could receive all my prescriptions for free, as opposed to £7.50. I asked my Citizens' Advice tutor about the rationale behind my new card. She explained that hypothyroidism, left untreated, is potentially fatal. I got a faint whiff of nanny state, but I paid plenty for the NHS. I was happy to accept any discounts in perpetuity.

All was well until I got to the pharmacist. She had a bubbly tone as we exchanged pleasantries before the transaction. But when I presented my card, she gave me a suspicious look and a muttered comment about my worthiness. I wondered why she doubted my sincerity—my doctor signed the application as proof of my condition. I could easily get more depressed and look extra portly if she needed more convincing. In the midst of her freeze-out, she stared at my paperwork.

"By the way, I see you live in The Rookery. Is your kitchen floor the color of flesh?"

Was it possible for her to judge me more?

On subsequent visits, she always asked if I'd be using my exemption card. Ben's theory was it rankled her that some foreign person was using a public benefit. Luckily, we moved away from her shop before she inquired about my yurt curtains.

In the year before we relocated to the UK, I managed to extrude a disc in my low back and endure six months of torture before pain-killing steroid shots got me barely functional again. My American physical therapist had me doing lots of cobra and child's poses from yoga, but my core was so weak I couldn't sit upright without serious propping from my arms.

After moving to England, I stumbled across the book *Back Sufferer's Bible* by Sarah Key, the one-time physiotherapist (physical therapist) to Prince Charles and the royal family. Using her exercises, my back started to improve. She trained other physios in her methods, and I found one on a farm about forty-five minutes away in rural Norfolk. My back protested such a long drive on the A170's firm seats, but I didn't want a repeat of my nontherapy in the States. The therapist had a spacious studio in a converted barn, filled with giant Swiss balls and leftover medieval torture instruments. When she realized I couldn't sit up without help, her tone reminded me of my driving instructor.

"Right. How did you slip through the cracks like this? We're going to have to sort you out."

She started me on a no-nonsense strengthening regime that restored my back, and graduated me into "clinical Pilates." It was a class of the walking wounded who exercised under professional supervision, but I rejoiced in its effectiveness. I paid out of pocket for her private therapy, but at £20 per session, it was far less than my deductible would have been for the semi-worthless American sessions I'd endured with "assistants," not therapists. Ben could tell which days I'd had physio because there was a delicious quiche for dinner—I could also buy farm-fresh eggs in her waiting room for the bargain price of £1 per half dozen.

—ele—

## The Aristocat

B EN AND I WERE cat people, but we somehow missed exchanging this
bit of getting-to-know-you information until later in our acquaintance. When I found out he actually liked cats, I was relieved. If I hadn't
gotten married, I would have wound up an old cat lady. Once I knew he
was feline-friendly, I could be an old, married cat lady.

I didn't realize just what kind of magical cat powers he had until we went
to our next-door neighbor's New Year's party. She had half a dozen indoor
cats, but her house looked and smelled remarkably cat-free to the casual
observer. Only a couple in the clowder had the nerve to join the party.
A tremendous twenty-pounder named Humby rejoiced on Ben's arrival,
bypassing the lap of his owner. Humby knew he was the Hulk Hogan of
the cat kingdom and he tested Ben's lap like a sumo wrestler on a frayed
rope bridge. Once Ben welcomed him with clicking and purring noises,
Humby settled in for the winter. His housemate, Sarah Elizabeth, ran out
to greet Ben as well. He had a feline fan club.

Ben talked about his mother's pet cats with the nostalgia old men reserve
for their war buddies.

"Monty was a great cat, a lovely, tortoise-shell tabby with long hair."
Based on tone of voice, I thought he was going to tell me how Monty had
taught him to shave, but instead he went on about his finer feline features.
I had childhood cats too, but Monty was the stuff of legend.

Britain was pet mad. Little metal signs showed silhouettes of dogs leaving
deposits, obscured by a large, red anti symbol. When I first read the phrase

"no dog fouling," I thought they weren't allowed to get involved in scuffles on the soccer field. It was easy to spot dog-friendly pubs by the water bowls they set out for canine patrons. I had pub lunch with a woman who surprised me by inviting her terrier, Tibby. He whined for attention the entire time, so my dining companion held him at table level to appease him. At one point, Tibby decided he had too much phlegm and flubbered doggie spittle right into my fresh pint of blackcurrant squash.

When it came to making friends with the neighborhood cats, plenty of feline strangers ran up to Ben like they hadn't seen him for years, blissfully rubbing against his legs. Some threw themselves at his feet without any shred of dignity. Either he naturally smelled of bacon or he was the modern cat Messiah.

This wasn't just a local phenomenon. We visited Blickling Hall in Norfolk, a Jacobean stately home where Anne Boleyn was born. As we walked up the grand, yew-lined front promenade, a black cat with a red collar laid outstretched on the pavement. I could sense his small disdain from fifty cat paces. Ben began his usual clicking and purring routine.

"He's an aristocat, Ben. No way he's going to give you the time of day."

Instead, the Blickling cat ran up to Ben and greeted him like an old friend. I was cruelly ignored. Feline Sir Blickling marked Ben as his property lavishly, then moved on to solicit pets from a little boy next to a delightful yew topiary.

We resisted getting a cat in England because we lived near busy streets. Ben got his cat fix vicariously. A coworker was telling me about her wicked Maine Coon, Donatello. I scrunched my nose at hearing his litany of sins, and recited them to Ben over dinner one evening.

"Maine Coons are lovely cats." He was defensive. "What exactly is it that makes this cat wicked?"

"Well, Susan walks by in her stocking legs, and Donatello picks that moment to spring on her. He keeps putting runs in her hosiery."

"He's probably been neglected for attention all day, and that's his last hope. What else has he done?"

"He nudges his food bowl toward the edge of the counter and threatens to drop it off unless he gets attention right away."

"Again, a cry for help. Anything else?"

"He likes to dive in their fishpond and swim, or worse yet, fish. Maine Coons like to swim, you know."

Ben smiled at the whimsy of a fluffy Maine Coon doing a swan dive into the back garden water feature and poking his head up among the lily pads. This final trait ushered the entire breed into Ben's feline hall of fame.

"She's being unreasonable. All this, it's just him being himself. He sounds like a very good cat."

I laughed that Ben so thoroughly defended a cat he'd never met. I reported back to my co-worker that Ben was ready to take on Donatello's animal rights case when and if needed. As a criminal lawyer, I thought getting assaulted from behind—in expensive legwear—was indefensible. Ben was resolute that, should we ever move to a cat-safe area, we should get a male Maine Coon. We should also move somewhere where the cat could do his own hunting and fishing, and perhaps we could build him a feline stately home. Engineers enjoy a project.

_ele_

# Hitting the Commute Button

A S PART OF MY everyday English life, I took the train to work in Cambridge. Driving into the city center would have been an unpredictable travel nightmare on one of the most congested roads in the country. If I did manage to arrive on time, there was the problem of finding a place to park in a town built by medieval pedestrians. The train was a fifty-minute ride, far more reliable for getting to work on time.

Commuting was an alternate universe. The people I saw every day were bound by an unwritten code of conduct that prohibited any more communication than the occasional sideways glance. The personality tests didn't know what to do with me—I was an introvert who craved meaningful human interaction. The world of commuting was lonely, made worse because I was surrounded by scores of other people. Most of the time, I tapped away on a tiny Netbook computer to make the time pass.

Once the train filled, commuters got testy. A middle-aged man barked, "Fine, you take it!" to a girl of seven who happened to beat him to the last seat. If he was this irate before 9 a.m., surely the rest of his day would be miserable. People felt free to bring their dogs on the train, tucking them under one of the table seats and feeding them bits of their bacon butty (sandwich). I heard other passengers clucking with disapproval about one dog in particular. I thought allowing any pets but service dogs on trains was asking for foul situations. But with more eavesdropping, the other passengers were merely offended the owner didn't ask the conductor's permission before bringing the dog aboard. I covered my open drink with my hand and hoped he wasn't a Yorkshire terrier named Tibby.

I noticed some people carrying bags that said "Bench" on them. One hipster wore a hooded sweatshirt labeled the same way. I thought it was some English, passive-aggressive attempt to reserve a seat wherever they were, but Ben told me "Bench" was a trendy urban brand, far too hip for me to recognize. That was a relief. The same went for "Superdry." That logo didn't help its wearers avoid the station benches sprinkled with mizzle.

Commuting became a mind-numbing pattern: drop off, ticket check, platform dash, wait. The air was filled with male voices making platform announcements, mostly unintelligible. When I could understand, they were made with such a blah-de-vivre that they sucked away my little enthusiasm like an emotional Dyson.

Once at work, I didn't find my job anything to get excited about either, because my vocational ego got in the way—in my mind, I was overqualified and underpaid. I was particularly ill-suited to my primary job function as a volunteer coordinator. Some were wonderful, but I was effectively the complaint desk for a few retired eccentrics who shrieked when any of their work could possibly conflict with the University of the Third Age walking group schedule or knitting club. I was used to handing out jail sentences, not feeling like I was serving one myself.

The station in Cambridge had an especially frightening women's loo. Someone decided to line the interior of each cubicle with stainless steel. They were kept remarkably clean, but it was like sitting down in front of an 180-degree mirror. Worse were the snippets of conversation I overheard from breathless commuters compelled to use their mobile phones while indisposed. The steel reverberated their voices like loudspeakers.

"I'm on the toilet!" one woman barked. "What do you want?" I wanted her to accidentally flush her phone in a spectacular whoosh of water. UK toilets were much higher flow than their US counterparts.

I was waiting at the platform one morning when the PA clicked on.

"The train now arriving at Platform 4 will form the 0-800 service to Norwich, calling at March, Ely, Thetford, and... braaaaaach!" My head happened to be within three feet of the nearest loudspeaker, so there was no mistaking what had happened. The announcer had just belched into the PA. My fellow commuters kept flicking through their phones, unfazed.

It was just another day at the office.

_ele_

# London Calling

M Y UK LIFE WAS teaching me some lessons that I didn't think would come up on the "Life in the UK" test, but were valuable nonetheless. I cringed every time an American politician or religious zealot referred to the United States as "the greatest nation in the world." By what standard? So many other cultures were beautiful or admirable. Their citizens loved their motherland, too. What was it about the United States that made us feel we could jump the worthiness queue? Maybe the stereotype was true and there is a certain hallmark American swagger where humility is an afterthought. By contrast, British stiff upper lips didn't appeal to me. I didn't like the idea of stifling enthusiasm for decorum's sake. Zeal and self-control appeared on the same continuum in the UK. I found it tricky to figure out.

I expected I'd have more American visitors pining to get free lodging and a chance to cavort around the British countryside with me, but only one friend took me up on that offer. On a visit back to the US, I learned that one potential visitor felt unsafe in Europe and would never darken my English doorstep. She'd seen decades of US news reports on terrorism and land war in Europe. The IRA bombings of The Troubles era left her afraid to take public transportation in London. Coupled with the submachine gun-clad guards at some European airports, she figured she'd be entering a war zone. I shrugged and gave up on American hospitality.

My truth was that I felt considerably safer living in the UK, where the populace didn't default to gun ownership, and violent crime was far lower.

The government tried to short-circuit any situation that might remotely promote violent crime. I brought a small, sheathed paring knife to work one day, intending to cut up an apple. One of the volunteers in the kitchen saw me take it out of my lunch bag and spoke up.

"You didn't bring that knife here on the train, did you?"

He explained that unless I was a chef and could prove it was a tool of my trade or had another valid reason, it was illegal to carry a knife in a public place unless it had a manual folding blade less than three inches long. I should have figured this out on my own in a country where the only weapons the police carried were batons and incapacitant spray. My mother mailed me what she thought was a thoughtful Christmas stocking stuffer: a pink, mock croc keychain pouch of pepper spray. In a bit of excellent luck, it had slipped undetected through postal inspection. Pepper spray was illegal for me to possess in the UK, never mind use. It was classed as a firearm. If I was caught with it, the offense carried the same penalty as gun possession: a minimum of five years imprisonment.

Compared to my US home, there was more petty crime in the UK per capita. That would explain Ben's vigilance in never leaving anything valuable in our cars. Lots of house door latches automatically locked when closed—a frustrating discovery in my early days of UK living.

But I couldn't remember the last time I'd read anything about anyone in the UK being shot, or held up at gunpoint. There were no reports of children shot by accident while playing with unsecured guns at home. Back in Peoria, I'd see those stories hit the news every month, or in a bad run, every day. I felt safe in my UK life. Not always comfortable, but my risk of meeting a violent end was statistically much lower.

I lost patience with my fellow Americans abroad sometimes, but I wasn't expecting my accountant back in the middle of Illinois to swim in the cultural shallow end. One of the most painful reminders that I couldn't ever leave the US behind was my yearly encounter with Uncle Sam at tax time. Even though I had no US earnings, I had to file a tax return with the US government anyway, showing my UK earnings were subject to the foreign-earned tax exemption. The US reserves the right to tax its citizens the world over, but I was already paying taxes in the UK, on fairly measly earnings. Like most lawyers, I had an aversion to any practice area that drop-kicked me out of my comfort zone. I could discuss plea deals until the cows came home, but taxes made my eyes water and my joints seize up. I read a bit about how to show my foreign earnings on a US tax return, but I thought I'd let my small-town American accountant take care of the rest.

I called the office at what would have been about 1 p.m. in Illinois. A male voice answered. "Leo's Taco Shack."

This man was allegedly a certified public accountant in the middle of corn and soybean fields. At best, his small town was a rural hamlet full of farmers. I would be shocked if they'd gone multicultural by incorporating a taco shack.

I stuttered. "I was calling for the tax service. Wrong number?"

"Oh no. Caller ID said you were international. I always answer that way when I don't know who it is."

I'd heard the new accountant was a bit quirky, but he'd passed the CPA exam, reportedly harder than the bar exam. He had to have some synapses firing. I explained my story, current location, and how I'd sold my old house in Illinois during the past tax year.

"I wouldn't even bother reporting that income."

The needle scratched across my mental record. Even I knew better than to lay quiet when the State of Illinois had a tax form stating exactly what proceeds I made and when. This conversation wasn't going terribly well. He was what Ben would call a "cowboy," and that was no compliment.

"Did you earn any US income?"

"No," I replied, "but…"

"Don't waste your time filing," he said dismissively.

"But I earned income in the UK."

"How many dollars was that?"

"Well, I don't know off the top of my head. They paid me in pounds. Just a second. I'll get my calculator and convert it."

He paused and exhaled into the phone.

"This is a bit outta my depth. I'm not gonna be able to help you."

I was not dealing with someone open to new experiences, namely typing the multiplication sign and 1.63 into his calculator to convert pounds to dollars that day. I started to wrap the conversation up but was interrupted.

"Hey! Are you calling from London right now?"

I'd already told him my location, but it took a while to sink in. Like many Americans who hadn't traveled much, he assumed everyone in England must live in London. At least he knew that city.

"No, I don't live in London. I live in a city called Peterborough."

"Where? Oh, never mind… It's just amazing! You sound like you're calling from next door!"

The modern marvels of fiber optics and satellites were a revelation to this goofball. He probably needed to sit down, like when he first saw sliced bread. I would have received far better tax advice at a genuine taco shack.

In the end, I bought myself TurboTax, muddled through the instructions, filed electronically, and celebrated with the biggest bottle of Ribena I could find.

# Part Six:

## The "Life in the UK" Test

*A mind that is stretched by a new experience can never go back to its old dimensions.*

– Oliver Wendell Holmes, American jurist

A FTER TWENTY-SIX MONTHS OF island living, the UK Border Agency, arbiter of imported and deported peoples, made me succumb to an official entrance exam in order to secure my residency. If I failed, I couldn't convert my visa to a permanent version and I could be deported. More precisely, I'd be denied "indefinite leave to remain." I knew to interpret "leave" as permission thanks to my former lawyering, but I couldn't help but wonder if the term was dreamed up by the same person who wrote the song, "Running to Stand Still." The "Life in the UK" test was used to vet both those who wanted to become citizens, and people like

me who just wanted to hang out on a long-term basis. I hoped there would
be fewer sheep involved than on the driving test.

I reported to the nearest bookstore and found the official *Life in the
UK Test Study Guide*, published by Her Majesty's Stationery Office. The
introductory paragraphs crowed that since the test's introduction in 2007,
the *Study Guide* had quickly become a national bestseller. That claim was
a bit insincere—every foreigner wishing to remain on the island was forced
to purchase this book if they wanted a chance at passing.

I guessed the test might focus on purely governmental questions, like
defining a constitutional monarchy, or perhaps some pithy factoids like the
date of Magna Carta. The church and state were comfortable bedfellows
in the UK, so I suspected at least one question on the Church of England.

I hoped the words to "God Save the Queen" would not be on the
test, either. I had a mental block on learning them. I wasn't particularly
interested in a group of people who held out their DNA as a calling card for
superiority, granting them access to vast real-estate portfolios and millions
of pounds from the British government. (According to the polls, most
young British people felt the same way.) I knew the melody to "God Save
the Queen" to be the same as "My Country, 'Tis of Thee"—Ben gripped
his chest and nearly fell down the first time he heard the American lyrics.
It was what he called melodic treason. The only British lyric I knew was
where the word "queen" appeared. When I felt pressure to sing along *en
masse,* my version usually went like, "Blah, blah, blah, blah-blah Queen;
Blah, blah, blah, blah-blah Queen; Queen, queen, queen, queen."

Thankfully, neither that tune, nor the enigma of a song called
"Jerusalem" would appear on the test. Since my island arrival, I'd read that
the general British population felt "Jerusalem" should take the place of
"God Save the Queen" as the national anthem. England liked to refer to
itself as a "green and pleasant land," which was straight out of "Jerusalem"

the song, not the Middle Eastern capital. Britain's version of "Jerusalem" was in heavy rotation at various national events, weddings, and football matches. It had a dramatic chorus that lent itself to interpretation by both Welsh male-voice choirs and emotional football fans.

I appreciated the melody, but I found its lyrical suggestions completely nuts. They were taken from an 1808 William Blake poem that described the green fields of England as the new Jerusalem. (Some of the Romantic poets got a bit loose with the opium as they put quill to parchment.) The lyric also floated the ancient conspiracy theory that Jesus visited England at some point in his life, most likely Glastonbury. Everybody knew Glastonbury was a dairy farm that became famous for hosting the craziest music festival in the UK, if not the world. It had a lesser stone circle than Stonehenge, but I couldn't see it as a tourist attraction for Palestinians of modest means. If the theory was true, the subtext would be the disappointment Jesus felt about traveling so far for just a few big rocks, artistically arranged. It was also doubtful he would have enjoyed the spectacle of crazy natives wading through mud to listen to a week's worth of cutting-edge pipe and drum acts nearly two millennia before the invention of wellies.

I dove into the guide and saw the bona fide test material. I did not expect a plethora of assorted general knowledge questions. The exam would be computerized, with the questions dealt at random like a poker hand. The answer to many multiple-choice questions on consumer help was, "Consult your nearest Citizens Advice Bureau." I worked for CAB and was familiar with the work it did, but it was news to me that CAB was the correct answer to, "What should you do if you have difficulty finding a dentist?" I'd never known a client to ask for that advice, but I did know that, occasionally, the government used Citizens Advice as a dumping ground for the disgruntled people it didn't have the time, staff, or inclination to help. I was fairly certain that bit of trivia wasn't going to be on the test.

Besides multiple choice, I'd have to navigate a few true or false questions. According to the guide, I might be asked to cough up statistics like the population of Wales, geography, various countries' patron saints and their feast days, and the ethnic demographics of the Greater London area. I prayed I'd be dealt the most painless questions, like what profession took care of sick pets, or the address of the Prime Minister's house in London.

I was caught off guard by a question on the UK film-rating system. Ben and I had gone to see a movie when I overheard one of the ushers say "Twelve A." I had been to that theater before, but I didn't remember any sub-theater numbering system. Maybe I'd missed it because it was magical, like Platform 9 ¾ at King's Cross Station in London.

"Wow. This theater is way bigger than I thought," I said.

As usual, Ben couldn't understand what I was talking about as he watched me trot around the lobby. I walked past theater 12, but 12a was nowhere to be found. Out of the corner of my eye, I caught an advertising display that said a film was rated 12a, meaning children under the age of twelve must be accompanied by an adult. I pretended to look for the ladies' loo—I'd found that excuse covered up all sorts of American confusion.

Failing the test was not an option, nor were regular flights across the Atlantic to maintain a commuter marriage. I sat through eighteen practice exams, which took me back to the day before my UK driving test when I plotted all thirty-one possible test routes on my Peterborough A–Z map. There would be twenty-four questions. I could miss six and still pass. I occasionally bungled the Muslim demographic statistics of London, so I hoped no more than six questions would require me to cough up population sizes.

On test day, the butterflies in my stomach flew in nauseating formation. I arrived at the test center and paid £15 for the privilege of being there. The UK Border Agency had caught on that, in an age of austerity, prospective immigrants were sitting ducks for fees on all manner of "services," including this exam. Ten people were scheduled in my group, but from what I overheard in the waiting area, only three of us were native English speakers. An Asian man took the chair beside me, firmly gripping his *Study Guide...* in Mandarin. Unless I had seriously misjudged all the test instructions, the exam would be in English. A flustered Asian girl flew in five minutes before exam start time and spoke in Chinese to the man with the Mandarin manual. She sailed out of the room and returned again, looking relieved. I guessed he'd given her some last-minute guidance, but for all I knew, he could have told her there was a sale on peaches at Aldi.

For all the respect British culture gave to following the rules, this test was going nowhere. Several more non-natives sauntered in at fifteen minutes past start time, and amazingly, the invigilator (proctor) let them in. The term "invigilator" conjured up images of upright citizens running around the airport, demanding to know who packed everyone's bags. My mood had migrated from anxious to peeved. I had gotten up extra early and struggled to find the venue's top-secret public car park. Despite the late-comers' countries of origin, clocks translated the world over. I just wanted the experience behind me.

After showing proof of purchase, all ten of us had to be individually ushered into the test room and registered on the Border Agency's website. The young woman who registered me was supervised by an older woman perched over her shoulder like a geriatric parrot, squawking directions without effect. We came to the part of the webpage that asked for my place of birth.

"Springfield, Illinois."

I smiled. I'd started off strong by answering a question correctly.

The woman looked hesitant.

"I-L-L-I..."

"How about I just put in 'Springfield?' " she interrupted.

I shot her my most citrus look. "That won't really help much. There are fifty-two different cities named Springfield in the United States. At least thirty-five states have one." I'd looked this fun fact up in childhood and it roosted in my memory, right next to the *Muppet Show* theme song.

"Oh. Then why don't I just put "Illinois?"

Did this test facility pay a premium per keystroke? What happened to the British penchant for doing things the right way? I sighed.

"Ah. Now you've narrowed it down to about thirteen million people."

She gazed back at me. It was like staring down a snowy television console.

"Look, I've filled out plenty of these forms before," I said. "They want the city and state. That's how Americans identify locations." I was trying to be helpful. Desperate, I looked for her old parrot to bail me out, but she was distracted helping a woman who had never encountered a computer mouse before.

"What? You've taken this test before?" My invigilator's voice was so loud, all the people who spoke decent English swiveled their heads to stare at me, the recently-outed flunkee.

"No! I mean I've filled out enough UK Border Agency forms in my time to know they're going to want the city and state."

She huffed and subjected herself to the tortuous spelling of "Illinois." Next, she picked up my passport to enter its number into another field.

"Now, I need you to verify the information I've typed in is correct."

I could see her reciting that line off a flashcard in her mind. I craned over the computer screen and reached for my passport to check she'd gotten the number right. I grasped it, but she snatched it away.

"No! I can't let you have that back!"

Incredulous and blinded by rage, I saw a heavy, English-manufactured steel hole punch within my wingspan. I wanted to use it to bludgeon her, but I needed the pass certificate she had the power to print for me. Simultaneous access to the "control" and "P" keys went directly to some people's heads.

Thankfully, her geriatric parrot fluttered back and interrupted my grievous bodily harm charge in progress.

"You need to give this woman her passport back *right now!*" Her squawk left no room for deviation. "She doesn't know her passport number off the top of her head. No one does!"

I wished the parrot would have added, "You fool!" in Mr. T tones, but it was still a moral victory. I felt a hand, and now the parrot had landed on my right shoulder.

"It's her first day," she whispered. My trainee sheepishly offered my passport back, and I retrieved it from her hand with a satisfying snap. I pitied the fool and concluded our business.

I TOOK MY PLACE at a computer next to a young man in the corner. He counted the lint balls under his mouse to pass the time. He was from New Zealand, and we gleefully dished on how absurd this test mandate was to those of us who spoke English as a first language.

We began the test. I was done in five minutes and wondered what I'd missed. I looked around to see everyone else beavering away. To avoid obvious hubris, I checked my answers. At the ten-minute mark, I could take no more and declared myself finished. Instead of going on my way, I was forced to loiter without my results for three hours. It was an utter waste

288 CLAIRE CRAIG EVANS

of time. I didn't think I was more worthy as a UK resident for knowing St. Andrew's Day was the 30th of November. I felt a bit resentful because besides eroding my stomach lining, learning this trivia displaced truly vital knowledge to my life in the UK, like which day to set out our wheelie bins.

I liked to live my life as if it were set to music, and I heard the orchestral chorus of "Jerusalem" swell in my head as my invigilator handed me written proof that I had passed the "Life in the UK" test. There was my claim check for months of lost confidence—easily taken for granted until the day it was gone. I felt tears of joy, just as when the courier van reunited me with my Samsonite after its trip to Delhi.

Despite the parrot, I resisted the urge to fold my certificate into a pirate hat. It would complement the eyepatch my invigilator would need one day when another aggrieved foreigner successfully put her eye out. For health and safety's sake, they needed to get rid of that industrial paper punch. Now I was thinking like a Brit.

A month later, the Border Agency clerk who approved my application for indefinite leave to remain told me I scored 100 percent on the test. I wasn't yet able to understand a Scouser directing me to the nearest bus stop, or hell for that matter, but I knew the distance from John O'Groats in the far north to Land's End in the southwest was approximately 870 miles, or 1,400 kilometers. The indefinite leave to remain visa in my passport cost £1,250, the most I'd ever paid to enter a high-stakes trivia contest. Thankfully, I'd won.

Too bad I was still hopeless at pub quiz.

# Acknowledgements

Truly, I feel grateful for everyone who came across my path and gave me something to think about, and later, write about. (On second thought, I send a big raspberry to the OAP selling tickets at Althorp House.) I treasure all the people who've encouraged my work through the years, whatever form it may take. Above all, I thank Ben for his patience, perspective, and chronic helpfulness.

I'm particularly indebted to Vicki Harris, who has been described as "the perfect editor." I cannot disagree. I gave her a shrub and she made it a topiary. I appreciate the keen eye of Dana Lee, proofreader extraordinaire. I'd like to thank Linda Pilla and Sandra Benn for consults on tricky Scottish accents, and Jonathan Thomas and Scott Hemmenway for their help tackling a dead language. *Gratias vobis ago.* [I give all of you my thanks.]

# Also by Claire...

B
UT WAIT, THERE'S MORE in 2024! Claire's next book is *Under Your Charms*, a sweet romantic comedy that made the semifinals for the Amazon Breakthrough Novel Award. Visit www.teawithclaire.com for more details and preorder information.

Besides writing, Claire is a sought-after virtual presenter to libraries and civic groups. She gives talks on these topics, with more added every year:

James Herriot: The Simple Life of the World's Most Famous Veterinarian

In Cod We Trust: A Deep Dive into the History of Fish and Chips

Britain's Hidden Treasures: Unearthing the Relics of an Ancient Past

The Great British Baking Tour (also available in Holiday Edition)

From Uptown Girls to Downton Abbey: How American Gilded Age Heiresses Invaded the British Aristocracy

Pottering Around the UK: Real Life Locations from the World of Harry Potter

The Politics of Tea: The East India Company and British Tea Culture

Steeped in Secrecy: The Boston Tea Party, 250 Years Later

From Merlin to Doc Martin: A Real-Life Travel Guide to the Best of England's Dramatic Cornwall

Mary Anning on England's Jurassic Coast: The Life and Times of the World's First Female Paleontologist

Happy Christmas at Home: Celebrating the Holiday, UK Style

Go to www.teawithclaire.com/events/ for the latest updates.